Raising a Champion

A Beginner's Guide
to Showing Dogs

A. Meredith John
Carole L. Richards

The Well Trained Dog

www.thewelltraineddog.com

Published by: **The Well Trained Dog**
www.thewelltraineddog.com
P.O. Box 2467   P.O. Box 516
Corvallis, OR 97339   Collingswood, NJ 08108

Disclaimer
The authors assume no responsibility for errors that may appear in this book or any damages that may arise from the use of the information given in this book.

Publisher's Cataloging-in-Publication
(Provided by Quality Books, Inc.)

John, A. Meredith.
    Raising a champion : a beginner's guide to showing
dogs / A. Meredith John, Carole L. Richards. -- 1st ed.
    p. cm.
    LCCN: 2001093305
    ISBN: 0971072205

    1. Dogs--Showing. 2. Dog shows. 3. Show dogs--
Handling.   I. Richards, Carole L.   II. Title.

SF425.J64 2001   636.7'0811
                        QBI01-201010

Printed in the United States of America

First Edition
10 9 8 7 6 5 4 3 2 1

Books are available at special discounts for bulk purchases for premiums, fund-raising, or educational use. For details, contact:
          The Well Trained Dog
          P.O. Box 516
          Collingswood, NJ 08108
          info@thewelltraineddog.com

Principal Photographer: John A. McCourt
Book design by A. Meredith John and Carole L. Richards
Cover design by Kate L. Jope

Cover photo *by John A. McCourt*: Ch. Zara's Zinderella, NSD NRD V

Raising a Champion
A Beginner's Guide to Showing Dogs

Table of Contents

Acknowledgements

The idea for this book was born in a whelping box. On a warm summer night a few years ago, we sat with our bitch Taupe as she leisurely whelped her first litter, taking an hour or more of rest between each of the six pups. We passed the time chatting about the new puppy owners. Some puppies would go to people who had been showing dogs for decades, and others would go to novice show homes; geographically, the homes were scattered across the country. What could we do to ensure a happy and successful experience for show novices, both locally and far away? We talked about our handling class students and the common problems, concerns and questions that all beginners invariably have. As we talked, we realized that there was a desperate need for a "user's manual" for novice handlers: a book that would explain, in a systematic fashion from the very beginning, how dog shows work and how to train a dog for the show ring, leaving no stone unturned.

And that's how our book writing adventure began.

To ensure that this book reflected more than our own perspectives on showing and on teaching others to show their own dogs, we talked to judges, handlers, breeders, AKC officials, trainers, first time exhibitors, and veterans of decades of dog shows. Our friends, puppy owners, and handling class students became our laboratory rats: they were quizzed about what helped or hindered as they trained and showed their dogs, what they wished they'd known when they started, and what still confused them. Without the help of dozens of people this book would lack much of the insight and advice we, in turn, offer our readers.

It's impossible to name everyone who assisted us in some form or another without inadvertently omitting someone; for that we apologize in advance. We would like to thank Susan Adams, Debbie Adamsbaum, Bobbie Anderson, Raymond Barclay, Nancy Ballerstedt, John Bonner, Bob and Beth Buchhofer, Karen Chamberlain, Roy and Anitra Cuneo, Terry DiPietro, Nancy DiSilva, Judic DeWitt, Tom Feneis, Lee and Terry Goldenberg, Debbie Hopkins, Barbara Kahn, Pat Klee, Carol Lewinski, Les and Mary Moore, Ann Pace, Barbara Pietrangelo, Kim Petri, Diana Pirner, Catherine Reed, Nancy Sowerbutts, Charlene Trost, and Lori Westling for their contributions, direct and indirect, to this project.

Our text is enhanced with photos that make training and showing dogs come alive, thanks primarily to Jack McCourt, who took over 2,000 pictures and patiently put up with our repetitive phrase, "This is good, but maybe ... ." Anyone who has taken photos of animals knows the patience and perseverance required to take a perfect picture, and we thank Jack for tracking down and shooting the photos. When he wasn't planning and taking photos, Jack edited text, served as a sounding board for our ideas, and helped us keep our focus, so that we wouldn't drift too far from our original purpose.

Special thanks go to Priscilla Gabosch, an AKC judge and delegate, who read our manuscript with the eye of an insider to the world of judges and ring stewards. Priscilla's sharp pencil and her eye for detail, coupled with years of practical experience as an exhibitor, judge, steward, and instructor, made her comments invaluable.

In addition to the photos taken at shows, matches, and training classes, there are sets of pictures that were taken in more formal photo sessions, so that we could clearly illustrate points that required a sequence of steps. We offer our heartfelt thanks to the people who let us use their dogs as models and who gave generously of their time during these photo sessions: Jackie McIlhenny of "Dynasty Dalmatians"; John and Kathy Yaninek of "Tanner's Vizslas"; Joyce Shaw of "Black Water Chesapeakes"; and Priscilla Gabosch of "Liberty."

Finally, when all the photos had been taken, the figures drawn, and the text written, our production team of Kate Jope, Sue Friedman, and Tracy McTernan tackled the technical aspects of our cover, manuscript and Web site with careful research, the ability to respond to our vision, and the perseverance to deal with the evolution of this project. The fact that they're all "dog people" made this project a labor of love for them, and that passion is reflected in their work.

Chapter 1 Introduction

"What a gorgeous puppy—are you going to show it?"

You've heard that dozens of times since you got your puppy. The question keeps playing over and over in your mind until you finally decide it's a *great* idea: you're going to take the plunge and enter the world of dog shows.

Or perhaps you decided before you got your puppy that you wanted to enter the dog show world, and you purchased your puppy from an experienced, reputable breeder with that goal in mind.

Showing dogs can be an exciting and rewarding hobby. At first, however, it may seem completely bewildering:

If you purchased your puppy as a show-prospect, then you've got your goal in sight. This book will help you get there.

- ❖ How does a dog show work?

- ❖ What makes one dog a "show-stopper" and another just a nice pet?

- ❖ What is the judge really looking for when he compares the dogs?

- ❖ How do you raise a puppy to be a show dog?

If these are the questions you're asking, then this book is for you.

Who Should Read This Book?

First, if you're new to dog showing and want to learn the basic skills for training and showing your puppy, this book is for you. It doesn't matter if you're planning to show your puppy yourself or if you're getting him ready to be shown by a more experienced person: this book explains the basic training you need to do to prepare your puppy for the show ring. If your dog is no longer a puppy, don't worry. The training techniques described here work just as well with an adult dog.

Watching a dog show is a great way to learn if you have a knowledgeable friend who will help you master the ins and outs of the sport.

Second, if you're a breeder who is launching a new show puppy with a novice owner, this book is for you and your new puppy owner. It gives your new owner a manual for basic show training and explains the rules and regulations governing dog shows. This book can help fill the gap when you're not available to answer the many questions a new owner has about showing dogs.

Third, this book is for you if you've trained or shown a dog before but want to improve your training skills and understanding of dog shows. It will add new training techniques to your tool kit and will increase your knowledge of the dog show judging process, making you a better trainer and more knowledgeable exhibitor.

What You Will Learn

Both you and your puppy will acquire new skills as you venture into the dog show world. This book will help you learn:

❖ how to teach a puppy to stand still in a show pose

❖ how to teach a puppy to move on a leash like a show dog

❖ how to teach a puppy to stand calmly when he is examined by a judge

❖ how *you* handle your dog in the show ring

You will learn how to teach young puppies (or adults) how to stand in a show pose using a positive, reward-based approach.

Learning to show a dog isn't just a matter of training your dog and mastering the skills needed for handling your dog in the ring. To be successful, you'll need to understand many other aspects of the sport:

❖ what basic equipment you need for showing a dog

❖ how to find dog shows in your area

❖ what the different classes at a dog show are

❖ how to enter a dog show

❖ how to read a judging schedule and a dog show catalog

❖ how to count the championship points earned at a dog show

❖ what the terms and jargon used by dog show people mean

❖ how to have fun showing your dog

This book will serve as your guide as you explore and master the intricacies of dog showing.

One Step at a Time

Very few people learn to swim by leaping into the deep end of a pool, hoping they'll float. The same is true about showing dogs; you can't learn to show dogs well just by entering shows and hoping you'll win. You'll need a plan for learning about dog shows, for learning the skills *you* will need in the ring, and for training your puppy.

What this book covers

Each chapter in this book builds on the ones before it, starting with the assumption that you know little or nothing about showing dogs.

❖ First, you'll learn how a dog show works, including the classes at a dog show, the sequence of judging, and the levels of competition. Along the way you'll pick up some of the jargon of the dog show world.

❖ You'll learn about your breed's "standard," which is the official description of the perfect example of each breed.

❖ Next, you'll learn about many things that you can begin doing right away, such as socializing your dog, locating a handling class, and getting books and magazines. You'll also learn about the leads and collars used in the show ring.

❖ At last, it's time to learn the basic skills of gaiting and

With patience and training, your show puppy can develop into a well-trained show dog and you can learn the ropes of showing dogs.

posing your dog! This part of the training will take most of your time and energy. It also is the most rewarding as you see your puppy blossoming into a trained show dog.

❖ When your puppy is trained, it's time to work on *your* skills and what *you* should do in the ring. You'll learn about the sequence of events that occurs in the show ring as a class of dogs is judged.

❖ You'll learn about "match shows" and how to get the most out of these dog show "dress rehearsals."

❖ Before you enter your first show, you'll learn how to find upcoming shows, how to read the pamphlet containing information about a show, and how to complete an entry form

❖ You'll learn how to check an entry confirmation, and how to read a judging schedule.

You'll learn about all the people and jobs involved in a dog show, including the judge and the ring steward.

❖ You'll learn about the planning you need to do before the day of the show. You'll also learn about the chores you must do when you arrive at the show, but *before* you enter the ring.

❖ You'll learn how to count the points your dog earns toward his championship, and how to keep accurate records of your dog's show career.

To supplement all of the above, you'll find FAQs—Frequently Asked Questions—at the end of the book. You'll also find a glossary of dog terms, and list of useful names and addresses.

What this book *doesn't* cover

This book was written for beginners—for people who know nothing about dog shows. There are a number of specialized topics that the book doesn't cover.

This book doesn't cover the acquisition of a potential show dog: we assume that you already have a dog, or have located a breeder from whom you plan to acquire a dog under terms with which you are both comfortable. If you're still searching for a dog, then you should visit dog shows and talk with exhibitors of the breeds that interest you. You should also contact your local kennel club, local and national breed clubs, and the American Kennel Club for referrals to reputable breeders.

This book covers only the judging procedures most frequently encountered when showing dogs—the "90 percent" rule, so to speak. Special circumstances aren't covered; this book focuses on things that apply to *most* breeds. *Breed-specific differences* in how dogs are shown are not addressed. For example,

❖ German Shepherd Dogs are posed differently than any other breed. Posing a German Shepherd isn't covered in this book.

❖ The spunky temperament of terriers is often displayed in the ring by having the dogs "spar" with each other, but since sparring is limited to terriers, it's not covered in this book.

In sparring, terriers are allowed to face each other and make eye contact, giving them the opportunity to challenge each other.

The procedures, rules, and methods we describe cover *only* the situations commonly encountered when exhibiting *most* breeds of dogs at conformation shows.

Similarly, grooming and grooming equipment are beyond the scope of this book, since grooming requirements vary among breeds. Proper grooming of your dog for the show ring should be learned from people who show your breed of dog, or from books and videotapes about grooming for the show ring.

Other quirks of this book

Where are the little dogs and the hairy dogs? Lots of pictures are used in this book to illustrate the basic dog showing skills (gaiting, stacking, and having your dog stand for a judge's examination). For lessons that require detailed pictures, medium or large, smooth coated dogs were photographed because they photograph well and because their short coats don't obscure the detailed points of the lesson. Everything said here, though, applies to small breeds and long-coated breeds, too.

Male or female? Throughout the book people are referred to as both "him" and "her" since this is a sport enjoyed by both men and women. With dogs, it's a little more complicated. When gender doesn't matter, "dog" can mean an animal of either sex, but when the gender of the animal is important, "dog" means male and "bitch" means female.

AKC? There are a number of kennel clubs in the United States but the vast majority of shows are conducted under the rules of the American Kennel Club (AKC). While the handling skills taught in this book are used at all dog shows, this book focuses on the rules and regulations of dog shows held under the auspices of the AKC.

It's hard to decide who is happier: the handler or the Standard Poodle!

Attitude is everything! A good show dog must be a happy dog. The training techniques presented in this book all use praise, encouragement, and reward– *never* punishment. Training is a slow process, and you must have the patience to take small, incremental steps, building your puppy's skills gradually on a solid foundation. Your ultimate goal is to have a happy dog that is thrilled to be in the show ring.

This is a great book *but*.... You should look for coaching and mentoring from other people to supplement what you learn from this book. For example, you may be able to get help from your dog's breeder, from members of your local kennel club, at handling classes, and from other people who show dogs. You can't learn how to show a dog just by reading a book: you also need to get "hands-on" experience.

Summary

There's so much to learn and enjoy about showing dogs!

Showing dogs may seem daunting at first, but once you've learned the ropes, you'll find showing dogs is fun and rewarding. Of course, there *is* a lot to juggle: you have to learn how to train your dog, you have to learn your role as a handler, and you have to understand the ins and outs of how a dog show works. But if you take it a step at a time, with this book to guide you along the way, you'll master the world of dog showing and avoid many of the errors and pitfalls that can discourage novice handlers.

Ask seasoned veterans of the dog show world, and most can name the first dog with which they earned a championship, even if it was long ago and subsequent dogs have blurred in their minds. Turning your first show dog into a champion is a rewarding, exciting, and memorable experience!

Dog showing should be an activity that *you* enjoy, that *your dog* enjoys, and that the two of you enjoy doing *together*.

<table>
<tr><td>

Chapter

2

</td><td>

Understanding Your Goal

</td></tr>
</table>

Showing your dog successfully requires a clear understanding of what happens at a dog show. In this chapter you'll get an overview of how a dog show works, learn what to look for when you attend a dog show, and how to set realistic goals.

The American Kennel Club

The American Kennel Club, headquartered in New York City, is virtually synonymous with "dog show" in the United States. Every year, dog events conducted under the rules of the AKC are televised to tens of thousands of viewers, both in the USA and abroad.

The AKC was founded to provide a registry of purebred dogs and to "sanction dog events that promote interest in, and sustain the process of, breeding for type and function of purebred dogs." In addition to registering dogs and sanctioning competitions, the AKC supports other activities that affect dogs and their owners, including monitoring state and national legislation, and conducting a public education campaign about responsible dog ownership.

The AKC sanctions more than 10,000 dog events each year, including obedience trials, agility trials, hunting tests and dog shows. In 2000, more than 3,400 dog shows were held under the rules of the AKC, and more than 20,000 dogs earned the title, "Champion." More than 4,000 affiliated clubs participate in the activities of the AKC.

Since the first purebred dog was registered by the AKC in 1878 (an English Setter named "Adonis"), the AKC has registered more than 35 million purebred dogs, and annual registrations top the one

In addition to promoting dog sports and supporting the breeding of purebred dogs, the AKC conducts major public education activities.

GROUP	DESCRIPTION	EXAMPLES
Sporting	Used to hunt land and water game birds	• Pointer • Irish Setter • Labrador Retriever • Cocker Spaniel
Hound	Used to hunt game by sight and scent	• Afghan Hound • Beagle • Greyhound • Whippet
Working	Used for guarding, pulling carts, and search and rescue	• Doberman Pinscher • Great Dane • St. Bernard • Siberian Husky
Terrier	Originally used for hunting vermin and, in the case of some of the larger terriers, for hunting game	• Airedale Terrier • Fox Terrier • Scottish Terrier • American Staffordshire Terrier
Toy	Bred to be companions valued for their small size	• Chihuahua • Papillon • Pug • Toy Poodle
Non-Sporting	A collection of breeds that do not neatly fit into the definitions of the other Groups	• Bulldog • Dalmatian • Lhasa Apso • Standard Poodle
Herding	Used to herd livestock	• Collie • German Shepherd Dog • Old English Sheepdog • Pembroke Welsh Corgi

Figure: Description of and examples from each of the seven AKC Groups.

million mark. The AKC now recognizes more than 150 breeds; new breeds are regularly added to the AKC's list. For example, Jack Russell Terriers became eligible for registration by the AKC in 1997. Border Collies became eligible for registration in 1995.

Breeds that are fully recognized by the AKC are assigned to one of seven Groups. The seven Groups are Sporting, Hound, Working, Terrier, Toy, Non-Sporting and Herding. The Groups—except for the Non-Sporting Group—are based on the original use for the breed of dog or on the breed's current function. For example, Dalmatians were historically bred to work with horse-drawn carriages, as "coaching dogs," but are now in the Non-Sporting Group.

How a Dog Show Works

A dog show is like a large "single elimination" tournament, in which a dog keeps competing until he is defeated. He must win during the current round of competition in order to progress to the next round of competition. The goal is to be the only dog in the show not defeated by another dog during the show, and therefore win the top honor: Best in Show.

At an all-breed dog show, there are three rounds of competition, starting with individual breed judging (several breeds are judged simultaneously, each in a different ring by a different judge), followed by the judging of the seven Groups (one Group at a time), and ending with the competition for Best in Show.

At each stage of the competition, dogs are judged against each other and against their breed's "standard": the official description of the perfect specimen of the breed. Thus, the question that the Standard Poodle judge asks himself is, "Does this Standard Poodle match the breed standard more closely than the other Standard Poodles here?"

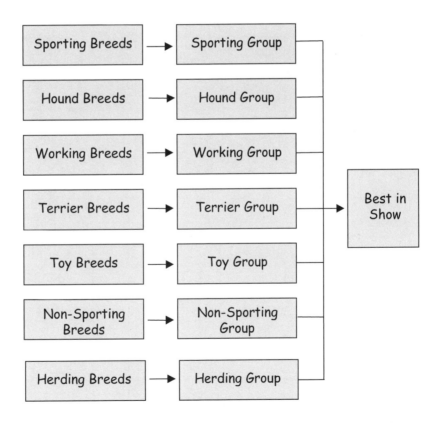

Figure: The progression of judging from individual breeds through Best in Show.

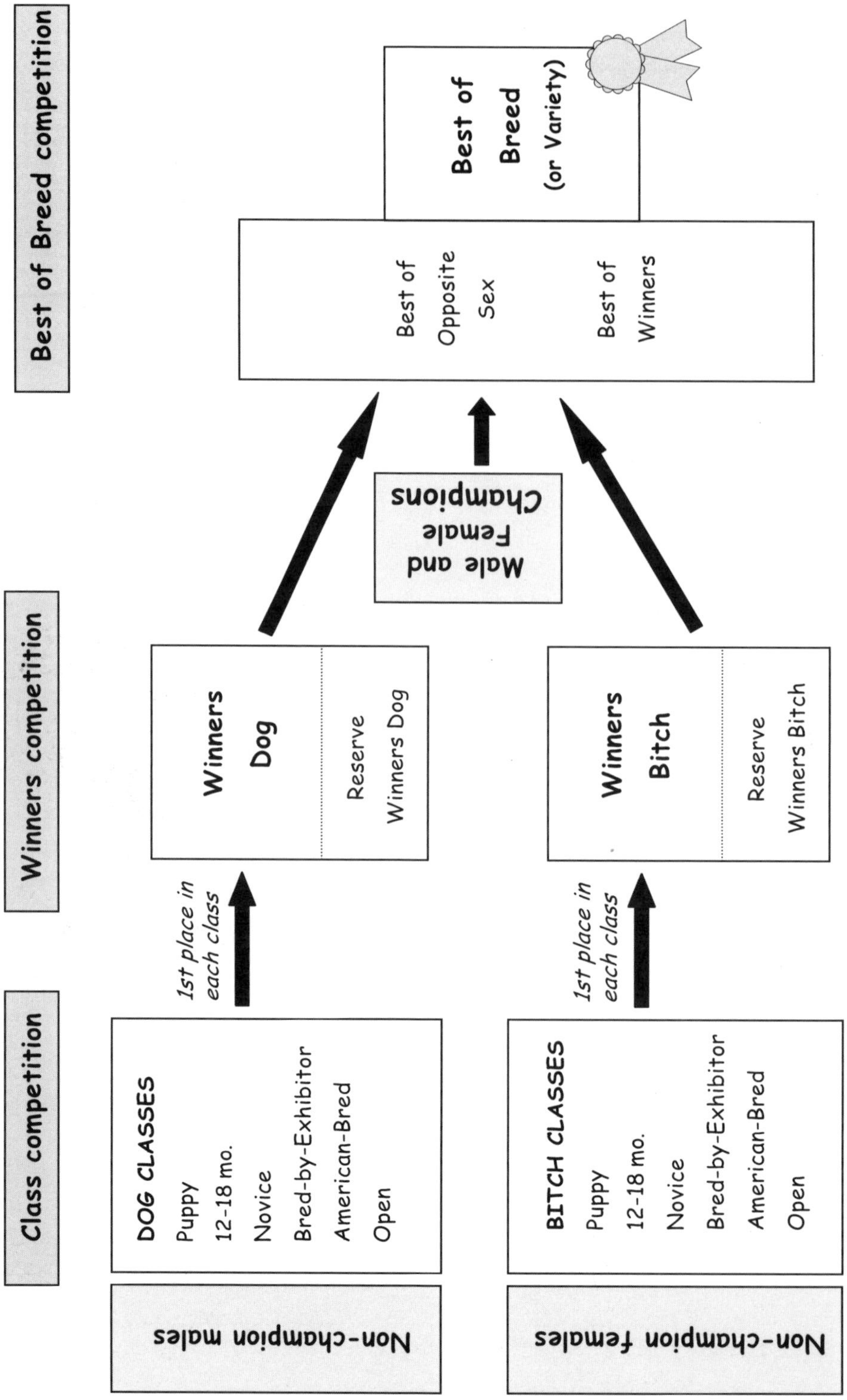

Best of Breed competition

Best of Breed (or Variety)

Best of Opposite Sex

Best of Winners

Male and Female Champions

Winners competition

Winners Dog

Reserve Winners Dog

Winners Bitch

Reserve Winners Bitch

1st place in each class

1st place in each class

Class competition

DOG CLASSES
Puppy
12-18 mo.
Novice
Bred-by-Exhibitor
American-Bred
Open

BITCH CLASSES
Puppy
12-18 mo.
Novice
Bred-by-Exhibitor
American-Bred
Open

Non-champion males

Non-champion females

Figure: Classes at the breed level of competition.

Breed or Variety competition

All dogs entered in a show—both champion and non-champion—must start at the breed level of competition, competing against dogs of their own breed.

Non-champion dogs compete at the breed level for points toward their championships. All of the dogs in the breed competition vie to be selected as Best of Breed. For example, among all the Rottweilers entered in the show, one is chosen as the best Rottweiler at the show—the Best of Breed. Either a champion or a non-champion may be selected as Best of Breed.

Some breeds are divided into "Varieties," which are judged separately, as though they were different breeds. For example, Collies have two varieties: Smooth Coated and Rough Coated. Two "Best of Variety" Collies are chosen: the best smooth-coated Collie and the best rough-coated Collie.

During breed judging, each dog is entered in *one* of several classes offered for non-champions; non-champion males and females are judged separately. The classes at a show are:

- ❖ Puppy (sometimes divided into classes for 6-9 month old puppies and 9-12 months old puppies)

- ❖ 12-to-18-Months

- ❖ Novice

- ❖ Bred-by-Exhibitor

- ❖ American-Bred

- ❖ Open

In the Puppy classes, puppies are judged against other dogs of the same breed at the same level of maturity.

In each breed, the non-champion male classes are judged first: Puppy, 12-to-18-Month, Novice, Bred-by-Exhibitor, American-Bred, and Open. The judge awards first through fourth place to dogs in each class.

Next, the first place winner of each class for males competes in the "Winners" class. One of these males is selected as "Winners Dog," who is the best non-champion male—the best among the first place winners. The Winners Dog earns points towards his championship, and continues to the next stage in breed competition. A runner-up, the "Reserve Winners Dog" is also chosen.

After the Winners Dog has been selected, the non-champion female classes are judged. The first place class winners then compete in the female Winners class to be named the

Winners Bitch, who earns points toward her championship and, along with the Winners Dog, proceeds to the next stage of competition. A Reserve Winners Bitch is also named.

In the next step of breed judging—the Best of Breed competition—the Winners Dog and Winners Bitch compete against the male and female champions to win Best of Breed (or Variety). A champion, Winners Dog, or Winners Bitch may be selected as "Best of Breed," which ends the competition at the breed level.

Two other awards are made during the Best of Breed competition: "Best of Opposite Sex" (if the Best of Breed is a male, then the Best of Opposite Sex is the best female, and vice versa), and "Best of Winners" (the better of Winners Dog and Winners Bitch).

The Best of Breed or Best of Variety winner continues to the next level of competition: the Group.

In breed competition, all dogs in the ring are the same breed and sex, except during Best of Breed class, which has both males and females.

Group competition

In the Group level of competition, each of the seven Groups is judged separately. For example, all Terrier Best of Breed winners are judged as a Group, all Toy Best of Breed winners are judged as a Group and so on. Within each group, the judge selects first through fourth place winners. Only the first place dog—the Group winner—advances to the final level of competition: Best in Show.

How does the judge make his decision when he is faced with as many as 25 different Terrier breeds in the Terrier Group, ranging from the large and noble Airedale Terrier to the small and spunky Smooth Fox Terrier?

After each breed in a Group is judged, the Best of Breed winners compete against each other in Group competition. Here the Working Group is being judged.

The judge compares each Best of Breed winner against the description of the ideal specimen of the breed, given in the breed's standard. Thus, the decision the judge makes during Group judging is whether the Best of Breed Airedale Terrier is closer to the "perfect" Airedale Terrier than the Best of Breed Smooth Fox Terrier is to the "perfect" Smooth Fox Terrier. The dog that is the closest to the standard of its breed is the Group winner.

Best in Show competition

Best in Show judging, the final event of the dog show, occurs late in the day after all of the Groups have been judged. Unlike the Group competition, in which first through fourth places are awarded, only one award is made during Best in Show judging: one dog is named Best in Show.

At most shows, the Group-winning dogs—the dogs competing for Best in Show—are top national competitors: exquisitely groomed, in peak physical condition and impeccably trained. They are outstanding representatives of their breeds.

How can the judge pick a Best in Show winner when faced with seven amazingly different and superb dogs? How can he decide between the Chihuahua and the Saint Bernard? Or between the Bloodhound and the Scottish Terrier? As during the Group competition, the judge compares each of the seven dogs to its breed standard, and picks the dog that is closest to the perfect example of its breed as the Best in Show winner.

In the Best in Show competition, the winner of each of the seven Groups—Sporting, Hound, Working, Terrier, Toy, Non-Sporting and Herding—competes for the top show honor.

Go to a Dog Show

Dog shows are usually held on weekends, although you may occasionally find weekday shows. A dog show usually lasts one day (however, there are a few two days shows). The logistic and business aspects of a show are carried out by companies—"dog show superintendents"—with whom the kennel club contracts for services.

There are several ways to locate a dog show near you:

❖ Your local kennel club may be able to direct you to a show in your area.

❖ The AKC's Web site (www.akc.org) has a current schedule of shows all over the country.

❖ Contact a show superintendent in your area and ask about upcoming shows, or search the superintendent's Web site for a schedule of shows (a list of superintendents is given at the back of this book).

Show logistics

Dog shows usually last all day. Breed judging takes place in the morning and early afternoon, starting between 8:00 and 9:00 a.m. Group judging usually starts in the early or mid-afternoon. Best in Show judging occurs in the late afternoon, after all seven of the Groups have been judged.

The show's judging schedule—the time each breed will be judged—is available about a week before the show. Contact the show's superintendent or check the superintendent's Web site for the show's judging schedule. If you can't get the schedule before the show, then arrive at the show early and pick up a judging schedule at the superintendent's desk, which is the command center of the show. The people there can help you locate the breeds you want to watch. There may also be an education booth near the superintendent's desk with information about dog events, dog care, training classes, local clubs, and upcoming shows.

Allow plenty of time at the show to observe everything. Leave your dog at home so that you can concentrate on the show.

Characteristics of the show

The number of breeds eligible to be entered at a show determines whether the show is an "all-breed" show or a "specialty"show. In an all-breed show, the most common form of dog show, all breeds recognized by the AKC are allowed to enter. As many as 150 different breeds may be present. A specialty show is an AKC-approved show in which the breeds that may be exhibited are limited, most often to one breed, or to the breeds in one group, such as Terriers.

At benched shows, exhibitors often decorate their benches in a theme appropriate to their breed. The bench for these Pharaoh Hounds is decorated with an Ancient Egyptian motif.

A dog show may be either "benched" or "unbenched." At *unbenched* shows the dogs are required to be present on the show grounds only while they are being judged. After they have been judged, they may leave. At *benched* shows the dogs are required to stay at the show all day in a designated spot (on their benches) so that the public may find and view the dogs at their leisure. Years ago many shows were benched but today only a handful remain.

Outdoor shows take place rain or shine, but are usually held in months with good weather.

Indoor shows take place year-round in heated or air-conditioned facilities.

Dog shows may be held indoors or outdoors. The variation among show sites is tremendous, ranging from urban convention centers, college stadiums, city parks, and recreation centers to county fairgrounds and rodeo arenas. The climate, time of year, show size, and availability of facilities all play a part in show site selection.

What to look for

As you wander around the show, talk to people and ask questions. Most dog show exhibitors are happy to explain what's going on and to answer questions about their breed. However, be careful about *when* you ask your questions. Don't interrupt exhibitors when they are about to go into the ring or are rushing to get their dogs ready. *Always* ask if it's a good time to talk.

As you watch the judging, there are several things you should look for:

Equipment

- What types of leads and collars are used for breeds that you're watching?
- How long is the lead?
- What is the lead made of: leather, nylon, braided cotton? How about the collar?
- Does the handler carry small toys or bits of food to keep the dog alert?

Grooming

- How is your breed groomed for the show ring?
- Is there a special area where the handlers do their pre-ring grooming?
- Are the dogs brushed in the ring while the judge is busy watching another dog?
- Where do the handlers carry their brushes or combs?

Presentation

- Does the handler place the dog's legs into position, or are the dogs shown standing naturally?
- Is the tail held in place or left free?
- Do the handlers stand or kneel when they pose their dogs?
- When the judge examines the dog, does the dog stand on the ground or on a table?

Movement

- How quickly do the dogs move? Do they walk or trot?
- How quickly do the handlers move? Do they walk or run?
- Does the dog move by the handler's side or ahead of the handler?
- How much space is there between the dogs when they move together?

The Three Basic Skills

As you watch the judging, you'll notice that there are three basic skills that are used over and over in the ring: gaiting (moving), stacking (standing in a formal pose), and standing still for the judge's examination.

Stacking. Dogs are posed for the judge as a group when they enter the ring, individually as the judge examines them, and as a group when he makes his final decisions.

Your dog must learn to stand perfectly still in a show pose, and you must learn how to pose him so he looks his best.

Gaiting. Dogs are moved in the show ring individually and as a group, at a pace appropriate for that breed.

You and your dog must learn how to gait properly, both alone and then as part of a group of dogs.

Being Examined. Every dog is examined by the judge, who uses his hands as well as his eyes to assess the structure of the dog. During the exam, the dog must stand perfectly still, and must not display any aggression or fear toward the judge.

You and your dog must learn how to behave during the judge's examination.

Setting Your Goals

Where do you and your dog—both complete beginners—fit into this picture?

While your dream may be for your dog to win Best in Show at the Westminster Kennel Club Show, your more immediate goals should be less ambitious, and should build upon each other in a logical sequence that can lead to your ultimate goal.

Your first goals are to learn how to show a dog, and to train your puppy to be a show dog. That's the focus of this book, which teaches you what you'll need to know to reach these goals.

When you've taught your puppy the three basic skills, and when you feel confident that you know your own role in the show ring, it will be time to show your dog. A logical progression of goals for you and your dog is:

❖   to win your class

❖   to win your Winners class, and earn points towards a championship

❖   to earn enough points that your dog becomes a champion

Your dog won't become a champion overnight, but if you set your goals realistically so that you don't get frustrated or discouraged, then in the long run, you'll succeed.

Summary

In the United States, most dog shows are run under the auspices of the American Kennel Club. These shows are large, single elimination tournaments, in which dogs progress through three rounds of judging, from individual breeds, through the seven Group, and finally to the Best in Show competition.

Dog showing involves three basic skills: gaiting (moving) your dog, stacking (posing) your dog, and presenting your dog for the judge's examination. All the actions in the ring are based on these three building blocks, and they form the foundation of every show dog's training.

Set your goals realistically. When you and your dog have learned the rules of showing dogs, have mastered the three basic skills—gaiting, stacking and being examined—and can confidently pull it together into a smooth show-ring routine, you'll be ready to launch into showing your dog, secure that you've got the skills and knowledge you'll need to be successful in the show ring.

<table>
<tr><td>Chapter
3</td><td># Getting Started</td></tr>
</table>

There are many things that you can do right away to start your adventure in dog showing. Even if you don't have your show puppy yet, there's a lot to do. In this chapter, you'll learn about socializing your puppy, selecting and using the right lead and collar for showing your dog, getting on mailing lists for show announcements, and finding resources that you can use to explore dog showing.

Socialize, Socialize, Socialize!

Can you imagine a successful show dog that cowers by his handler, shaking like a leaf, or who won't let the judge do a hands-on examination, or that is aggressive toward or scared of other dogs? A dog that isn't well-socialized—accustomed to a variety of places, sounds, smells and people—simply *cannot* be a successful show dog.

A successful show dog must be able to cope with:

❖ *Strange places*. Shows can be indoors or outdoors, in crowded gymnasiums with slick floors or in echoing convention centers, on college campuses or in rodeo arenas.

❖ *Strange noises.* Public address systems blare and squawk, crates and exercise pens crash as they are folded up, and dogs bark and howl.

❖ *Strange people*. Judges and ring stewards come in all shapes and sizes, as do other exhibitors and spectators.

❖ *Strange dogs*. In the ring and ringside, a show dog is very close to other dogs, which may be much larger, smaller or more dominant than he is.

Your first task as a dog exhibitor and as a responsible dog owner is to socialize your dog so that he can cope with crowds, noise, and unfamiliar people and dogs. Socializing your puppy should be a high priority *early* in your dog's life so he becomes a companion that you will enjoy every day, long after his show career is over.

There are all sorts of opportunities for socializing your puppy, *when he has had his vaccinations*.

❖ Take your puppy to a "puppy kindergarten" class so that he can socialize with strange dogs his own age in a controlled environment. (However, be *very* careful if you take your puppy or dog to a public dog park—you don't know which of the other dogs might be aggressive or might not be vaccinated.)

A puppy kindergarten class is a good place to socialize your puppy in a safe, controlled environment.

❖ If your dog is too old for puppy kindergarten, take him to an obedience class—one taught with positive reinforcement rather than punishment—so that your dog learns to be relaxed and comfortable around other dogs and to pay attention to you when other dogs are present.

❖ Take your dog to youth soccer games and other sporting events, and let people pet him. Be careful, however, that small children don't scare your puppy with abrupt movements or rough petting.

❖ Take your puppy to pet stores. They generally welcome four-footed customers, and they have wonderfully strange sounds and smells. Your puppy is also likely to encounter other dogs in the non-threatening environment of the store.

❖ Walk your puppy downtown or at a shopping mall, and let strangers pet him. If he's a little shy, give a stranger a treat to feed to your puppy while petting him.

❖ If you can find a class for your dog—obedience, tricks, conformation—that meets *indoors*, grab the opportunity to introduce your dog to "indoor" show conditions.

If you don't have your puppy yet, start planning ahead for his arrival by looking for opportunities to socialize him, investigating puppy kindergarten and training classes, and getting on class waiting lists if necessary.

In any socializing activity, the goal is to make the experience a happy one for you and your dog. You cannot over-socialize a dog—and socializing your puppy is a great way to have fun with your dog!

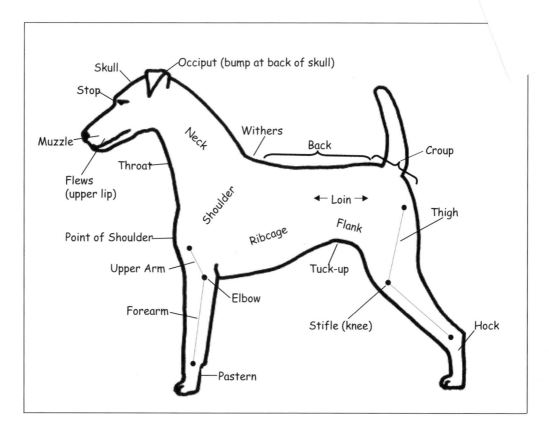

Figure: The basic parts of a dog, with terminology commonly found in breed standards.

Your Breed's Standard

Before you begin showing your dog, you should read and understand the *standard* for your breed. A breed's standard describes the *ideal* specimen of a breed, giving a detailed description of the size, coat, color, temperament, gait, and so on. A breed's standard is used by dog show judges as the benchmark against which to evaluate dogs.

The Complete Dog Book, published by the American Kennel Club, contains the official standard for all AKC recognized breeds and varieties. Breed standards are also available on the AKC's Web site. *The Complete Dog Book* can be purchased at or ordered from most major bookstores or ordered directly from the AKC.

In order to understand a breed standard, you will need to learn some basic dog anatomy. For example, you will find terms like "stifle," "croup," and "pastern" in breed standards. Many of the words encountered in breed standards are defined in the glossary of this book or in *The Complete Dog Book*.

If possible, discuss your breed's standard with dog's breeder. You may also wish to purchase the AKC video for your breed to help you learn the breed standard. Make sure that you understand the standard, and that you begin to develop a picture in your mind of the *perfect* specimen of your breed.

In addition to describing the perfect specimen of each breed, the breed standard also lists characteristics that disqualify a dog from being eligible to show, such as a Bull Terrier with blue eyes, or a Dalmatian with both black and brown spots, or a Rhodesian Ridgeback without a ridge. You should know the disqualifying faults for your breed, and make sure that your puppy is free of such faults.

Equipment

Dog showing involves all sorts of equipment: grooming tools, tables, crates, exercise pens, and more. Much of this equipment is breed-specific. For example, Dalmatian owners don't need a heavy-duty hair dryer or a collection of brushes and combs, but these are absolutely necessary for Poodle owners. This book focuses on the basic equipment needed by *every* breed: leads, collars, and bait.

Leads

All dogs are shown wearing a lead and a collar, which may be separate items or an "all-in-one" unit. There are several collar and lead styles. Consult your mentor about the type of lead that is generally used with your breed, or pay close attention as you watch your breed being shown.

You'll have several choices to make about material, weight, and length of your lead. Vendors at dog show sell a wide variety of lead types.

A show lead can be made of leather, waxed cotton, or nylon. It is important that the material be flexible and can be easily gathered into a ball small enough to hold comfortably in your hand. The lead should be as thin as will *safely* hold your dog if he spooks. Never use a lead made of chain. Try several materials until you find one that you like.

A lightweight white lead and collar are a very good choice for showing this French Bulldog; the lead's weight and color do not detract from the dog.

The lead's snap should be as small as possible to do the job–not a large piece of hardware. The lead's color should be compatible with the color of your dog: if you have a black Labrador Retriever, use a black lead, not a red one! The lead should "vanish" from the judge's eye, not leap out at him. Black, brown, or white are good choices for most breeds.

Your lead should be short enough that, when wadded up, it makes a small ball that fits easily in your closed hand. The lead should be long enough so your dog can move beside you at a trot: with a little slack in the lead when your dog is slightly ahead of you. Leads about four feet long are good for medium and large dogs, while longer leads are used for smaller dogs. If your lead is longer than you need, simply trim it to make it shorter.

This Dalmatian is shown using a black nylon slip collar and a black lead with a small snap.

Collars

There are three basic types of collars used in conformation showing. Some collars are separate from leads, and some are combined into a single lead-and-collar unit. Always use a collar that blends with the color of your dog. Depending on the style of the collar, you may need to buy several collars before your puppy becomes an adult. Don't buy an adult-size collar for a puppy; it won't fit properly and will thwart your training efforts.

Martingale. A martingale can either be a separate martingale collar plus a lead, or an "all-in-one" unit. "Martingale" refers to the collar style. The martingale collar has two loops. The larger loop almost completely circles the dog's neck and the smaller loop creates a bridge across the rings of the larger loop. The smaller loop attaches to the lead (or is one piece with the lead). A martingale is used with sight hounds, such as Borzois, and with well-trained dogs requiring little collar control.

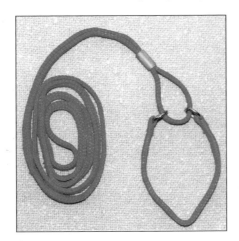

This all-in-one martingale combines the martingale collar and the lead into a single piece of equipment.

The large loop of the martingale collar is placed over the Saluki's head. The small loop creates the tightening/releasing action.

Noose. The one-piece noose is a combination collar and lead. The collar portion is held in place by a small slide or slip lock. The size of the collar is adjusted by placing the noose around the dog's neck and sliding the lock towards the dog's head. A noose is frequently used with setters, spaniels, and small breeds.

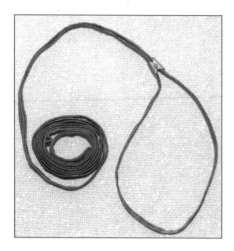

The one-piece noose lead has a "collar" that is made larger or smaller by moving the clip. This collar has no slip action.

The noose collar is worn up high on this Longhaired Dachshund's neck, behind her ear, and is adjusted to give the collar a bit of ease.

Slip collar. The slip collar is commonly used for medium and large breeds because it gives the handler more control of a dog than does a martingale or a noose.

Slip collars may be made of metal, nylon, or leather. If you choose a metal collar, select one with small oval links that are heavy enough to hold the dog but are not large and clunky, and which move smoothly as the collar tightens and releases. The collar should fit easily, but not sloppily, over the dog's head. Your mentor or an equipment vendor at a dog show can help you select a slip collar that fits your dog correctly.

There's a right way and a wrong way to put on a slip collar. In fact, a slip collar is sometimes called a "choke" collar because, when it is put on incorrectly, it chokes the dog. When it is put on correctly, the slip collar can tighten and release quickly and does *not* choke the dog.

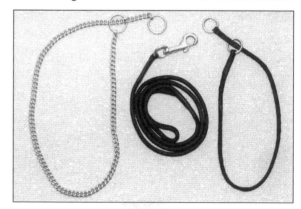

Slip collars can be made of fine metal links or nylon. The lead is attached to the collar with a *small* bridle snap.

To put on the collar correctly, remember the phrase, "P is for puppy." Hold the collar in front of you and make a "P" with the collar. Stand facing your dog, and put the loop of the "P" over your dog's head. When you stand on your dog's right side (so he's on your left), the ring attached to the lead will be near his right ear. If, however, you put the collar on *backwards*, the lead ring will come up from under his chin.

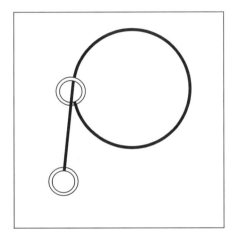

The first step in putting a slip collar on correctly is to form a "P is for Puppy" with the collar as you stand facing your dog.

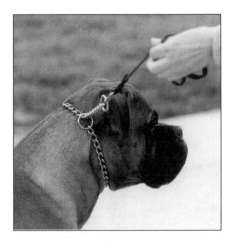

When the loop of the "P" is placed over your dog's head, the moving end should pass over his neck when he stands on your left side.

Bait

Bait is used to keep the dog's attention in the ring and to reward good behavior. Bait may either be a small piece of food or a small toy. Since bait is carried in the handler's pocket, it can't be messy or crumbly food or a large toy.

The type of bait you use will depend on what works best with your dog. Some dogs will react only to food, while others react to toys. Some are equally keen on either. Experiment to see what type of bait gives you the *controlled* behavior you want from your dog.

This Irish Terrier is very alert and focused on the small piece of bait that his handler is holding.

Some foods commonly used for bait include roast chicken, hot dog slices, cubes of cheese and soft dog treats. Many people bake beef liver with garlic powder until the liver is slightly dried and rubbery. Some show vendors sell cooked liver to use for bait at show. Actually, any food can be used as bait as long as your dog likes it and it can be chewed and swallowed quickly.

Handling a Lead

Before you begin training your dog, you need to learn how to handle a show lead. A correctly handled lead should never be noticed when your dog is shown; it shouldn't distract the judge's attention from the dog, either because it gets in the dog's way or because the handler fumbles with it. You need to learn to bundle up and let out your lead quickly with small movements of your hand and arm, so that you're always working with the most appropriate amount of lead.

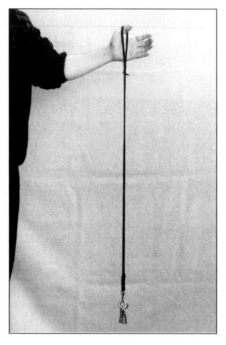

Your starting point: your lead fully extended with a weight on the end.

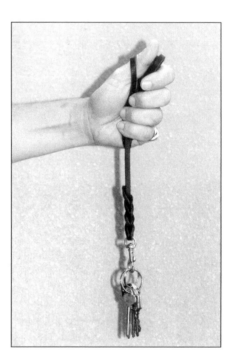

Your goal: the lead neatly folded in your palm.

For this exercise, you'll need your show lead (or lead and collar unit, if they're combined) and a weight, like a set of keys. Attach the weight to your lead, either by using the snap or by tying the collar portion of your combination lead and collar to the weight.

Start with your show lead dangling its full length from your *left* hand, as though your dog were at the end of his lead. Gather the lead up into your hand using only a rocking motion of your left hand–sort of a back-and-forth wrist motion. It's awkward at first, but with practice you'll learn to do it easily and quickly.

You'll have to tinker with the exercise, experimenting with which fingers to use to anchor the lead, figuring out how to wiggle your index finger loose, and deciding how tightly to loop and anchor each lead fold. Figure out what's comfortable for you. If your show lead is new and stiff, the exercise will be more difficult, but this is a great way to break in your new lead so that it becomes soft and pliable.

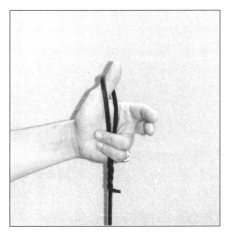

1. Put the lead loop over your left thumb. Fold one or two fingers over your lead to anchor it.

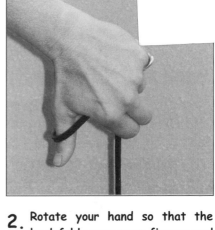

2. Rotate your hand so that the lead folds over your fingers and your thumb points down.

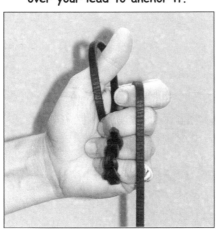

3. Anchor the lead with your index finger. Rotate your hand back to its starting position.

4. Wiggle your fingers free so that you hold three folds of the lead in your fist.

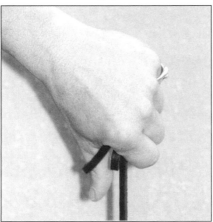

5. Flip your hand over, and again anchor the lead with your index finger.

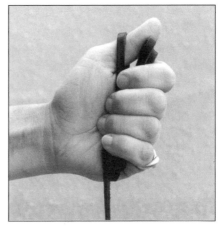

6. Turn you hand back upright and wiggle your index finger free. You now have five folds of the lead in your hand.

Practice bundling up and letting out your lead until you can do it very quickly. Carry your lead in your pocket and practice this exercise in odd snatches of time—while waiting in a line, for example, or taking a coffee break, watching TV, or walking around your neighborhood. The neighbors may think you're a bit strange as you play with a lead and an "invisible dog", but it's worth it: you're learning a valuable skill in your spare time.

Learning More

There are lots of resources available to help you learn about dog shows and showing your own dog. You should take advantage of as many of them as you can since you'll learn different aspects of the sport from each resource.

Publications

You can't learn to handle a dog by just reading, but books serve as invaluable supplements to handling classes and discussions with knowledgeable dog show exhibitors and breeders. This book will be your introductory handbook about showing dogs. As your skills improve, you'll undoubtedly acquire more advanced books on dog showing; several excellent books are available.

The American Kennel Club publishes two monthly magazines which contain articles about dog sports and a calendar of upcoming events.

The AKC publishes a monthly magazine, *The AKC Gazette*, which contains a wealth of information about showing dogs, news about changes to AKC rules, veterinary information, training tips, and breed news. Included with a subscription to *The AKC Gazette* is a supplemental magazine, *The AKC Events Calendar*, which lists upcoming conformation shows and other dog-related events throughout the country, and is very helpful in planning which shows you wish to attend.

A number of very useful publications are available from the AKC at no charge. You should order a copy of each of the following:

❖ *Rules Applying to Dog Shows*

❖ *Match Regulations*

❖ *Purebred Dog—General Information Booklet*

❖ *You, the AKC and the World of Purebred Dogs*

❖ *Rules for Registration and Discipline*

To purchase *The Complete Dog Book*, to subscribe to *The AKC Gazette*, or to request free publications, contact the AKC by mail, e-mail, or phone at:

AKC Order Desk
5580 Centerview Drive
Raleigh, NC 27606-3390
e-mail: orderdesk@akc.org
(919) 233-9767

Handling classes

At conformation handling classes *you* learn how to handle a dog in the show ring, and *your dog* gets experience practicing with other dogs and people. You should try to supplement what you learn from this book by taking a handling class.

Many kennel clubs offer handling classes to their members and to the public. Contact the AKC by mail, phone, or the Internet for help locating the kennel club nearest you.

Many obedience training clubs offer conformation handling classes in addition to obedience and puppy kindergarten classes. Again, the AKC can help you locate obedience training clubs in your area.

Finally, non-AKC affiliated groups, such as obedience schools and boarding/training kennels, may offer handling classes. Consult the yellow pages for your area, call the Humane Society, and check with local pet supply stores for tips on finding classes.

At a handling class, you will learn how to train your dog for the ring. You'll also learn the skills *you* need to show your dog.

Before you sign up for a class, observe a session or two if possible to assess the class size and format, how the class is conducted, and whether you'd be comfortable in it. Find out whether the class is structured (a lesson planned for each week over, for example, an eight week session) or if it is a ring practice session with little or no instruction.

❖ Find a class in which the instructor will teach you *and* your dog so you can both acquire the skills you'll need in the ring. Unless you find a class specifically designed for beginners, there may be a wide variety of skill and experience levels in the class. Don't be discouraged—just make sure the instructor is willing to accept *and teach* complete beginners in a mixed-experience class.

❖ Find an instructor who has experience showing your breed or similar breeds, knows the rules governing dog shows, and has the ability to teach you the skills you'll need in the show ring. For example, if you have a toy breed, make sure the instructor knows how to exhibit small dogs.

❖ Find a class where there is a *positive* approach toward training dogs using encouragement and rewards. Remember: attitude is everything in a show dog!

Before signing up for any class, discuss your goals with the instructor, if possible, so that the instructor understands what you need and you understand what the instructor is offering.

Mentors

A mentor is a well-informed person who is willing to instruct and advise you as you enter the world of dog showing. A mentor can be a person who has experience with your breed (for example, the breeder of your dog or another person who shows your breed) or an experienced exhibitor of other breeds (for example, a member of your local kennel club).

You may end up with several mentors. For example, if you show Standard Poodles, you may find one person who will teach you how to groom your dog for the show ring, and another—perhaps with expertise in other breeds—who will be your mentor in the training and showing of your dog.

A mentor can be anyone who is willing to help you learn about one or more aspects of showing dogs.

Clubs

Every breed recognized by the AKC has a national club—such as the Vizsla Club of America—that will be a valuable source of information to you. Most national clubs distribute information packages about their breeds, including a copy of the breed's standard. Many national breed clubs also have web sites, which contain a wealth of information. Contact the AKC or check the AKC's web site for help in locating your national breed club's secretary or web site.

National clubs are also called "parent" clubs because they oversee a network of affiliated local or regional breed clubs. Local breed clubs hold meetings, conduct dog events, and provide educational information to the public. Club members are usually supportive of new dog show enthusiasts. The national club for your dog's breed can help you locate the local breed club in your area.

Televised dog shows

Dog shows are occasionally broadcast on TV, usually on cable channels. The televised version of a dog show reveals only a small part of what occurs at a show, but it will give you the flavor of how dogs are shown. Some television broadcasts also include interviews with judges, exhibitors, and kennel club officials.

The Internet

Start with a visit to the AKC's Web site for a comprehensive view of the world of the purebred dog; the AKC Web site will link you to many other sites. The Web sites of national breed clubs vary from simple to complex. Browse the sites of several breeds; you may find information about dog showing that applies to *all* breeds. Many individuals have wonderful personal Web sites about showing dogs. Use phrases such as "dog show," "show dogs," and "showing dogs" in your Internet search.

Contacting Superintendents

When a kennel club holds a show, it contracts with a "show superintendent" to help run the show. A superintendent is a individual whose company manages the business and logistical aspects of a dog show, including providing information about the show, accepting entries, and supplying rings and equipment.

Contact superintendents who serve your area by calling, writing or visiting their Web sites, and request *premium lists* for upcoming shows near you. A premium list is a brochure that gives information about a show, including its date and location. The premium list also contains the entry form for the show. A list of superintendents can be found at the end of this book.

Your Puppy's Training Plan

When you're ready, you'll need to make a training for teaching your puppy to stack, to gait, and to accept the judge's examination. You *may* teach your puppy to gait and to stack concurrently, but you should teach the skills in separate, short training sessions:

❖ The attention span and stamina of a puppy are short, and if you try to pack too much into a single training session, the puppy will become bored and uncooperative. Several short training sessions each day are better than one long session.

❖ The skills of gaiting and stacking are *opposites*: in one, you ask the puppy to move briskly, and in the other you ask the puppy to be perfectly still. Teach the skills separately until the puppy understands each one, or he will become confused.

Never train a puppy until he is so tired that he quits. Your puppy should look forward to every training session, and each session should end on a happy note.

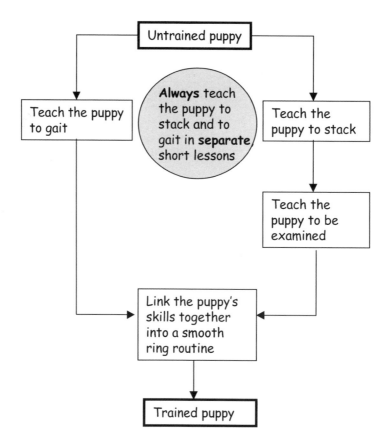

Figure: Flowchart for training a puppy for the show ring.

Summary

It takes time and patience to learn dog showing skills, and lots and lots of practice! But here are plenty of resources available to help you learn to show your dog successfully: this book, the AKC, handling classes, mentors, Web sites, videos, and lots of other publications.

Understanding your breed's standard is an important part of getting started. Read the standard, discuss it with your mentor, or watch the AKC video.

Having the right basic equipment is important to every sport. Make sure that your collar fits your puppy, and expect to buy larger collars, if necessary, as your puppy grows.

The importance of socializing your puppy can't be over emphasized. Socializing your puppy should be fun, and everything you do with your puppy will help build the strong, lasting relationship that you'll build on as you train him to be a show dog.

Chapter 4

The Perfectly Stacked Dog

One of the three basic skills of dog showing is stacking, or posing, a dog. Before you can stack your dog well, you must have a clear picture of your breed when it is perfectly stacked, and you must understand how small changes in a stack can "make or break" the picture. In this chapter, you'll learn to recognize a correctly stacked dog and to identify some common errors in stacking a dog.

The Perfect Stack

[The] neck should be of moderate length and thickness gradually widening towards the shoulders…Shoulders long and sloping well into the back…Back should be short, strong and level….Forelegs should be perfectly straight…elbows should be perpendicular to the body…stifles [should be] well bent, not turned either in or out…hocks [should be] parallel with each other when viewed from behind…the feet should [not] be turned either in or out.

(from the Airedale Terrier standard)

It is the Airedale handler's job to stack his dog so that it looks as much like the perfect Airedale Terrier as possible. He must place the front legs so that the feet are directly under the dog's shoulders, position the rear legs so that the stifles are "well bent," and place the feet so that they point forward, with toes "not turned either in or out."

In this chapter you'll find a series of photographs that illustrate correctly and incorrectly stacked dogs. A description of the change in the dog's position and an explanation of how the changed position affects the stack accompany each picture.

Within each series of photographs, the same breed is used to illustrate correct and incorrect stacks. The contrast is remarkable; slight changes in the stack can render the dog almost unrecognizable. To help you identify the crucial changes in the dog's position, some pictures include graphics illustrating the key differences.

The Correctly Stacked Dog

When a dog stands naturally, his weight is distributed evenly among his four legs, and his feet are placed so that he is comfortable and balanced when he stands. When a dog is correctly stacked, he should also be balanced, with his weight evenly distributed.

When correctly stacked, the dog's front legs are positioned so that a line dropped directly from the shoulder runs straight through the front legs. The rear legs are placed so that the hocks are perpendicular to the ground.

The front legs of the dog are set at the same width as the dog's shoulders. The middle toes on each front foot point straight ahead. The head faces forward.

The rear legs are set slightly wider than the width of the hips so the dog is balanced and stable. The middle toes on each foot point straight ahead.

Stacking Mistakes Visible from the Side

Correct. This dog is correctly stacked, with the rear feet set far enough back so that the hocks are perpendicular to the ground, and so that the dog's weight is distributed evenly among the four legs.

Overstretched. The rear feet are set too far behind the dog so that the hocks are not perpendicular to the ground, and the legs do not bear a balanced share of the dog's weight. The dog's back is no longer level.

Understretched. The rear feet are set too far forward under the dog, so that the hocks are not perpendicular to the ground. The dog's back and croup may appear to be rounded rather than level when the dog is understretched.

Correct. This dog is correctly stacked, with the front legs dropping directly from the shoulders, and the rear legs set so that the hocks are perpendicular to the ground. The dog's weight is evenly distributed among the four legs.

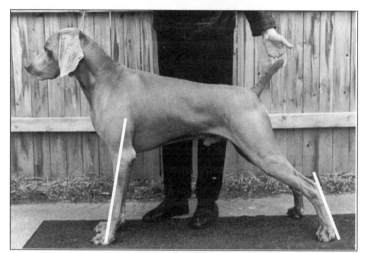

A-framing. Also called "hobby horsing." The front feet are set ahead of a line dropped straight down from the shoulder, and the rear legs are over-stretched, so the dog looks like an "A" with a wider base than top.

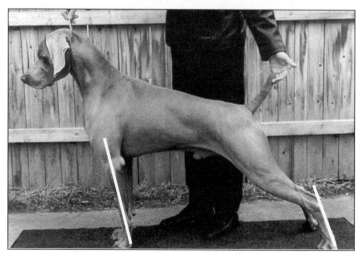

Diving. The front feet are set too far under the body, behind a line dropped from the shoulder. The rear legs are pulled too far back, so that the dog looks as though he is about to dive forward onto his nose.

Stacking Mistakes Visible from the Front

Correct. The legs are set directly under the shoulders with the middle toes of each foot pointing straight ahead.

Too wide. The legs are set wider than the shoulders, giving the impression that the dog is too stocky.

Too narrow. The legs are set narrower than the shoulders, giving the front a "pinched" look and making the dog unstable.

Toes out, elbows in. Also called "east-west." The toes point outward, making the elbows push in and pinch the front.

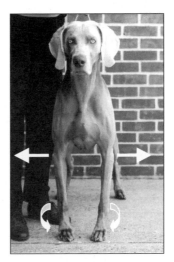

Toes in, elbows out. Also called "toeing in." The toes point inward, making the elbows pop out to the sides.

Stacking Mistakes Visible from the Rear

Correct. The rear feet are set slightly wider than the width of the hips, so the dog is balanced and stable. The middle toes point straight forward.

Set too wide. The rear feet are set much wider than the hips. As a result, the hocks turn inward (cow-hock) and are no longer parallel.

Set too narrow. The rear feet are set directly under, or narrower than, the hips. As a result, the dog's hocks may twist outward, and the dog will be unstable.

Other Mistakes in Foot and Leg Placement

Two types of errors in foot and leg placement have been illustrated:

❖ Setting the dog's front legs ahead of or behind his shoulders, and setting the dog's rear legs so that the hocks are not perpendicular to the ground. These errors result in overstretching, understretching, A-framing, and diving. The opposite of diving is "rocking back" or "bracing", in which the dog's front legs are ahead of his shoulders and his rear legs are understretched.

❖ Setting the dog's feet too wide or too narrow. These errors can actually create the appearance of a structural fault that *is not* present: a pinched front, popping elbows, bow legs or cow hocks.

Another common but less dramatic error in foot placement occurs when the front feet or the back feet are staggered, with one foot slightly ahead of the other. In this case, one of the legs must be incorrectly positioned: either one of the front legs is too far forward or too far back, or one of the hocks isn't perpendicular to the ground. When a dog is correctly stacked, the middle toes of the front legs should point forward and the feet should be aligned; the same is true for the rear feet.

Mistakes in Positioning the Head

Correct. The head is held in a relaxed, neutral position corresponding to the way in which the dog holds his head naturally when he is calm but alert.

Head pulled forward. The line of the neck and the transition into the shoulders becomes poorly defined. If the head is pulled extremely far forward the dog may brace back on his front legs in order to remain balanced.

Head jammed back. The line of the neck into the body forms almost a 90° angle, creating an abrupt transition from the neck to the shoulders. If the head is jammed far back, a break, dip or roll of wrinkled skin may appear over the shoulder.

Summary

When a dog is correctly set, the front legs drop directly from the shoulder, and the feet are centered under the dog's shoulder, set at the same width as the dog's shoulders. The rear legs are pulled back just far enough so that the hocks are perpendicular to the ground, and the feet are set so that they are slightly wider than the width of the dog's hips. The middle toes of the front and back feet face forward. The head is held in a relaxed, neutral position.

You must have a clear image in your mind of how your breed looks when it is correctly stacked. Subtle differences in how the feet of a dog are set, or in how the head of the dog is held, can make monumental differences in the dog's appearance. The difference between a correct stack and an incorrect stack can be a matter of a fraction of an inch. Once you know what a correct stack looks like, and what a correct stack *feels* like as you are setting your dog, you'll be well on your way to being able to stack your dog like a pro.

A correctly stacked dog, with front legs dropping straight from the shoulders, toes pointing forward and rear feet set slightly wider than the hips, is a pleasure to behold.

<table>
<tr><td>Chapter
5</td><td># Stacking a Dog</td></tr>
</table>

When stacking a dog, the handler's job is to make the dog look as much as possible like the ideal described in its breed standard. The actions of the handler must be smooth and efficient so that the judge sees a posed dog every time he looks, not a work in progress. In this chapter, you will learn how to stack a dog quickly and effectively, using the sequence of steps customarily used by handlers.

Overview of Stacking a Dog

When you watch a professional handler stack a dog, it often appears as though he is on auto-pilot; his hands seem to know exactly where to go and what to do, and it takes him only a few seconds to stack his dog. How does he do it?

This handler systematically sets the front legs of his dog, followed by the rear legs.

Once the feet are set, he positions the head and the tail to finish his presentation.

The answer is that he stacks his dog by rote. He has practiced stacking his dog in exactly the same way, thousands of times, one step after another. Thus, when the handler is in the ring, he doesn't have to think, "What do I do next?" He knows, for example, that every time he stacks a dog, he will position, or "set" the left front leg first, using his left hand.

Because he does not have to think about the *mechanics* of stacking his dog, he can concentrate on the subtle details of the stack so that his dog looks its best.

The standard procedure for stacking a dog follows simple rules:

❖ Set both front legs of the dog and then both back legs.

❖ When setting the front legs (or the back legs), set the leg on the judge's side (the dog's left) first, and then set the leg closest to you.

❖ Use your right hand to set the right front leg. Use your left hand for everything else.

These guidelines mean that you will position the dog's legs in the following order:

❖ left front (use your left hand)

❖ right front (use your right hand)

❖ left rear (use your left hand)

❖ right rear (use your left hand)

The front feet should be set directly under the dog's shoulders, so that they are shoulders' width apart. The rear feet should be set so that the hocks are perpendicular to the ground, and the distance between the feet is slightly wider than the hips.

However, stacking a dog isn't just a matter of simply placing the feet in the right order and in the right place. As you stack the dog, you will need to control his head so that he is *always* looking straight ahead, even when you are picking up his rear feet. If the dog can swing his head around to watch you as you set his rear feet, his front feet will be twisted out of position.

Stacking a dog correctly may seem complicated, but fortunately, if you practice setting your dog the same way every time, it becomes second nature, like playing scales on the piano or riding a bicycle. Once you have learned the "feel" of stacking your dog, using the same steps over and over, you will be able to stack your dog very quickly, without having to think about each step in the process.

Stacking a dog by positioning his feet is sometimes called "hand-stacking" or "hard-stacking," to distinguish it from "free-stacking" in which the handler does not place the dog's feet. Instead, in free-stacking, the dogs are presented to the judge standing naturally. Many of the herding breeds are free-stacked rather than hand-stacked. However, free-stacking is beyond the scope of this book since most breeds are presented to the judge hand-stacked.

Stacking a Dog

Step 1. Have your dog on your left side, either on a table or on the ground. Slide the collar up high on your dog's neck, just under his jaw and behind his ears. Having the collar under the jaw and ears allows you to control your dog's head so that he cannot twist out of position.

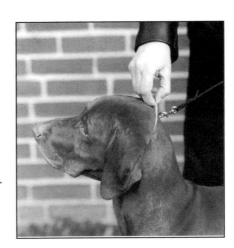

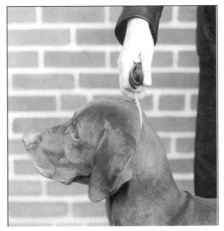

Step 2. Gather the lead in your right hand, or, if your dog is on a table, drape the lead around your neck.

Slip the fingers of your right hand through your dog's collar behind his head, fingers pointing to the rear. The collar should be loose enough that you can easily slip your fingers under it, but snug enough that you can control your dog's head.

Step 3. With your left hand, reach over your dog and grasp the left elbow.

Use your hand to keep the elbow locked. Lean your dog slightly into you, and lift his left foot slightly off the ground.

Set the left foot directly under your dog's shoulder, and put his weight back on the leg.

Be careful that you do not drag your dog's foot as you position it.

Step 4. If you are holding your gathered-up lead in your right hand (rather than draped around your neck), transfer it to your left hand.

Slip the fingers of your left hand under the collar, fingers pointing to the front. Your right hand is now free to set the right front leg.

The right front leg is the *only* leg you set with your right hand. Everything else is set with your left hand.

Step 5. With your right hand, grasp your dog's right elbow. Use your right hand to keep the elbow locked. Push your dog slightly away from you so that his right foot lifts slightly off the ground. Set the right foot directly under his shoulder, and put your dog's weight back on the leg. The feet should be shoulders' width apart.

Step 6. If you are holding your gathered-up lead in your left hand (rather than draped around your neck), transfer it back to your right hand.

Slip the fingers of your right hand back under your dog's collar, fingers pointing to the rear. This frees your left hand to set your dog's rear legs and position his tail.

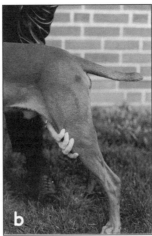

Step 7. Set the dog's left rear leg with your left hand by:

a) reaching behind your dog and grasping the hock , or

b) reaching under your dog and grasping the stifle.

Use your hand to lock the joint. Lift the leg slightly and set the foot so that the hock is perpendicular to the ground.

Step 8. Set the right rear leg with your left hand by:

a) grasping the hock, or

b) grasping the stifle.

Use your hand to lock the joint. Lift the leg slightly and set the foot so that the hock is perpendicular to the ground. The feet should be set slightly wider than the hips.

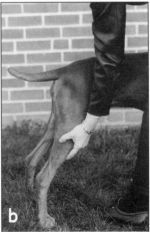

How do you decide which method to use when setting your dog's rear legs?

❖ The dog's size and your size may be factors. A small person may be unable to set a large dog's left rear leg by reaching underneath the dog, while a little dog may be too close to the ground to make reaching underneath feasible.

❖ One dog may be more cooperative when you grasp his hock, while another might be more relaxed when you grasp his stifle.

❖ *You* may have a preference. Grasping the hock may be faster and feel more comfortable to you than holding the stifle, or vice versa.

Experiment with both ways of setting the rear legs to discover which works best for you and your dog.

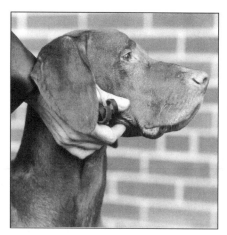

Step 9. Use your right hand to position your dog's head, either by holding the collar up high under your dog's ears, as shown in earlier steps, or by grasping your dog's right cheek and jaw. Use the method that gives you the best control of your dog's head. He should be looking directly forward.

Step 10. Use your left hand to position your dog's tail if appropriate for your breed. If, for your breed, the handler does *not* position the tail, you may put your left hand in your dog's collar, freeing your right hand to hold your dog's jaw and steady his head.

Summary

Most dogs are stacked in exactly the same way: the handler first sets the left front leg, and then sets the right front leg. Next, he sets the left rear leg and finally he sets the right rear leg. By setting the dog using the same sequence of actions over and over, both the handler and the dog learn exactly what to expect. The handler doesn't have to think "All right, that leg is set, so now what's next?" The dog knows exactly what the handler will do, and won't be startled by any unusual moves.

By the time you've stacked your dog hundreds of times, you'll be able to do it quickly and correctly, and your dog will be happy and cooperative. As a result, when you're in the ring and the chips are down, the judge will see your dog standing perfectly rather than you fumbling to stack your dog.

<table>
<tr>
<td>

Chapter

6

</td>
<td>

Teaching a Puppy to Stack

</td>
</tr>
</table>

Stacking a trained dog requires methodically setting his legs in a predictable order. How do you train your puppy to accept being stacked, and to stand like a statue? In this chapter you'll learn how to teach your puppy to stack, first on a table and then on the ground.

Preliminary Considerations

You will need the following equipment when you train your puppy to stack:

❖ *Collar*: a soft nylon collar that fits your puppy well and which you can hold easily. A nylon buckle or slip collar is a good choice for a young puppy.

❖ *Stacking table:* an elevated surface like a grooming table, a picnic bench, or even a large sturdy box. Your "stacking table" must be very stable. If your puppy is large, your table may be relatively low—say, 12"-18" tall. The table should be tall enough that the pup knows he is "up on something" and therefore that his mobility is limited.

This Dalmatian puppy is being trained to stack on a bathroom rug placed on the dining table.

❖ *Non-slip surface:* a rubber bath mat, small rug, a bath towel, or any material that gives your puppy firm footing on your stacking "table." Some tables, like grooming tables, will not require an additional mat or towel.

❖ *Bait:* a tasty treat that can be fed to your puppy in a series of nibbles, such as a jerky strip, a stick of string cheese, or a hot dog sliced into quarters lengthwise.

Your puppy should accept having his feet and legs touched, held and moved without pulling away. Many puppies are ticklish. You can condition your puppy to having his legs positioned by moving his legs as he eats his meals. Put his bowl on a brick or a stack of books so that it is at shoulder height. Then sit or kneel on the floor next to him while he eats and move his legs as though you were stacking him. Gently grasp his elbows to move his front feet a tiny bit, or position his rear feet by holding a hock gently. If he pulls his foot away, don't scold him. Just hold the elbow or hock gently again, and move the foot again as he is distracted by his meal. Eventually, he will ignore you as you position his feet and he eats his dinner.

Your puppy should be accustomed to wearing a collar and should accept gentle collar restraint without throwing a tantrum. If you're teaching your puppy to gait at the same time that you're teaching him to stack, then your puppy will already be used to his collar. If your puppy isn't "collar broken" then follow the instructions for introducing your puppy to his collar given in the chapter on teaching your puppy to gait.

If you are teaching gaiting and stacking at the same time, it is *very important* that you practice these skills in *short, separate sessions*. If you teach stacking and gaiting in the same session, you'll confuse your puppy: in one skill you ask him to be still, and in the other you ask him to move briskly. If your puppy is very young, you may also exhaust him. Instead, you should plan, for example, a brief stacking session in the morning, a gaiting session at midday, and another brief stacking session in the evening.

Teaching Your Puppy to Stack

When teaching your puppy to stack, use food for distraction, encouragement, and reward. The positive association of stacking with food works well for most puppies, resulting in a puppy that is happy to be handled and stacked. If, on the other hand, you try to *force* a puppy to stack and stand still, you'll create a dog that resents stacking and won't be happy in the ring.

Ground rules for training

As you train your puppy to stack, expect to do *many short repetitions* of every step. Remember, the attention span of a puppy is very limited.

❖ Repeat each step—or a sequence of two or three steps—over and over until your puppy shows by cooperating that he understands what to do. Be patient: your puppy doesn't

Patience and repetition are key to teaching a puppy to stack. Keep the lessons short and upbeat: your puppy should enjoy stacking.

have any idea of what you want when you introduce each step.

❖ Expect backsliding. Your puppy may appear to be making steady progress in learning to stack, and then suddenly seem to forget everything. Be patient, and start at the beginning again. He will catch on quickly.

❖ If your puppy that becomes uncontrollably *wild* in the presence of food, or is completely uninterested in food, you may need to use a toy or quiet verbal praise as the positive motivator.

❖ The attention span of a puppy is very short. Never push a puppy to his limit, so that he becomes cranky and uncooperative. Several short sessions, each a few minutes long, are far better than one long training session each day.

Initial steps

The goal in the first phase of stack training is to have your puppy stand still on a stacking table while you hold his collar and position his feet, using bait to distract and reward him. At this stage, the goal is *not* a perfectly stacked dog or a dog that will hold his pose for several minutes.

Step 1. Put your puppy on the stacking table. Let him sniff and explore. Your puppy must become familiar with his strange new environment so that he will not worry as you train him to stack. If your puppy seems very fearful on the table, try feeding him his meals on the table for a week (closely supervised so that he does not fall off). When your puppy accepts being on the table without any signs of fear, proceed to the next step.

Step 2. Get your puppy to stand up. Put your left arm between your puppy's hind legs or across his back, steadying him with your left hand on his belly. Hold your right hand across his chest or in his collar. With this grip, your puppy is safely restrained. Some puppies stand confidently on the table, while others need the reassurance of a hand supporting them. When your puppy will stand calmly on the table as you hold him very lightly, proceed to the next step.

Step 3. Using a piece of bait, get your puppy to move forward, toward the table's edge. While cradling your puppy securely with your left hand offer him a piece of bait, held in your right hand. Hold the bait directly in front of your puppy's mouth, so that your puppy can nibble on it easily. Next, move your bait hand forward *slowly* as your puppy continues to nibble. Continue to move the bait forward slowly until he takes a step toward the edge of the table.

Step 4. As your puppy moves toward the bait, let one foot go off the table edge. Letting your puppy find the table edge and experience a mild "falling" sensation helps teach him not to move forward.

Gently move your puppy back from the edge while he nibbles on a piece of bait. Have him stand, and give your stacking command ("stand") while offering him bait. Hold the bait at your puppy's mouth so he can nibble without moving forward.

If your puppy moves forward, hide the bait in your hand, gently reposition him on the table while saying "stand" and give him a bit of bait. If he moves again, repeat the sequence. Reinforce the association between getting bait and not moving forward.

It is *very important* that your puppy understands that he is on a table and that his mobility is limited. In the next steps, you will no longer restrain your puppy with your left hand.

Step 5. Set your puppy's front legs using your left hand. While your puppy nibbles on bait held in your right hand, reach over the puppy with your left arm and grasp his left elbow with your hand. Move his left foot until it is approximately under his shoulder. If he moves his foot out of position, reset it. Next, position his right front leg either using your left hand, or by switching the bait to your left hand and grasping his right elbow with your right hand.

Step 6. Use your left hand to position his rear legs. Keep your puppy's front feet in place by letting him nibble on bait. Next, gently grasp his left hock with your left hand and position his leg so that the hock is approximately perpendicular to the ground. Say "stand" as you position his leg. Don't fine-tune the leg placement. If your puppy moves his foot, patiently reposition it and repeat "stand." Set his right hind leg using your left hand.

When your puppy will let you set both his hind feet and will keep them in place for several seconds while he nibbles on bait, proceed to the next step.

Step 7. While baiting your puppy, run your hand along his back. As your puppy continues to nibble on bait held in your right hand, run your left hand over your puppy's back and legs. Your puppy will probably move his feet as you run your hand over him. Simply withhold the bait briefly, reset his foot and repeat your stacking command while giving him the bait again. By doing this, you reinforce the association between keeping his feet in place and receiving a reward.

Step 8. As your puppy stands still while nibbling on bait, hold his collar. With your left hand, gently move the collar up under his jaw, behind his ears.

Next, move the bait an inch or two away from his mouth, wait *a second or two*, and then move it back so that he can nibble again. If he moves, reset his feet and try again. Reward him with a nibble of bait if he stays still when you briefly pull the bait away.

After two or three repetitions of withholding bait for a couple of seconds and then rewarding him with another nibble, release him, play with him, and repeat the stacking sequence.

Once you are comfortable with this sequence of steps, it should be easy to sneak several quick stacking sessions into your day. If your stacking table is always available, you'll be able to do a quick training session before your puppy's meal and as you do chores around the house. Remember, several quick, happy sessions during the day will be far more effective than one long training session.

Next Steps

The next step in teaching your puppy to stack is to repeat the training that you did on the table with your puppy on the ground. Although small breeds are stacked on a table for the judge's exam, they are stacked on the ground at all other times. Therefore, all breeds must learn to stack on the ground.

When your puppy will let you position his feet without fussing, and will stand for several seconds on the table, watching bait held in front of him without moving his feet, you are ready to begin the transition to stacking on the ground. If your puppy cannot yet hold a stack on the table for several seconds, continue to practice stacking on the table.

You may teach your dog to stack on the ground either indoors or outdoors. Choose a training location that is relatively quiet and free of distractions. Remember, you will no longer have the table to limit your puppy's mobility. If you train outdoors, attach a light leash to your puppy's collar,

When your puppy will stand still for several seconds without nibbling bait, he's ready to stack on the ground.

drop the leash on the ground and step on it, just in case your puppy decides it's time to run and play.

Make sure your puppy has secure footing. If you are indoors on a slippery floor, use a piece of matting or a rubber backed bathroom rug. If you are outdoors choose a level area with closely cropped grass, asphalt, or lightly textured concrete.

Training your puppy to stack on the ground requires repeating the stacking steps that you followed to train him on the table: use bait to distract him, set his front legs, set his back legs, and run your hands over his body. If he moves a foot, then reset it. When he will keep his feet in place, slowly lengthen the time between nibbles on the bait.

Use bait to keep your puppy's attention while you set the front legs by grasping each elbow. When the front legs are set, position the rear legs.

When your puppy's feet are set, move your left hand to his collar, and slowly lengthen the interval between each nibble on the bait.

When your puppy will hold a stack for several seconds while you kneel beside him, move in front of him and lengthen the time between each nibble of bait.

If your puppy has learned his lessons well on the table, the transition to stacking on the ground should go smoothly.

Stack your puppy and bait him from the front. Bait only often enough to keep his attention, *slowly* stretching the time between nibbles on the bait.

If you train slowly and carefully, you will soon have a perfectly stacked puppy waiting patiently for the next piece of bait.

Summary

Teaching a puppy to stack requires patience and bait. Your puppy should first be taught to stack on a table, and then on the ground. In the early stages of stack training, don't worry about perfect placement of the feet. Your goal is to teach your puppy to accept having his feet positioned and to stand still.

Once your puppy has learned to stand still, you can fine-tune your stacking skills by stacking your puppy in front of a large wall mirror, window or sliding glass door so that you can see what the judge sees.

Chapter 7

The Moving Dog

If you watch carefully at a dog show, you'll see that not all dogs move alike. Some dogs, like the Scottish Deerhound, have light, springy movement, while others, like the Newfoundland, have a powerful, rhythmic gait. The sprightly Manchester Terrier moves with high, quick steps; the Bulldog has a solid, rolling gait. In this chapter you'll learn why movement is an important part of the judging process, what defines "correct" movement, and how a dog's movement is judged.

Why Judge Movement?

The way in which a dog moves reveals a lot about a dog. A discerning judge can tell much about a dog's structure by the way a dog moves; a judge can also evaluate whether or not a dog would be capable of doing the work for which it was bred. Movement demonstrates a dog's coordination, the balance of his body's parts, and his overall soundness.

Movement is discussed in many breed standards. Movement is also called "gait," "carriage," or "action" in some breed standards. Many standards include a gait or movement section, while in other breed standards—such as the Irish Terrier standard— the discussion of gait is included in the "Legs" section.

Movement to show structure

Although a perfectly stacked dog may appear to have correct structure, as soon as the dog moves, faults in his structure will be come evident. For example, a dog may appear to have a strong level topline when he is stacked, but when he moves, a sagging or roached topline may be revealed. Or, a stacked dog's front may appear true, but when he begins to move, he may pop out at the elbows or flip at the pasterns.

"Movement, or action, is the crucial test of conformation."

(the Airedale Terrier standard)

Quite simply, if a dog isn't put together well, then he can't move correctly. Many breed standards concur with the notion that movement reveals a considerable amount about the underlying skeletal and muscular structure of a dog:

> "A short choppy movement or high knee action indicates a straight shoulder; paddling indicates long, weak pasterns, and a short stilted rear gait indicates a straight rear assembly; all are serious faults."
>
> *(the Labrador Retriever standard)*

"The gait … is steady, balanced and powerful. He is agile for his size and build." (*the Alaskan Malamute standard*)

> "Desired movement cannot be maintained without sufficient angulation and firm slimness of body."
>
> *(the Kuvasz standard)*

> "Proper movement is the crucial test of proper conformation and soundness. It must be sound, straight moving, agile, brief, quick and powerful, never lumbering. … The front and rear assemblies must be in dynamic equilibrium."
>
> *(the Chow Chow standard)*

A dog's skeletal structure is a major determinant of his ability to move well. For example, a dog with straight shoulders and a well-angulated rear will tend to move slightly sideways (to "sidewind" or "crab"), or will pace in order to keep his front and rear feet from colliding.

> "Balance is a prerequisite to good movement. The front and rear assemblies must be equivalent in angulation and muscular development for the gait to be smooth and effortless."
>
> *(the English Springer Spaniel standard)*

> "The worst possible form of hindquarters consists of a short second thigh and a straight stifle, a combination which causes the hind legs to acts as props rather than instruments of propulsion."
>
> *(the Wire Fox Terrier standard)*

> "Essential to good movement is the balance of correct front and rear assemblies."
>
> *(the Newfoundland standard)*

Movement to show original function

Occasionally you may hear someone say, "That's a movement breed." Of course, movement is important for *all* breeds, since it reveals so much about a dog's underlying structure. However, in many breeds movement serves an additional role. Movement demonstrates whether the dog would be capable of serving the function for which it was originally bred. The breed standards of sporting dogs, herding dogs, hounds, and terriers often refer to the original function of a breed in their discussions of movement: sporting dogs should be able to run for hours, herding dogs should be able to change direction quickly, and earthdogs should be able to dig.

> "The dual function of the Curly as both waterfowl retriever and upland game hunter demands a dog who moves with strength and power yet is quick and agile."
>
> *(the Curly-Coated Retriever standard)*

> "In keeping with the Dalmatian's historical use as a coach dog, gait and endurance are of great importance. Movement is steady and effortless."
>
> *(the Dalmatian standard)*

> "The well-constructed Briard is a marvel of supple power. His movement has been described as "quicksilver," permitting him to make abrupt turns, springing starts and sudden stops required of the shepherding dog."
>
> *(the Briard standard)*

What is "Correct" Movement?

Not all breeds move alike. A Greyhound should not move like a Newfoundland; a Chihuahua should not move like a Pekingese. Some breed standards, such as the Lhasa Apso standard, have no discussion of correct movement for the breed. Other breed standards are *very* specific, describing precisely how the dog should move, particularly when a distinctive or unusual gait is characteristic of the breed:

> "The style and carriage are peculiar, his gait being a loose-jointed, shuffling, sidewise motion, giving the characteristic "roll." The action must, however, be unrestrained, free and vigorous."
>
> *(the Bulldog standard)*

> "... [c]haracteristic of the Otterhound gait is a very loose, shambling walk, which springs immediately into a loose and very long striding, sound, active trot with natural extension of the head... Otterhounds do not lift

"Free, straight and easy all around. It is a distinctive gait, not stilted, but powerful, with reach and drive." (*the West Highland White Terrier standard*)

their feet high off the ground and may shuffle when they walk or move at a slow trot."

(the Otterhound standard)

"The gait is unhurried and dignified, with a slight roll over the shoulders. The rolling gait is caused by the bowed front legs and heavier, wider forequarters pivoting on the tapered waist and the lighter, straight hindquarters. The rolling motion is smooth and effortless and is as free as possible from bouncing, prancing or jarring."

(the Pekingese standard)

"The Affinpinscher has a light, sound, balanced, confident gait and tents to carry itself with comic seriousness."

(the Affinpinscher standard)

"[Movement] should be free, light-footed, lively and straightforward. Hindquarters should have strong propelling power." *(the Silky Terrier standard)*

Thus, the notion of "correct" movement is very breed-specific; movement that is correct for one breed may be completely incorrect for another. In fact, gaits that are highly desirable in one breed may be definite *faults* in another.

For example, a Boston Terrier's legs should swing straight and true along the line he's travelling, but a Scottish Terrier's legs should angle in as he moves:

"The gait of the Boston Terrier is that of a sure footed, straight gaited dog, forelegs and hind legs moving straight ahead in line with perfect rhythm, each step indicating grace and power."

(the Boston Terrier standard)

"The gait of the Scottish Terrier is very characteristic of the breed. It is not the square trot or walk desirable in the long-legged breeds. The forelegs do not move in exact parallel planes; rather, in reaching out, the forelegs incline slightly inward because of the deep broad forechest."

(the Scottish Terrier standard).

So, a Boston Terrier whose legs converged toward the centerline of his body when he moved, or a Scottish Terrier whose legs moved straight ahead, would have faulty movement, most probably the result of faulty structure.

Another example is a "rolling" gait, which is required in some breeds and penalized in others:

"The proper Clumber roll occurs when the dog with correct proportion reaches forward with rear legs toward the center line of travel and rotates the hip downward while the back remains level and straight."

(the Clumber Spaniel standard)

"Movement faults include...crabbing and moving with the feet wide, the latter giving roll or swing to the body."

(the English Springer Spaniel standard)

Yet another example is the stylized, prancing gait called a "hackney" gait, which is considered proper movement for the Miniature Pinscher, but is a fault in other breeds:

"The hackney-like action is a high-stepping, reaching, free and easy gait in which the front leg moves straightforward and in front of the body, and the foot bends at the wrist."

(the Miniature Pinscher standard)

"Padding, hackneying, weaving, crabbing and similar movement faults are to be penalized according to the degree to which they interfere with the ability of the dog to work."

(the Belgian Tervuren standard)

"Hackney gait must be faulted."

(the Pointer standard)

Read your breed's standard to learn how your breed should move. Your Poodle should move like a Poodle, not like your friend's Bulldog! Watch your breed being shown, study the AKC video about your breed, and discuss proper movement for your breed with your mentor or handling class instructor.

Judging Movement

Judges are required to assess the movement of *all* dogs that they judge. The judge will evaluate the movement of the dogs as they move together as a class, and individually as they perform individual gaiting patterns. In order to evaluate a dog's movement, the judge will observe him from the front, the side, and the rear as he moves.

Movement in a group

When they enter the ring, the dogs may be gaited as a group counterclockwise around the ring's perimeter. As they move together, the judge can form a general impression of the dogs, comparing one against the other, and determine if any dog is lame. Later, after the dogs have all been examined and moved individually, they may again be moved as a group around the ring's perimeter, so that the judge can evaluate them further.

Movement as an individual

After the judge has done a hands-on examination of a dog, he will have the handler move the dog around the ring following one of several standard patterns. The purpose of the gaiting patterns is to give the judge a chance to observe the dog's movement from the side, the front, and the rear:

> "…you must individually gait and observe the dog going away, from the side and returning…."
>
> *(AKC's Guidelines for Conformation Dog Show Judges)*

When the judge watches the dog move directly toward her, she can see how well his legs move under him.

When seen from the side, the dog's "reach" and "drive"—how efficiently he covers ground—can be evaluated.

By observing the dog going away and returning, the judge can see whether the dog's legs move in parallel planes or tend to converge (or "single track") under the dog as the dog moves. He can also observe whether the dog flips its wrists as it moves, or pops out at the elbows, or a host of other faults. As the dog moves around the ring's perimeter, the judge can observe the dog's side movement, assessing, for example, the balance of the dog's reach and drive. Some breed standards are quite clear about what judges should observe when judging movement:

> "When viewed from the side, there should be good reach with no restrictions of movement in the front and plenty of drive in the rear, with good flexion of the stifle and jock joints. Coming at you, there should be no sign of elbows being out. When the Chesapeake is moving away from you, there should be no sign of cowhockness from the rear."
>
> *(the Chesapeake Bay Retrieve standard)*

"Comes and goes at a trot moving in a straight line."

(the Chinese Crested standard)

"When viewed from the side, the movement exhibits a good length of stride, and viewed from the front and rear it is straight and true, resulting from straight-boned fronts and properly made and muscled hindquarters."

(the Cavalier King Charles Spaniel standard)

The movement portion of judging is *not* a race. Dogs that are moved too quickly cannot be judged properly:

"Movement at a trot is free, precise and effortless ... Coming and going, his movement is precise and true." (*the Bichon Frise standard*)

"Do not allow the dogs to be moved at excessive speed. Do not hesitate to tell an exhibitor exactly how you want a dog moved and controlled."

(AKC's Guidelines for Conformation Dog Show Judges)

Most dogs are shown at a moderate trot. Some breed standard stipulate the correct, or incorrect, speed at which the dog should be shown:

"... excessive animation should not be mistaken for proper gait."

(the Cocker Spaniel standard)

"The breed should be shown on a loose lead so that its natural gait is evident."

(the Sussex Spaniel standard)

Stopping

Oddly enough, standing still is an important part of judging movement!

As noted earlier, although a dog may appear to be correctly structured when stacked by his handler, several faults may become apparent when the dog begins to move—apparently straight hocks may be revealed as cow-hocks, a level topline may roach, a good tailset may deteriorate.

Similarly, when a dog comes to a stop after movement and stands naturally, both faults and strengths will be revealed. A dog that sets his

The "stop" gives the judge a chance to see the dog stand naturally.

front naturally straight and true without the assistance of a handler demonstrates good underlying structure, whereas a dog that stops with an "east-west" front reveals an underlying skeletal problem. Similar issues with a dog's topline and rear structure can be revealed by the way that he stands when he comes to a stop.

At the end of the individual gaiting pattern, the dog should stop about six feet away from the judge, so that the judge can observe the dog standing naturally. After the judge has studied the dog as he stands still, the handler may be asked to gait his dog to the end of the line around the ring's perimeter, giving the judge another opportunity to judge the dog's side movement.

Summary

Movement is an important component of evaluating a dog. The manner in which a dog moves is a direct function of how the dog is constructed. A dog that is put together correctly may move well, whereas a dog that is not well-built cannot move well. The way in which a dog moves may also show whether the dog would be capable of doing the work for which it was bred.

There is substantial variation in how the different breeds should move. Most breed standards include a description of the correct gait for that breed. When evaluating movement, a judge will observe the dog from the front, the side, and the rear—both individually and in a group—to ascertain whether each dog's movement conforms to the description in the breed standard.

Teaching a Puppy to Gait

How do you transform your bouncing, playful puppy into a smoothly gaiting show dog? How do you harness your puppy's energy and channel it into controlled movement? In this chapter, you'll learn how to leash-break your puppy and how to teach him to move at your side calmly—a great skill for show dog and pet alike. Then you'll teach your puppy to change speed, turn and halt on cue. Finally, you'll pick up the pace and teach your puppy all these skills at a trot.

Preliminary Considerations

Think about the following:

- ❖ A puppy has a very short attention span.

- ❖ A very young puppy tires very quickly.

- ❖ If it's not *fun* a puppy won't do it willingly.

- ❖ A puppy will respond to positive motivation.

Teaching a puppy to stack requires the *passive* cooperation of your puppy, since you can physically restrain your puppy until he cooperates and stands still. On the other hand, teaching a puppy to gait requires a puppy's *active* cooperation; dragging a reluctant puppy on a lead does more harm than good.

As a result, gaiting lessons need to be especially happy and upbeat to encourage your puppy's active cooperation. Use lots of rewards and praise when you teach your puppy to move happily at your side. Your lessons should be *very short*— a few minutes long, once or twice a day, so that your puppy doesn't wear out. If you're training a *very* young puppy to move on a lead, be especially aware of signs of fatigue.

If you are also teaching your puppy to stack, do *not* teach stacking and gaiting in the same lesson—that will confuse your puppy. Instead, teach stacking and gaiting in separate, short sessions, letting your puppy rest in between lessons.

Finally, if your puppy is between four months and seven months old, you may need to postpone your puppy's leash training. At that age, puppies teeth; adult teeth push out baby teeth, and molars begin to cut through the puppy's gums. During teething, the puppy's gums and mouth may be very sore, and some puppies become extremely sensitive to collar pressure. If your puppy is teething and suddenly becomes uncooperative when you put a leash and collar on him, suspend your training until his gums, mouth, and jaws are no longer sore. For most puppies, teething is complete when they're about six or seven months old.

Leash Breaking Your Puppy

Learning to gait begins with simply learning to walk calmly on a lead. This is an important skill for both pets and show dogs.

Wearing a collar

If your puppy is not accustomed to wearing a collar, then teaching him to tolerate a collar is your first step. Use a flat buckle collar or a slip collar. Even if you will use a martingale or noose lead and collar for your *trained* dog in the ring, training a puppy is much easier with a simple buckle collar or a slip collar.

Never leave a slip collar on a puppy. If your puppy wears a collar all the time, it should be a buckle collar.

There's great variation in how a puppy will tolerate a collar. Some won't even notice the collar, and others will throw a tantrum. Quietly put the collar on your puppy, and give him a treat as soon as the collar is on. The collar should be tight enough that he can't pull it off, but not so tight that it chokes him: you should be able to slip a finger under the collar easily. (If your puppy wears a buckle collar all the time, be sure to loosen the collar as he grows.)

When your puppy accepts a collar and a lead, and tolerates light pressure on a lead, you're ready to try walking on a lead.

If your puppy scratches the collar or shakes his head and then ignores the collar, you don't have a problem. If your puppy has a tantrum, *don't* take the collar off. Instead, either ignore him or try to distract him with a favorite toy or a piece of food. When he calms down and forgets about the collar, you may remove the collar if he is not going to wear it full time. Each time you put his collar back on, give him a treat.

When your puppy no longer notices that he's wearing a collar, you're ready to move on.

Next, your puppy must get used to light pressure—like the gentle tugging of a lead—on the collar. With your puppy next to you, pull gently on the collar with your fingers. If your puppy ignores the pressure on the collar, then you don't have an issue. If your puppy resists, then use treats and praise to convince your puppy that pressure on his collar is acceptable.

When your puppy accepts light pressure on his collar without having a tantrum, you're ready to start leash-breaking your puppy.

Walking on a lead

Your first goal is to teach your puppy to move beside you calmly as you walk at a "stroll-around-the-block" speed.

If using a slip collar, hook the lead's snap on the ring that doesn't move.

If you're using a flat collar, attach a light lead to the ring on the collar's buckle. If you're using a slip collar, attach the lead to the "dead" ring of the collar—the ring that does not tighten the collar. Have a toy or treats in your right pocket.

Begin with your puppy standing or sitting on your left side. There should be a little slack in the lead, but not enough to trip your puppy. Gather up any excess lead in your left hand. Give your puppy a verbal cue that you are about to start moving, such as "Let's go," or "Move." Use just a word or two—nothing long or complicated such as, "OK, Rover, c'mon, here we go, good job buddy, let's go!"

Take a few small steps forward while pulling *gently* on the lead, and watch your puppy's reaction. One of three things can happen:

1. *Your puppy won't budge.*

   Do not tug on the lead to force your puppy to move. Instead, lure him forward using a treat or toy held in your right hand. Hold the toy in front of your puppy and encourage him to move forward, cheerfully repeating "Let's go … good boy … let's go." Your puppy should move toward the treat. As soon your puppy moves, praise him and give him the treat or toy.

This Chesapeake Bay Retriever puppy is confused. A few encouraging words, a toy, or a piece of food will get him moving.

2. *Your puppy lunges ahead.*

If your puppy takes off like a rocket, stand still and gently stop your puppy's forward motion with the lead. When your puppy settles down, try taking a few small steps again. If your puppy lunges forward again, stop again. Eventually, your puppy will understand that the only time that he will be allowed to move forward is when he does *not* lunge.

This puppy is wild. Hold your ground—*only* allow him to move forward when he is calm.

3. *Your puppy moves with you.*

Count your blessings and say a few encouraging words to your puppy such as, "Good boy ... that's right." Walk on for a few yards, quietly encouraging and praising your puppy. Stop and reward your puppy with a treat.

This is the behavior you want: a puppy that will move calmly on your *left* side.

When your puppy will move forward without lunging, lagging, or throwing a tantrum, adjust your pace to a speed at which your puppy will move calmly and happily at your side. Imagine taking a walk around the block with your dog. Big dogs will probably walk next to you, while little dogs may use a very brisk walk, or even a trot, to keep up with you as you stroll. If you select a pace that is comfortable for you and for your puppy, he will move nicely at your side.

Teaching your puppy to move calmly on a lead can take a few minutes or it can take several short training sessions. Keep your puppy's lessons short—just a few minutes, a couple of times a day. Never train when *you* are tired and can't be positive and encouraging, and when you can't control your emotions when your puppy is less than perfect.

More Lead Skills

When your puppy will move calmly at your left side for a *reasonable* distance— ~~~, feet for a 10-week-old puppy, and around the block for a 4-month-old puppy—it's time to introduce more skills and vocabulary to your puppy.

Your puppy needs to learn to change his speed on command, to turn right and left without tripping you, and to stop and stand still. As you teach these skills to your puppy, introduce them one at a time. Do not try to teach your puppy several new skills at once, or he will become confused.

Changing speed

Your puppy must learn to slow down and speed up on cue. For example, your puppy will need to slow down when you turn left, because he will be on the inside of the turn. Your puppy will also need to slow down as you approach the judge in the ring, so that you don't run into the judge.

To teach the "Slow" or "Easy" command to your puppy, begin with your puppy moving calmly at your left side at a normal speed. Then slow down slightly while gently saying "Slow" or "Easy." If your puppy slows down with you, praise him, walk slowly for a few more paces, and then speed up to your normal walking pace with your "Let's go" command. Again, if your puppy comes with you, praise and reward. Repeat the normal—slow—normal sequence until your puppy understands "Easy."

If your puppy does not stay with you when you slow down, repeat "Easy," tug gently on the lead and say "Easy" again. If your puppy slows, then praise him and give him a treat. If your puppy ignores the tug, then stop, get your puppy back by your side, and start the normal–slow–normal sequence again.

"Easy" is a wonderful everyday skill for your dog. When you're walking your dog on a crowded street or on an icy sidewalk, your dog will be much easier to control if he understands "Easy."

Turns

In the ring, your puppy must turn to the right, to the left, and completely around (180°) without tripping you. For example, imagine moving counterclockwise around the ring with your dog; he will make a left turn at each corner. Or, imagine moving your dog away from the judge, turning around, and returning directly the judge; your dog turns 180° when he turns around.

Left turn. Before you teach your puppy to turn left, your puppy should understand "Easy." During a left turn, your puppy must slow down because he will be on the *inside* of the turn. After he has made the turn, his speed should return to normal.

To teach the left turn to your puppy, begin with your puppy moving calmly at your left side. Slow down slightly while commanding, "Easy". After a step or two of moving slowly, repeat "Easy" and turn to the left. Your turn should be a rounded corner—not a squared-off military corner. As you come out of the turn, praise your puppy, say "Let's go" and pick up your speed again.

Repeat the slow–turn–normal sequence several times, making a counterclockwise square with several steps of calm walking at a normal speed on each side.

Right turn. During a turn to the right, your puppy must speed up slightly because he will be on the *outside* of the turn. After he has made the turn, his speed should return to normal.

To teach the right turn, begin with your puppy moving calmly at your left side. Have a treat or toy in your right hand. As you approach your corner, say "Hurry" and turn to the right. Hold the toy or treat in front of your puppy to encourage him to speed up slightly as he makes the turn. *Don't* tug on the lead to make him speed up. Your turn should be a rounded corner—not a squared-off military corner. As you come out of the turn, praise your puppy and give him his reward.

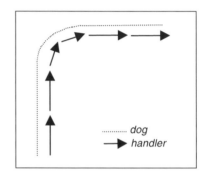

In the left turn, the dog is on the inside of the turn and must slow down.

In the right turn, the dog is on the outside of the turn and must speed up.

When your puppy understands that he must speed up slightly on a right turn, add two or three steps at a normal speed *after* the turn before you give him his reward. Finally, link several right turns together to make a large clockwise square.

About-turn. An about-turn is just an exaggerated right turn. Your puppy is on the outside of the turn, and so he must speed up even more while making the turn.

Teach the about-turn to the right exactly as you taught the right turn, using the same command and a treat or toy to encourage your puppy to speed up through the complete turn.

Small dogs will also need to learn a "left about-turn," which is just an exaggerated left turn. Teach this exactly the way you taught the left turn.

When your puppy has mastered the left turn, the right turn and the about-turns, link them together in a fun sequence so that your puppy doesn't get bored. For example, do a left turn, then a right turn, and finally an about turn. Stop, praise, and reward your dog. If your puppy is young, be careful not to string too many turns together; you'll wear your puppy out.

Finally, to reinforce your puppy's turning skills, and to teach him to read your body language as you turn, practice making complete circles to the left and circles to the right.

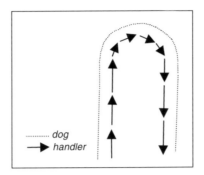

An about-turn is an extension of the right turn.

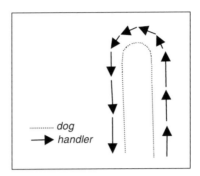

A left about-turn turn is an exaggerated left turn.

The circles should be about four to six feet in diameter, depending on the size of your puppy. This exercise will help your puppy learn to stay with you as you turn, to read your body movement, and to stay out of your way.

Halting

The next step is to teach your puppy to halt and stand still. He shouldn't sit when you stop, and he shouldn't keep moving.

The key to successful halting is gradual transitions. If you hit the brakes, your puppy will be confused, and may sit or may lunge ahead of you, causing an unfair leash correction. If, on the other hand, you slow down for two or three steps before you stop, your puppy will have a clearer picture of what you want.

To teach your puppy to halt, begin with your puppy moving calmly at your left side at a normal speed, with your lead in your left hand. Have a treat in your right hand. Slow down slightly while commanding "Easy". After two or three slow steps, say "Whoa" or "Stand," then stop, pull back *gently* on the lead (gently so that your puppy does not sit), and quickly bring the treat to your puppy's face, instantly rewarding him for stopping. As he stands still eating his treat, praise him and repeat his stopping command: "Good boy … stand … good boy."

Repeat the walking–"Easy"–halt sequence several times. If your puppy sits, gently stand him before you give him his reward, repeating your stopping command as he stands up. Only reward him when he stands.

Eventually, as your puppy learns what you want, you will be able to drop the "Easy" command, and just say "Whoa" or "Stand" as you glide to a halt. As your puppy becomes more skilled at halting and standing still, increase the wait between stopping and his reward *by a few seconds*, so that he learns to remain still until you release him.

Gaiting

When your puppy has learned to move calmly at your side at a normal speed, to change speed, to halt and stand still, and to make left turns, right turns, and about turns without tripping you, lagging behind you, or forging ahead of you, it's time to teach your puppy to gait.

Most dogs are shown moving at a trot, although there are a few exceptions such as the Bulldog.

Gaiting is very similar to moving calmly at your side while you walk. When gaiting, the dog moves at a calm, controlled *trot,* while the handler walks or runs to match the dog's speed. Small dogs that learned their earlier lessons at a brisk walk will have very little difficulty transitioning to gaiting. Large dogs will notice a bigger difference as they move from a walk to a trot, and as their handlers run rather walk beside them.

With large dogs, the handler must run as the dog trots.

With small dogs, the handler walks briskly as the dog trots.

Gaiting can be very exciting for a puppy, especially when his owner runs. When you start training your puppy to gait, pick a location that is safe and free of distractions. Much later, when your puppy knows how to behave, you should practice in locations with distractions. If you live on a safe, quiet street, practice gaiting on the sidewalk in front of your home. Empty parking lots are wonderful places to practice: parking lot stripes can help you move in a straight line and make good turns. Empty tennis and basketball courts are also good places to practice.

Slide your puppy's collar high up on his neck, right behind the ears. Gather up any excess lead in your left hand, so that there is just a little bit of slack in the lead. Hold your hand at waist-height—not up at your shoulder or dangling down at your side. Your hand should be held away from your body, centered over your dog's head.

Begin with your puppy moving calmly at your left side at a brisk walk, just as he learned in his earlier lesson. After several steps of calm movement at a walk, *slowly and smoothly* increase your speed until your dog is trotting, repeating your "Let's go" command. If you

This Bichon Frise's collar is up high on his neck, behind his ears. The handler's hand is held at waist-height, over the dog's head.

have a small breed, you may simply need to walk more briskly in order to get your puppy to trot. With a larger breed, you may need to jog in order to get your dog to trot. If you jog, use relatively short strides rather than a long, loping gait.

If your puppy speeds ups and begins trotting calmly at your side, praise him! Continue to have your puppy trot for several more steps and then stop and reward him. If, as you speed up, your puppy breaks into a gallop or starts bouncing and jumping next to you, simply halt. Do *not* make corrections with the lead! Let your puppy calm down, and then start over again: walk calmly for several steps, and then accelerate smoothly to a gentle trot.

As your puppy gaits, there should be a little slack in the lead, and your arm should "float" over your puppy's head. If you hold your arm stiffly, then each step will jerk the lead. If you swing your arm back and forth as if you were running, each step will jerk the lead. If your hand is always centered over your puppy's head, there will be a light, even pressure on his lead and collar.

When your puppy will gait at your side without going crazy, it's time to practice his other skills: decelerating to a slow trot and then accelerating back to a normal trot, turning left, right and about, making right and left circles, and gliding smoothly into a stop. Teach these skills at a trot in exactly the same way you taught them at a walk, and your puppy will learn quickly.

This handler holds her hand away from her body over her dog, so that the light pressure from the lead is straight up, not sideways, and her hand floats over her dog's head.

Summary

A good show dog will move at a controlled trot on a *loose* lead; the handler shouldn't pull on the lead to make the dog behave. A dog that has learned to move at a controlled trot on a loose lead can show his movement and structure at its best.

The expression "You must walk before you can run" really applies to gaiting. Your puppy should first learn his skills—moving calmly, changing speeds, turning and stopping—as you walk at a comfortable speed. Then, when your puppy has good leash manners, you can increase your speed so that your puppy is trotting at your side. When your puppy knows how to change speed, turn, and stop at a trot, you're well on your way to having a dog that can gait properly in the show ring.

Once of the nicest benefits of teaching your dog to gait is that by laying a foundation of good leash manners, you'll create an enjoyable companion in addition to training your show dog.

More About Gaiting

When your puppy will gait reliably at a steady trot, and can change speed, turn, and come to a halt, it's time to pull these skills together into a smooth show-ring routine. In this chapter, you'll learn some of the standard gaiting patterns used in the show ring, how to do a "stop," and some of the finer points of gaiting, such as finding a target and using the mats to your advantage.

Gaiting Patterns

A "gaiting pattern" is a standard movement pattern, selected by the judge and used by each handler in the class to show the individual movement of his dog. Each dog in the class uses the same gaiting pattern.

The most frequently used gaiting patterns are the "go-'round," the "out-and-back," and the "triangle." Other, less frequently used patterns are the "L" and the "T." These gaiting patterns incorporate the skills that your puppy has already learned: gaiting in a straight line, turning left, turning in a circle to the right, doing an about-turn, and coming to a halt.

The go-'round

The "go-'round" is simply a squared-off, counterclockwise circle along the sides of the ring. The go-'round is used during group movement and as you take your dog to the end of the line after the judge has watched your individual gaiting pattern.

The judge's direction for this pattern is usually, "Take the dogs around," (when

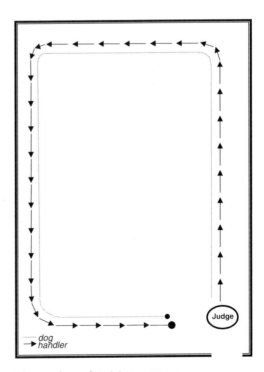

The go-'round gaiting pattern.

moving in a group) or "Go to the end of the line," or "Take him around" (at the end of the individual gaiting pattern).

The primary purpose of the go-'round is to give the judge the opportunity to observe the movement of your dog from the *side*.

The out-and-back

In the "out-and-back" the dog gaits in a straight line away from the judge, does an about-turn, and returns to the judge. Depending on the ring's size, the out-and-back may be done on the ring's diagonal or along the side of the ring.

There are two ways for small dogs to turn at the far end of the out-and-back: they can turn to the left, with the dog on the inside of the turn, or they can turn to the right, with the dog on the outside of the turn. Large dogs always make a right about-turn, with the dog on the outside of the turn. Making an about-turn to the left, so that the dog is on the inside of the turn, is too cramped and awkward with a large dog.

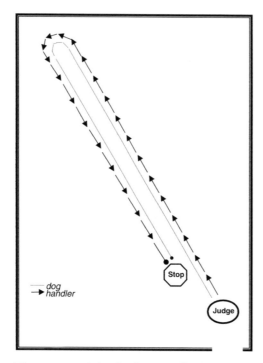
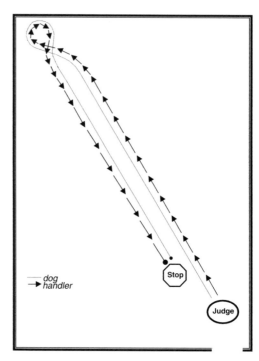

The out-and-back for small dogs (left about-turn).

The out-and-back for large or small dogs (right about-turn).

Before you start the out-and-back pattern, the judge may say, "Take your dog to the corner and back," "To the corner and back," or simply "Out and back." He may also point at the corner to which he wishes you to go. Watch the individual movement of the dogs judged before you so that you know what the judge wants.

The out-and-back pattern gives the judge an opportunity to observe your dog's movement from the *rear* as you move away and from the *front* as you return to the judge.

The triangle

The "triangle" is a cross between the go-'round and the out-and-back: it starts like the first two legs of the go-'round and then finishes with the return leg of the out-and-back.

In the triangle, the dog and handler usually move away from the judge along the right side of the ring, turn left and move along the far side of the ring, and then, in the far corner of the ring, turn to come back to the judge along the ring diagonal.

As in the out-and-back, small dogs may turn either right or left when starting the final leg; large dogs always turn right, making a three-quarters circle before they head back along the diagonal to the judge. Making a left turn in the far corner with a large dog is very awkward: after a left turn, a large dog requires several steps along the final leg of the pattern to regain his balance and gait smoothly.

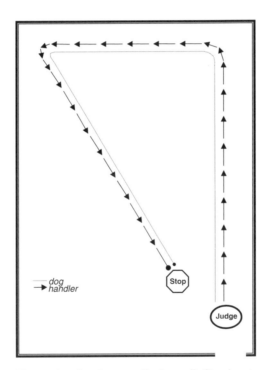

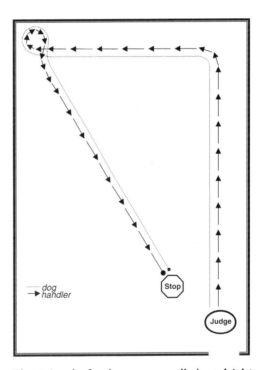

The triangle for small dogs (left about-turn).

The triangle for large or small dogs (right about-turn).

As you begin your individual gaiting pattern, the instructions from the judge may be, "Do a triangle," or just "Triangle." The judge may point in the direction he wishes you to go for the first leg. Again, watch the dogs ahead of you so that you know which gaiting pattern the judge has chosen.

The triangle pattern gives the judge a good look at your dog's *rear* movement (as you do the first leg of the triangle), at his *side* movement (as you do the second leg of the triangle) and finally at his *front* movement (as you come in on the diagonal).

The Stop

Every gaiting pattern brings you back to the judge where your dog must halt and pose so that the judge can observe him standing naturally. This is called coming to a *stop*. When executing a stop, your dog should come to a halt with his legs positioned exactly as they would have been if you had stacked him by hand.

Watch handlers as they execute a stop in front of the judge. As they come toward the judge, the handlers begin to slow down a few steps before a mental "stop target"—a point five or six feet in front of the judge. By decelerating smoothly, the handlers allow their dogs to walk into a perfect, comfortable stance without crowding the judge.

This West Highland White Terrier and handler have executed a beautiful stop.

Teaching your puppy to stop

Your puppy knows how to gait at your side and how to halt on command when you stop moving. The next step is to transform the halt into a stop. A stop is really nothing more than a halt in which the puppy faces the handler and sets his feet into position.

There are two ways to teach the stop. In the first, the handler steps in front of the puppy while telling him to halt. In the second, the handler swings the puppy around to face the handler while giving the halt command. Which one you use will depend on whether your puppy is gaiting at your side or out in front of you, and on how quickly you are moving.

Alternative 1 — handler steps in front of the puppy (puppy gaiting beside handler):

❖ Take several steps of good reliable gaiting. Have bait or a toy in your right hand.

❖ Slow down for a few strides, saying "easy" if necessary.

❖ Step out directly in front of your puppy while giving the halt command.

❖ If your puppy stops extremely close to you, take a small step backward to

Step 1. The puppy gaits by the handler's side for several steps.

make space between you and your puppy, repeating your halt command to keep your puppy from moving forward.

❖ Show your puppy the treat or toy, repeating either your halt command or "Stay" to keep him from moving forward.

❖ When the puppy has been still for a few seconds while facing you and watching his treat, release him with an "OK!" and give him his reward.

Alternative 2 — puppy turns to face the handler (puppy gaiting slightly ahead of handler):

❖ Take several steps of good reliable gaiting. Have bait or a toy in your right hand.

❖ Slow down for a few strides, saying "Easy" if necessary.

Step 2. The handler steps in front of the puppy, offering the puppy a treat to get him to stop, *or* the handler steps backward, using the treat to lure the puppy to turn and stop.

Step 3. The handler steps back slightly from the puppy, repeating his stop command.

❖ Call your puppy's name and take a step or two backwards. As he turns toward you, use your halt command. If he turns his entire body to face you, good! If he turns just his head to watch you and then stops, take a step or two backward, luring him with the bait or toy to turn his entire body toward you.

❖ Show your puppy the treat or toy, repeating either your halt command or "Stay" to keep him from moving forward.

❖ When your puppy has been still for a few seconds while facing you and watching his treat, release him with an "OK!" and give him his reward.

When the puppy shows that he understands that his halt command now means "turn, face me and stand still," you should:

❖ Gradually increase the time that the puppy will stand still looking at you or at a treat. Your goal is to have him stand still long enough for the judge to have a good look at him.

❖ Gradually shift your position so that your properly executed stop presents your dog's profile to the judge.

By keeping your movements slow and smooth as you come into a stop, your dog should be able to "walk" into perfect placement of his feet. If you stop abruptly, his feet wil be skewed, but if you stop smoothly, he will be able to place his feet squarely and comfortably.

Fixing a crooked stop

When everything goes right with a stop, all of your dog's legs should be positioned exactly as though you had stacked him by hand, with feet pointing forward and the correct distance apart.

What do you do if the dog's feet aren't properly positioned? You need to teach your dog to take a step forward and "fix his feet" on command. Fixing a stop is most important if your dog's front feet are crooked; crooked back feet are less critical.

Although this Bullmastiff has set his front feet well in this stop, his rear feet are staggered.

The handler takes a step back and baits the dog to step forward, setting all four feet correctly.

Begin by gaiting your dog and then executing a stop. If your dog stops with his feet perfectly set, praise him lavishly and reward him. If your dog stops with either his front feet or back feet staggered, then take a step backward, pull *gently* on the lead, and tell him "Step" or "Fix it". The gentle tug on the lead will pull your dog off-center—he's already unbalanced because his feet are staggered—and he should step forward and set himself squarely. If he squares his feet successfully, praise him and give him a reward. If his feet are still staggered, try it again: take a small step backward, tug on the lead and say "Fix it". This may take several repetitions, but when he *does* stop with his feet square, praise him lavishly and reward him.

Teaching a dog to fix his feet on command is a slow process; he won't learn this as quickly as he learned to turn or to come to a halt. Simply be patient, and fix his feet every time he comes into a crooked stop.

Finer Points of Gaiting

Gaiting properly in the show ring is much more than simply trotting under control following the judge's directions. The purpose of gaiting is to display your dog's movement and structure at its best. There are several factors that can have a profound effect on how well your dog moves in the ring.

Tight or loose lead?

Most breeds are shown on a loose lead (a lead with a *little bit* of slack in it). Many standards actually stipulate that the breed should be shown on a loose lead rather than a tight lead:

"The Otterhound should be shown on a loose lead."

(the Otterhound standard)

"It is recommended that dogs be shown on a loose lead to reflect true gait."

(the Golden Retriever standard)

"The breed should be shown on a loose lead so that its natural gait is evident."

(the Sussex Spaniel standard)

"In the show ring, the Shiba is gaited on a loose lead at a brisk trot."

(the Shiba Inu standard)

"The Shih Tzu … must be shown … *neither raced nor strung up*, to evaluate its smooth, flowing, effortless movement …"

(the Shih Tzu standard)

If a dog is shown on a tight lead, or "strung up," the balance of the dog is destroyed: he cannot put his full weight on his front feet when he moves. As a result, the movement of the dog cannot be accurately judged.

There are exceptions to the loose lead rule. For example, Cocker Spaniels are shown pulling on their leads to demonstrate their balance and drive. Some Terrier breeds are also shown on a tight lead. Watch your breed being shown, and observe whether it is shown on a tight or loose lead.

Breed-appropriate speed

Gaiting a dog in the ring isn't a race; no AKC rule says that the fastest dog wins. Some breeds are shown moving quickly, while others are shown at a slower pace. Many breed standards specify the speed at which dogs should be shown, ranging from "swift" to "unhurried:"

"Swift, tireless trot."

(the Basenji standard)

"When on a loose lead, the Afghan can trot at a fast pace."

(the Afghan Hound standard)

"The Chihuahua should move swiftly …"

(the Chihuahua standard)

"The dog should be evaluated at a moderate gait."

(the German Wirehaired Pointer standard)

"The natural working gait of the Bernese Mountain Dog is a slow trot."

(the Bernese Mountain Dog standard)

"The gait is unhurried and dignified …" *(the Pekinese standard)*

The best way to determine the appropriate speed for your breed is to study your breed's standard, to observe your breed being shown, and to talk to people who show your breed.

Moving in a group

When moving in a group, you should follow the dog ahead of you, never pass him, and never come so close that you interfere with his movement. There should be three to six feet between dogs as they move in a group—less for small dogs, more for big dogs.

When starting, let the dog ahead of you move out at least two full strides before you begin to move. If you start too soon, you will be right on the heels of the dog ahead of you. If you start too late, there will be a big gap between the dogs, making it difficult for the judge to compare their movement.

If you catch up to the dog ahead of you as you move, slow slightly and move a little closer to the ring gates. This will give you a slightly larger circle to travel, so you won't have to slow down significantly.

Some dogs like to be first in line. Some dogs worry about other dogs "chasing" them. Some dogs are content to follow a leader while others try to catch the dog ahead. Practice moving in a group with other dogs and handlers so that your

When the first Weimaraner has moved two or three strides, the second dog begins to move. The other dogs wait to begin moving.

dog learns to move in any position in the group line-up.

Using a target

When you gait your dog, it is important to move in a straight line. If you drift to the right or to the left as you move, your dog's movement cannot be true: he will have to drift as well, and may appear to "crab" or "sidewind."

People usually drift when they concentrate on their dogs as they move rather than looking up, watching where they're going. The simplest way to move in a straight line is to pick a "target" and to aim for it as you move, shifting your gaze back and forth between your target and your dog.

Just before you start each leg of your gaiting pattern, glance up in the direction you are going and pick out a person or object as a target, such as someone sitting at the ring corner to which you are headed. As you move your dog, keep shifting your glance between your dog and the target, so that you move in a straight line. On the final leg of the gaiting pattern, the judge will be your target.

Using the mats

At indoor shows, the rings are usually covered with rubber mats to give the dogs and handlers good footing. The matting is generally laid around the perimeter of the ring and across the diagonal. This matting configuration accommodates the basic gaiting patterns: out-and-back, triangle, and go-'round.

Your *dog* should always move on the mat. The purpose of the mat is to give the *dog* secure footing so that his movement is true. The only time your dog should move off the mat is at the corners if they have not been adequately matted.

If the mats are narrow, there may not be room for both the handler and the dog on the mat. The mat is there to help the *dog*; if necessary, the handler should move on the unmatted surface.

This Greyhound is gaited along the mat's center while the handler runs beside the mat.

The mats can help you and your dog move in a straight line. A dog that gaits along the mat's edge will tend to move in a straight line since he will avoid stepping off the mat. The handler can watch the edge of the mat in his peripheral vision, using it as a guide for straight movement.

Stopping at the right spot

The stop at the end of your individual gaiting pattern gives the judge a chance to look at your dog standing naturally. If your dog is right under the judge's nose, or if your dog is halfway across the ring, the judge can't evaluate your dog properly. So, it's important to stop your dog in the right place.

The general rule of thumb is to pick a "stop target" on the final leg of your gaiting pattern about five feet in front of the judge. This gives the judge a good angle for observing your dog and gives you a little maneuvering room if you have to take a step or two to fix your dog's stop.

This Cocker Spaniel has been stopped too close to the judge, and the toy is being held over his head rather than in front of him.

This English Springer Spaniel has been stopped about six feet from the judge so that she can have a good look at the dog.

Troubleshooting

Even when you've trained your dog well and you feel comfortable with your job as the human half of your team, things can go wrong as you display your dog's movement to the judge. You should know how to repair these gaiting problems on the fly.

Pacing

Pacing and trotting are both "two-beat" gaits. In a trot, the dog's *diagonal* pairs of legs move together. The left front and right hind feet hit the ground together, and then the right front and left hind feet strike the ground. Most dogs are moved at a trot in the show ring.

In a pace, the legs on the *same* side of the body move forward simultaneously: the two left legs move simultaneously, followed by the two right legs. The result is a rolling motion of the body as the dog lurches first to the left and then to the right.

No breeds should be shown pacing. In fact, some breed standards state explicitly that pacing is not correct:

"The American Eskimo Dog shall trot, not pace."

(the American Eskimo Dog standard)

Pacing is a very lazy, comfortable gait and some dogs simply prefer it to trotting. Other dogs—particularly those with short backs and long legs—pace because their hind feet and front feet don't collide when they pace.

To prevent pacing, move quickly and, if necessary, throw your dog *slightly* off balance as he starts to move; an unbalanced dog is more likely to recover into a trot than a pace. Try taking a "skipping" step or two as you start moving to unbalance your dog slightly, and then settle into the normal speed for your breed. A *light* pop on the lead, to throw your dog's front slightly off balance, can also help prevent or correct pacing. A courtesy turn—a small, clockwise turn in front of the judge—at the beginning of your gaiting pattern may also help prevent pacing.

In a trot, diagonally *opposite* legs move together. This trotting Bullmastiff's left front and right hind feet strike the ground at the same time.

Puppies go through growth spurts and may suddenly start pacing because of uneven growth, especially when they're in the "all legs" phase. Don't let your puppy get into the habit of pacing—encourage him to trot—but don't panic: another growth spurt may signal the end of pacing.

Refusing to move

If your dog goes on strike and refuses to move in the ring, you have two choices. You can try a quick, firm tug on the lead coupled with your gaiting command to get your dog moving. Alternatively, you can try enticing your dog to move forward with food or a toy. Under *no* circumstances try to drag your dog around the ring. If you can't get your dog to gait in the ring after two or three attempts, simply ask the judge to excuse you.

If your dog "puts on the brakes" and refuses to move more than once, you have a training issue. Go back to the steps for teaching a puppy to gait and reinforce the lessons enthusiastically with praise and rewards until your dog gaits reliably and happily, both alone and in a group, and at home and in strange environments.

Racing or pulling

Racing or pulling is a sure sign that your dog hasn't learned to move properly on a leash. Go back to the steps for training a puppy to gait, individually and in a group.

If your dog goes wild in the ring, then stop, collect your wits, calm your dog, and start gaiting again. Make sure that his collar is up under his ears snugly, and that you have a short, taut lead. If he is wild again, then stop, calm your dog, and start again. If you still cannot control your dog, then quietly ask the judge to excuse you. Go home and train your dog to gait properly around other dogs and in strange places.

The 1/3—2/3 rule

What if *everything* goes wrong?

Sometimes, your dog will take off at a gallop. Sometimes, your dog will start off in a pace. Occasionally *you* will head off in the wrong direction, doing an out-and-back instead of a triangle. Sometimes you and your dog just "get off on the wrong foot." Can you start over? It depends.

There's a standard rule-of-thumb for dealing with situations likes these. If everything is falling apart as you move your dog, then:

❖ Don't get flustered—keep your cool as you assess and repair the situation.

❖ If you have started gaiting and have not gone more that *one third* of the pattern's leg, return to the leg's starting point and give it another try.

❖ If you've gotten beyond the first third of the leg of the gaiting pattern, you've made the commitment to finish the leg. You can stop and get your dog under control *there,* to salvage the rest of the leg, but *don't* return to the leg's starting point.

So, if you don't like the way your gaiting pattern has *started out*—for example, if your dog is pacing or galloping—then assess the situation *quickly*. If you're in the "first third return zone," calmly return to the judge and start over. Don't attempt to apologize to the judge or explain what's happening—he will understand what you are doing and will appreciate your *quick*, calm professional actions.

Summary

Gaiting a dog well is more than just moving your dog around the ring at a trot. Once your dog has learned the basic mechanics of gaiting, you'll need to know the standard ring patterns for gaiting, how to execute a "stop" in the ring, and how to move your dog at the correct speed for his breed. You can add polish to your performance by knowing how to use targets and mats to move in a straight line, how to pick the perfect spot for your stop, and how (and when) to fix gaiting patterns that have gotten off on the wrong foot.

<table>
<tr><td>

Chapter

10
</td><td>

The Exam
</td></tr>
</table>

The judge's hands-on examination is a required part of judging. The judge must evaluate each dog's structure using both his hands and his eyes. In turn, the dog must cooperate by standing perfectly still. The handler must stay out of the judge's way during the exam while controlling the dog. In this chapter, you'll learn the steps involved in the examination and what *you* should do during the exam.

Overview of the Exam

There are things in every breed's standard that only can be evaluated by close inspection. During the examination, the judge assesses the texture of the dog's coat, the number and alignment of teeth, the dog's muscular condition, his underlying bone structure, the pigmentation around the eyes and nose, and the proportions of the head, among other things, and compares these against the breed's standard:

> "Coat—Hard and weather-resistant. Must be double-coated with profuse harsh outer coat and short, soft, close furry undercoat."
>
> *(the Cairn Terrier standard)*

> "Eyes dark in color, wide apart, set low down in the skull, ... of moderate size, neither sunken nor bulging. ... No haw and no white of the eye showing when looking forward."
>
> *(the French Bulldog standard)*

> "Serious fault—hairless eye rim ..."
>
> *(the Rottweiler standard)*

> "... a two-tone or butterfly nose should be penalized."
>
> *(the Brittany standard)*

> "Incomplete pigmentation of the eye rims is a major fault ... incomplete nose pigmentation is a major fault."
>
> *(the Dalmatian standard)*

Your breed's standard will indicate what judges will be looking for during the examination.

Many breed standards also specify the ideal—and unacceptable—temperament for the breed. *No breed* should exhibit fear of the judge or excessive shyness. Dogs that cannot be examined or that are aggressive will be excused or disqualified; the personal safety of the judge during the exam is paramount.

The Basic Examination

The standard procedure for examining dogs is used by most judges. As suggested by the AKC,

> "Examine every dog in approximately the same systematic manner … Approach dogs calmly. Examine with gentleness of touch and with no sudden, surprising gestures … begin with the mouth and head, then systematically work down the neck, front, shoulders, body and hindquarters."

> *(AKC Guidelines for Conformation Dog Show Judges)*

Most breeds are examined when stacked on the ground. Some of the smaller breeds—often called "table breeds"—are stacked on a table for their examination, such as Papillons, Toy Poodles, and Yorkshire Terriers. The table used for the exam is usually a standard grooming table. Some breeds, such as the Whippet, may be examined either on a table or on the ground, according to the judge's preference.

A few breeds are so short that examining them on the ground is difficult, but because they are so heavy, lifting them onto a table is out of the question. These breeds may be judged on a *ramp*: a low table with a ramp that the dog walks up. "Ramp breeds" include Basset Hounds and Bulldogs. The use of a ramp is at the discretion of the judge.

Large, short-legged breeds such as the Bulldog may be examined on a low table called a "ramp."

Dogs that are examined on the table or a ramp are stacked at the *front* of the table—exactly where you taught your puppy to stack. Watch experienced handlers of your breed as they lift and place their dogs on the table.

Steps in the exam

Step 1. The dog is stacked on the table, and, in this case, her attention is focused on a piece of bait. From a distance, the judge looks at the dog from the side, assessing proportion and balance, and then moves around to the front to look at her head, chest, and front legs.

Step 2. The judge approaches the dog from the front and examines her head, looking at details such as eye color, nose pigmentation, and position of the eyes and ears on her head.

The handler steadies the dog by holding the collar in her left hand and, if necessary, by putting her right hand at the back of the dog's skull (not shown here).

Step 3. Next, the judge examines the dog's bite. The extent of the mouth exam varies among breeds: some require a simple exam of the bite (shown here) while others require the judge to open the dog's mouth and count teeth or look at pigmentation.

The handler controls the dog's head so that she doesn't move during the judge's exam.

Step 4. After examining the bite, the judge moves to the side of the dog and begins to examine the dog's neck, shoulder and front structure, assessing, for example how the neck fits the shoulder structure, and checking the width and depth of the dog's chest.

The handler controls the dog's head so that she looks forward rather than twisting to watch the judge.

Step 5. The judge continues to work her way toward the dog's rear, assessing proportions and angles of shoulder structure, and length of rib cage and loin. The judge may reach over the dog's back with her right hand in order to feel both sides of the dog's body.

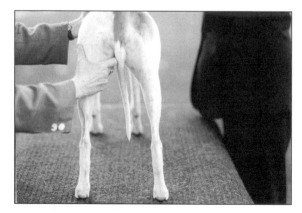

 Step 6. When the judge reaches the dog's back end, she assesses the musculature of the dog's thighs and, if appropriate, checks the tail set and length.

The handler continues to control the dog's head, and may move to stand in front of the dog if necessary to keep the dog steady.

Step 7. The judge checks the angles and proportions of the dog's rear skeletal structure. If examining a male, the judge will count the dog's testes.

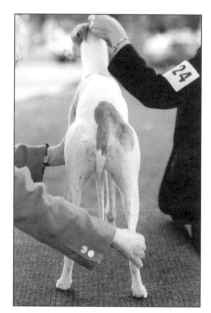

Step 8. The judge examines the dog's hocks, determining whether the dog is cow-hocked or turns out at the hocks. The judge may move the dog's rear feet, either to reposition an incorrectly set foot, or to help her evaluate the dog's structure.

Step 9. After examining the dog's rear, the judge will step back to take a final look at the dog. The handler moves back to the dog's side and quickly resets any feet that have moved, if necessary, in order to present a correctly stacked dog.

The mouth exam

An examination of the bite, and possibly of the tongue or the roof of the mouth, is always part of the judge's exam. Breeds vary in their requirements for teeth (for example, the number of molars), bite (the way the upper and lower jaws come together), and mouth pigmentation (for example, black, pink, or mottled). Some breed standards have lengthy discussions of the mouth and bite while others say little:

"A full complement of white teeth, with a strong, sound scissors bite."

(the Standard Schnauzer standard)

"There must be six incisor teeth between the canines of both lower and upper jaws. An occasional missing premolar is acceptable."

(the West Highland White Terrier standard)

"Dentition: Teeth 42 in number (20 upper, 22 lower) …"

(the Rottweiler standard)

"The Boxer bite is undershot; the lower jaw protrudes beyond the upper and curves slightly upward."

(the Boxer standard)

"Edges of the lips black, tissues of the mouth mostly black, gums preferably black. A solid black mouth is ideal … Disqualifying fault—the top surface of edges of the tongue red or pink or with one or more spots of red or pink."

(the Chow Chow standard)

To examine a bite, the judge approaches the dog from the front and cradles the dog's head in one hand, his other hand over the muzzle, pulling back the upper and lower lips to expose the front teeth. During the exam, the handler must keep the dog's head still by holding one hand on the collar and the other on the back of the dog's head or by holding the cheek and lower jaw.

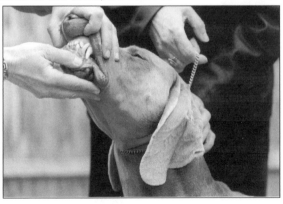

The judge examines the dog's bite while the handler controls the dog's head using one hand on the collar and the other on the back of the head.

Sometimes the judge will ask the handler to show the dog's bite. Use the same technique as the judge: put your right hand under the dog's chin, and your left hand over his muzzle. Use your index finger and thumb on each hand to pull back the lips, displaying the bite.

Some breed standards require the judge to examine or even to count the molars as well as the front teeth. To examine the side teeth, either the judge will ask to the handler to show the teeth by pulling back the lips, or the judge will move to the dog's side and pull back the lips to expose the teeth.

Watch the mouth exam as your breed is being judged so that you have a good idea of what will be expected of you and your dog.

To examine the molars, the judge moves to the dog's side and pulls back the lips. The handler holds the dog's jaw to control his head.

More About the Exam

The basic mechanics of the exam are always the same: the judge begins by examining the dog's head and mouth, and then works his way to the dog's rear. The handler's job during the exam is to keep the dog steady so that the judge can examine it, to keep out of the judge's way, and to present the dog in the best possible manner.

Bait

If used correctly, you may use bait to steady the dog during the judge's exam. However, bait must *never* interfere with the judge's ability to examine the dog. If the judge asks you to stop baiting your dog during the exam, follow his instructions *immediately*.

As the judge approaches this Pug, the handler will step aside and stop feeding the dog bait so that the judge can examine the Pug's head and mouth.

You may hold bait in front of your dog as the judge takes his initial look. As the judge moves toward the dog to begin his examination of the head, *do not feed the dog bait!* A judge cannot examine the mouth of a dog that is chewing, and a dog with food in its mouth may try to bite anyone attempting to examine his teeth.

After the mouth exam, as the judge moves to the left side of the dog, you may use bait to stabilize and distract the dog so that it remains steady for the rest of the exam.

Hold your bait carefully so that your dog does not stretch out of position to reach the bait, thereby interfering with the judge's ability to examine him.

Do not drop small pieces of bait on the ground in front of your dog; small pieces of bait are impossible to pick up, and create an unfair situation for the dogs examined after yours. For the same reason, do not toss crumbly bait on the ground. If your bait cannot be *completely* cleaned up, don't toss it on the ground.

Repositioning your dog's feet

No matter how carefully you've trained your dog, and no matter how steady he usually is during the exam, someday he will move during the judge's examination.

When you dog moves, your response will depend on which foot moves and where the judge is. The overriding rule is to *stay out of the judge's way*. If, for example, your dog moves a front foot as the judge is examining the shoulders, do not attempt to fix it. If the judge does not reset the foot, then you may reset it *after* the judge moves to the rear of the dog. Similarly, if the dog moves a hind foot while the judge examines the front, fix it if you can do so easily, but if the judge is examining the rear when the foot moves, leave it alone. As the judge steps back for his final look, you may *quickly* reset any feet that have moved.

The handler repositions the rear foot, being careful not to interfere with the judge as he examines the dog's front.

Occasionally the judge will reposition a dog's feet even if the dog has not moved them. The judge usually does this if the feet have been incorrectly positioned by the handler. If a judge repositions your dog's feet, leave them where the judge puts them, even if you don't like it: the judge is showing you how *he* wants your dog to be presented to him. In fact, many judges are also excellent handlers who know exactly how a dog should be set, so pay close attention when a judge resets your dog.

Where does the handler stand?

The handler's job is to control the dog during the examination without limiting the judge's ability to examine the dog. Where you stand during the exam depends on your breed, the behavior of your dog, and the actions of the judge.

In the initial presentation for the judge's exam, the handler is on the dog's right side, giving the judge an unobstructed view. The handler may stand or kneel, depending on the size of the dog.

As the exam progresses, the handler should quietly reposition himself to stay out of the judge's way. If the judge stays on one side of the dog and simply reaches across the dog to feel its right side, the handler may be able to remain at the dog's side without impeding the judge. If, on the other hand, the judge leans over the dog to examine its midsection or

With this tall Pointer, the handler stands at the side of the dog, controlling the head and holding the tail. The handler's position does not interfere with the judge's ability to do the exam.

With this shorter Welsh Springer Spaniel, the handler kneels during the exam, staying out of the way of the judge while controlling the dog's head.

rear, the handler may need to move quietly to the head of the dog in order to stay out of the judge's way while controlling the dog. If the handler moves during the exam, then, when the judge steps away for a final look, the handler should move back to the dog's right side.

Troubleshooting

Occasionally you may have problems with your dog during the judge's exam, particularly if the dog is relatively new to showing. Many of these problems can easily be handled in the ring.

Dog kneels or sinks down during exam. If your dog tries to kneel or to sink down in the rear as the judge examines him, hold the collar in your right hand, and place your left hand lightly under the dog's belly. Be careful not to push up on the dog's belly—you might create the appearance of a roached back. Alternatively, instead of putting your left hand under the dog's belly, you can try holding the dog's right knee with your left hand, locking it so that he can't kneel. Above all, any action that you take should not interfere with the judge during the exam.

Dog swings into or leans on handler as judge moves to rear. If your dog tends to lean into you as the judge moves along the dog's side, then hold the dog's collar in your right hand and gently poke your left index finger into the dog's right flank: most dogs will find it uncomfortable to press into your finger.

Dog swings head around to watch judge. If your dog tries to swing his head around to watch the judge during the exam, hold his collar in your left hand and use your right hand to hold his right jawbone, with your thumb on his cheek and fingers pressing into the soft

"V" formed by the lower jaw. If your dog swings his head to look at the judge when the judge is standing away from the dog, use both hands to control the dog's head if you don't need to position the tail with your left hand. If you must hold the tail with your left hand, then use one or two of the fingers of your right hand, while holding the collar, to push on the back of the dog's skull so that he looks forward.

Dog shows fear or can't be examined. Is this an isolated incident? Is the dog usually well behaved during the exam? If so, then try to identify the factor that has spooked your dog. Is the judge wearing a hat or a flapping coat? Are the weather conditions unusual—say, gusting winds or rain? Is the judge a smoker, and is the dog not familiar with the smell of smoke?

The handler of this Australian Cattle Dog controls the dog's head with both hands while the judge examines the body and rear.

If the dog won't cooperate in the exam, *don't* have a battle of wills with the dog in the ring; a struggle could turn an isolated incident into a long-term problem with the exam. Simply apologize to the judge and ask to be excused.

If your dog frequently shows fear or shyness during the exam, then your dog isn't ready to show. Begin retraining your dog to accept the exam, taking it slowly, and exposing your dog to lots of people he doesn't know, in lots of different places. *Never* fight with the dog during the exam if he is scared—that will only make the dog's problem worse. The exam should be a pleasant experience for the dog.

Bitch in season. You may show a bitch in season in conformation classes. Simply tell the judge, "She's in season" as he examines her head. Be aware that some bitches won't let judges examine their rears when they are in season, and will try to move away or sit. Don't worry about the behavior—judges understand bitches in season can be skittish.

Summary

The judge's hands-on examination is a crucial part of the judging process; every dog in each class must be examined by the judge. It is important that you know what the judge is evaluating when he examines your dog, so you must read your breed standard to understand the exam.

Most exams follow the same general procedure: the judge starts by examining the head and bite, and then moves to examine the body and rear end of the dog. The handler's responsibility during the exam is to control the dog and to stay out of the judge's way.

Chapter 11

Teaching a Puppy to Be Examined

If your puppy practically turns himself inside out wiggling with happiness when anyone pets him, you may wonder if he'll ever learn to stand still for the judge's exam. In this chapter you'll learn basic skills that will be useful in your puppy's daily life and will be the foundation for the judge's exam. When your puppy has mastered these skills and, in separate lessons, has learned to stack, you'll combine them into training for the examination.

Laying the Foundation

The easiest way to teach your puppy to accept an examination by a stranger is to teach a number of little skills that will be the building blocks for the examination. The added benefit of many of these building blocks is that they're good "life skills" for your puppy. For example, teaching your puppy to let you hold his head and open his mouth will make it easier for you to clean his teeth. Teaching your puppy to sit or stand calmly while a stranger feels his body will make visits to the veterinarian and the groomer easier.

All of the foundation exercises are *informal*, and many can be done as you socialize your young puppy in your neighborhood or as you sit at home, watching television. Some puppies will find these foundation skills very easy, and will progress through them quickly, while others will need a bit more practice at each skill. You can teach the foundation skills to your puppy *before* he can hold a stack reliably.

The sitting exam

The first step is to teach your puppy "emotional control" when a stranger touches him. Some puppies will wiggle and jump in delight when a stranger pets them, others will remain still and calm, and some will shrink away, not entirely confident of the stranger. If you've socialized your puppy well, then he should not be afraid of strangers. If he is afraid of strangers, your first step will be to socialize your puppy more.

It's easiest to teach a puppy to be calm when petted by a stranger if he's sitting; a sitting puppy is more secure, less exuberant, and easier to control than a standing puppy.

Teach your puppy to sit calmly while you stroke his head and run your hands firmly down his back.

Begin with your puppy sitting, either on a table or on the ground. Hold your puppy's collar or leash with your right hand, and run your left hand lightly but firmly down your puppy's head, neck, and back. Try to imitate the long, firm stroking motions a judge might use. If your puppy remains sitting, praise him. If your puppy struggles or stands up, don't correct him; simply make him sit again, run your hand down his body, and praise him.

When your puppy will sit still as you stroke him, ask a helper to be the "judge."

Have your puppy sitting at your left side, on a table or on the ground. Hold his collar or lead. The helper should approach your puppy from the front, just as a judge would do in an exam. If your puppy is still, praise him. If your puppy is excited or fearful, have the helper stand by your puppy's head until he relaxes; then praise your puppy and reward him with a treat.

Next, the helper should pet your puppy lightly but firmly on the top of his head. If your puppy accepts this, then the helper should give your puppy a treat. If your puppy is excited, the helper should pause briefly, let your puppy calm down, and then repeat the petting. If your puppy is calm—or at least, not as excited—the helper should give your puppy a treat and walk away. Release your puppy from his sit and praise him. When your puppy will sit still as his head is petted, the helper should also add lightly touching the top or side of the muzzle with his fingertips.

If your puppy is afraid of being touched by a stranger, don't force the issue. Instead, stop the exam training and work on socializing your dog.

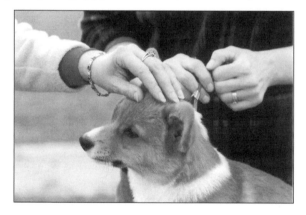

Have a helper pet your sitting puppy on the head. The puppy should be calm, and should not stand up, show fear, or shy away from the helper.

When your puppy will sit calmly while his head is petted, the helper should next move to the left side of your puppy and run both his hands firmly but lightly down your puppy's body. Hold your puppy's collar and prevent him from standing up during the "exam." If your puppy accepts the helper's body exam, then reward him with a treat and praise, and release him.

The helper moves to the sitting puppy's side and strokes his body firmly.

Your goal at this stage is for your puppy to accept the firm stroking of a stranger while sitting calmly.

When your puppy has mastered this skill with helpers he knows, have strangers stroke and pet your puppy's head and body as he sits—this is a great thing to do as you socialize your puppy! Have each "judge" give the puppy a treat *after* he is petted to reward him for his good behavior.

The standing exam

When your puppy accepts the light, firm stroking of a stranger while sitting calmly, repeat the process with your puppy standing at your side.

This is *not* to be done in a formal stack; the purpose of this exercise is to teach your puppy emotional control and to accept the hands of strangers. If your puppy moves his feet a little bit, it isn't important. If your puppy takes *several* steps toward or away from the "judge," you will need to practice the sitting exam some more.

Repeat the steps that you used when teaching your puppy to sit calmly while being stroked by a stranger:

- ❖ With your puppy standing at your left side, have a helper approach from the front. If your puppy stands still, the helper should give your puppy a treat.

- ❖ The helper next pets your puppy gently but firmly on the head. If your puppy is calm, the helper may also touch the muzzle lightly. If your puppy behaves well, the helper should reward him with a treat.

Your puppy should stand calmly while your helper pets his head and strokes his body. He should not be overly excited, or nor show any fear.

- ❖ The helper moves to the puppy's side and run both hands firmly down the puppy's back and sides as the handler holds the collar or lead.

❖   The helper then runs his hands down the hind legs of your puppy—something he couldn't do when your puppy was sitting! If your puppy behaves well, reward him with a treat.

Holding the head and muzzle

The foundation work for the mouth exam begins with teaching your puppy to let you hold his muzzle, lift his lips and open his mouth. You can condition your puppy to accept being held like this in dozens of quick sessions during the day as you watch television or play with your puppy.

The first step is to condition your puppy to having your right hand under his chin with the thumb across the muzzle—basically, holding the muzzle with a very light grip.

While sitting, standing, or kneeling next to your puppy, slip your left hand into his collar. Then support your puppy's head with your right hand under the jaw for a couple of seconds. Say "good boy" and take your hands away, releasing him. Repeat once or twice—the entire training session will take less than 10 seconds. You can do this any time you are playing with or petting your puppy. As you sit on the floor, watching TV with your puppy lying calmly at your side, take the opportunity to practice cradling his muzzle in your hand.

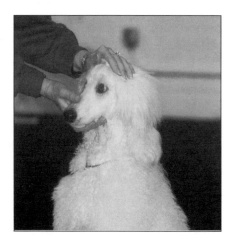

Hold your thumb gently over your puppy's muzzle while cradling his chin in your hand.

Ultimately, you will be able to grip your dog's muzzle to control his head as you stack him.

When your puppy accepts and enjoys resting his muzzle in your right hand, gently lay your right thumb *lightly* over the top of the muzzle. Some puppies won't care, and some will protest, since holding the muzzle this way, even very lightly, is a dominance action. Repeat this action, with the right thumb *lightly* on top of the muzzle while you control the dog with the collar in your left hand, dozens of times a day, for no more than a few seconds each time. Remember to praise your puppy liberally *while* you're holding his muzzle, not after you let go!

When your puppy accepts your right thumb on top of his muzzle, slowly increase the pressure until your puppy will tolerate a *light but firm* grip on the muzzle. Holding your puppy's muzzle will eventually be a tool for keeping your puppy from swinging his head.

Next, condition your puppy to having two hands hold his muzzle: put your right hand on the bottom, left hand on the top, to make a "muzzle sandwich." This is how the judge—or you—will hold the muzzle during the mouth exam. Again, praise your puppy *while* you hold his muzzle, not after you let go.

When your puppy will let you cradle his muzzle in your right hand with your left hand on top, practice lifting your puppy's upper lips with the index finger and thumb of your left hand. Praise your puppy while you lift his lips.

Finally, when your puppy will accept having his muzzle held, slowly incorporate muzzle cradling and holding by another person into your sitting and standing petting practice.

All of these muzzle exercises can be mixed in with playing and petting your puppy, dozens of times a day—you don't have to set aside special "muzzle training" time. If you handle his muzzle every time you pet your puppy's head and rub his ears, he'll learn to enjoy having his muzzle held.

Your puppy should allow a stranger to cradle his muzzle in two hands; this is the basis of the mouth examination.

If your puppy suddenly objects to having his muzzle held, check to see whether he is teething, which usually occurs when puppies are four to seven months old. If your puppy is teething, stop handling his muzzle until the teething is complete, and his mouth no longer hurts.

Counting testes

Male puppies must accept having their testes counted. In a show a judge is required to confirm that males have two testes by *lightly and briefly* feeling the scrotum; the skin is so thin that a *light* touch allows the judge to count the testes.

The simplest way to condition a male puppy to having his testes examined is simply to incorporate touching his scrotum into your everyday playing and grooming. When you pet your puppy, touch his scrotum. When you groom your puppy, touch his scrotum, and hold it lightly in your fingers for a couple of seconds. When your puppy is sleeping next to you as you watch TV, scratch lightly around his scrotum. If he is especially ticklish, then distract him: as he stands eating his meal, touch his scrotum.

The Formal Exam

By now, your puppy should have mastered all his foundation skills for the exam, taught in very brief sessions, intermingled with play, grooming, and socialization. At this point, your puppy should:

❖ sit calmly, under emotional control, while a stranger pets his head, holds his muzzle lightly, and strokes his back firmly while standing beside or behind him

❖ stand calmly while a stranger pets his head, holds his muzzle lightly, and strokes his back and hind legs firmly while standing beside or behind him

❖ if your puppy is male, allow a stranger to lightly touch his scrotum

If your puppy can do all these things, and if your puppy can hold a formal stack for 15 seconds or more, it's time to combine the skills into a formal exam. If, however, your puppy is *not* solid on these foundation skills, do not try to do a formal exam, since you could create problems with a steady stack if your puppy is not ready to be examined by a stranger.

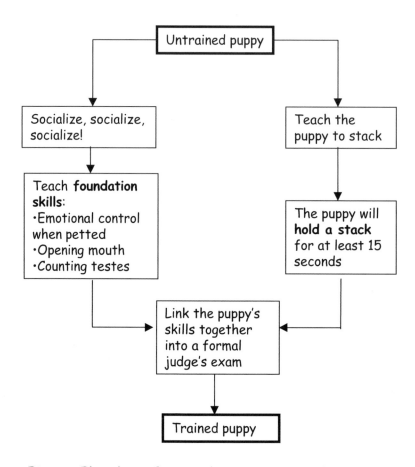

Figure: Flowchart for teaching a puppy to be examined.

The first step in training your puppy for a formal exam is for *you* to examine him:

❖ Stack your puppy on a table or on the ground.

❖ Hold his collar in one hand, and, using the other hand, go through the motions of an exam: pet the top of his head, hold his muzzle, lift up his lips, stroke his body, run your hands down his front legs and rear legs, and if male, count his testes.

Your touch should be light but firm. If your puppy moves a foot as you "examine" him, simply reset the foot while repeating your stack command, and continue with your exam. Then release your puppy with praise and a reward.

When your puppy will hold his stack through your examination, it's time to enlist a helper to play "judge." Make sure your helper knows the steps in the exam—head and mouth, then body and finally rear—and understands that his touch should be light but firm.

❖ Stack your puppy on the table or on the ground, with your helper standing two or three steps in front of your puppy.

❖ Next, the helper walks up to your puppy and offers him a piece of bait.

❖ The helper then examines your puppy's head, letting the muzzle rest on one hand.

❖ Finally, the helper moves to your puppy's side and rear, continuing his examination while you distract your puppy with bait.

Stack your puppy and stand by his left side. The helper approaches the puppy from the front and examines the puppy's head and body.

If your puppy moves a foot during the exam, then reset it while repeating your stack command. If your puppy moves substantially out of position, then stop the exam, release your puppy, and start over with a fresh stack.

If your puppy repeatedly moves or "breaks his stack" during the exam, then quit; he's not ready for a formal exam yet. Your puppy should *not* learn that it's OK to break his stack during an exam. Go back to your foundation work: have your puppy practice standing still, not in a formal stack, while a stranger pets him. When your puppy will stand still *reliably* while a stranger pets him, then try the examination in a formal stack again.

The first few times your helper examines your puppy, *do not* attempt a mouth exam. When your puppy is completely steady when examined by several different helpers, add the mouth exam; just lift the lips *briefly* to examine the bite. If your breed has a more extensive mouth exam—for example, counting teeth—practice it *separately* from the formal exam.

Summary

Teaching your puppy to accept a judge's examination begins with teaching him a number of skills that are useful both in and out of the show ring. You can begin working on these foundation skills right away, before your puppy knows how to hold a formal stack. Work on the foundation skills as you socialize your puppy, as you play with your puppy, and as your puppy rests quietly with you as you read, chat or watch television. Dozens of brief training sessions—each less than a minute long—scattered throughout the day will be more effective than one long training session.

When your puppy has mastered these foundation skills, and when your puppy can reliably hold a formal stack for at least 15 seconds, you're ready to combine the skills into a formal exam. The transition should be relatively simple, since you're not introducing any new skills to your puppy—you're just combining things he already knows. If your puppy has difficulty at any point, then don't push it—go back a few steps and work on his basic skills.

<table>
<tr><td>

Chapter

12
</td><td>

Putting It All Together
</td></tr>
</table>

In the ring, dogs must alternate between standing still and moving. Now that your dog has mastered the two basic skills of stacking and gaiting, you'll need to combine these skills. In this chapter you'll learn how to teach your dog make smooth transitions between standing still and moving. You'll also learn about the sequence of events usually followed in the ring, and what you should do when you're in the ring.

Making Transitions

Making a smooth transition between standing and moving is a skill which should be practiced, just as you practiced the other skills. The key is to make the transition *smooth*, so that your dog always appears at his best.

From still to moving

Stack your dog, with your lead gathered in your left hand, and the collar up under your dog's ears. After a few seconds, stand up, make sure there's a little bit of slack in your lead, and give your dog his gaiting command.

Start moving slowly. The goal is to make a smooth transition from being still to gaiting. *Don't* jerk your dog into motion with the lead while you take off with a flying leap; an off-balance dog is not what you want the judge to see. Instead, use two or three steps to *slowly and smoothly accelerate* to a trot.

As you begin this transition training, only go a few steps at a trot before rewarding your dog with praise and a treat. When your dog understands how to make the transition from stacking to gaiting, practice a complete gaiting pattern, starting from a stack with a smooth and graceful transition to gaiting.

From moving to still

Start by gaiting your dog for a few yards. As you approach the spot at which you plan to stack your dog, slowly decelerate as you give your dog his halting or stopping command. Your last couple of steps in motion should be at a walk, and you should try to *walk your dog into a stack*.

Walking your dog into a stack isn't as difficult as it sounds. In fact, walking your dog into a stack very similar to having your dog execute a stop while standing next to you, rather than facing you. As you slow to a walk and then to a halt, your dog should place his feet close to the correctly stacked position. Then, when you stack your dog, you should only need to make minor adjustments to one or two feet, and your dog will be set.

The first Clumber Spaniel was walked into his stack and is ready when the judge looks. The second dog is still being stacked: the judge sees a rounded topline and a low tailset.

Again, smoothness is key in making the transition. As you slow down and give your dog his stopping command, think about walking your dog into a stack, and be aware of how he places his feet.

The Ring Procedure

Almost without exception, judges conduct their classes following the same general sequence:

* ❖ evaluate the dogs as a group (stacked and moving together)

* ❖ evaluate each individually (examination and moving individually)

* ❖ evaluate them again as a group (stacked and moving together)

The ring procedure used is thus reasonably predictable, and is a sequence with which you must become familiar.

Entering and the initial stack

When the dogs and handlers enter the ring at the beginning of a class, the dogs are stacked quickly in a line so that the judge can check armband numbers, look at the class, and form an initial impression of the dogs.

Have your lead coiled and your dog's collar in position *as the previous class is receiving its ribbons*. Do not enter the ring until your dog and your equipment are ready.

As you reach the spot for your initial presentation, slow down and walk your dog into a stack, so that you have to adjust only one or two of his feet.

If you are not at the head of the line, do not crowd the dog stacked ahead of you. A rough rule of thumb is to leave a body and tail's length between each dog in line. If you are

When a class enters the ring, the dogs are stacked in a line for the initial presentation to the judge.

Next, the dogs are moved once or twice around the ring as a group so that the judge can form an initial impression of their movement.

showing a breed with a long tail, leave ample space between dogs or your dog will be smacked in the face by the tail of the dog ahead of him.

If your class is called into the ring in catalog order but the dog ahead of you enters the ring *after* you do, leave a gap in the line-up for the missing dog. Otherwise, you may have to move your stacked dog because the dog ahead of you, entering the ring late, needs room to stack.

Other things to remember when your dog is stacked in a group are:

❖ Stack your dog for the exam so that you have clearance around canopy poles and ropes, and the steward's table; the judge should have a clear view of your dog.

❖ Stack your dog on a level, even surface with good footing—if outdoors, do not stack your dog uphill or downhill, or with one foot in a hole; if indoors, do not stack your dog with feet off the mat.

Do not to stack your dog behind a pole or other object that will obstruct the judge's view.

Once stacked, don't fuss with your dog, making minor adjustments. You should stack your dog *quickly* and then *hold* the stack so the judge will see your dog, rather than see you bending over to make a tiny adjustment to the placement of a foot.

Moving in a group

After the initial presentation, the dogs are gaited around the ring once or twice together, so that the judge can check for lameness and form an initial impression of their movement, looking at their strengths and weaknesses in comparison to each other. The group movement ends as the first dog in line nears the spot where the judge will do the individual examination—usually by the ring entrance and judge's table.

During the group movement:

❖ Don't crowd the dog ahead of you. If you do, you'll create the illusion that your dog's movement is restricted because your dog won't be able to move out properly.

❖ Don't start moving the instant the dog in front of you takes off. Let the dog ahead of you move for a couple of strides before you begin.

❖ As you move around the ring, maintain four to six feet between dogs, depending on the breed's size.

❖ As the group movement ends, watch the handler ahead of you and slow down so that you don't collide with the handler and his dog.

The exam

After the dogs move as a group, the judge will examine and move each dog individually. The individual exam takes only 20 or 30 seconds, and yet it can be the make-or-break element in the judge's decision.

The exam is usually done near the table where the judge and ring steward do their paperwork. The judge may indicate to the first person in line where he wants the dogs to be stacked for the exam. If possible, watch earlier classes and see where the judge does his exam.

As soon as the group movement is complete, the first dog in line should be stacked on the table or at the spot designated by the judge. If you are first in line, immediately go to the table or to the place indicated by the judge and set your dog for the exam.

During the individual evaluation, the judge examines each dog. The judge may examine the dog's bite herself, or ask the handler to show the dog's bite.

If you are not first in line, wait until the dog ahead of you starts his individual gaiting pattern. As soon as he begins moving, go to the spot for the exam and stack your dog, so that he is set and ready when the judge turns to face you.

During the individual exam, you should:

- ❖ have your dog stacked, ready for the exam, while the judge is looking at the movement of the dog ahead of you

- ❖ keep your dog under control so that the judge is able to do the examination

- ❖ comply with requests from the judge, such as a request to show the dog's bite

- ❖ answer promptly with your dog's age if asked

- ❖ keep out of the judge's way so that he can do his exam

When this judge turns around after watching the previous dog gait, he will see the next dog already stacked and ready to be examined.

Occasionally a judge will engage in a little conversation as he approaches or examines your dog. Often the judge is trying to make the handler feel at ease. Be polite—respond pleasantly and *briefly*. Don't volunteer information about your dog unless she is a bitch in season—then simply say, "She's in season" as the judge begins his individual exam.

A judge may reset the feet of your dog during the examination, often to correct your placement of the feet. If the judge moves the dog's feet into a new position do not reset the feet unless the dog moves—and then put the feet back where the *judge* placed them: the judge has shown you how he wants to see your dog.

This Dalmatian has turned her head to look at someone, creating the misleading impression that her elbow pops out from her body.

Never let your dog turn his head to watch the judge during the exam. This causes his shoulders and spine twist out of alignment, with the net effect that the dog "pops out an elbow", making it appear as though the dog has space between the elbow and chest, when in fact the space between the elbows may be nicely filled by the dog's chest.

After completing the individual examination, the judge may step back to have a final look at your stacked dog. If your dog moved a foot during the exam, quickly reset it so that the picture the judge sees is perfect.

Individual movement

After the hands-on examination, the judge will evaluate the dog's movement, and will tell the handler which gaiting pattern to use—the triangle, the out-and-back, or another. The dog should be gaited at the speed appropriate for the breed so that the judge can assess the dog's front, rear and side movement.

As the dog and handler return to the judge on the final leg of the gaiting pattern, the dog should stop a few feet away from the judge so that he can see how the dog sets his feet naturally. After the judge briefly studies the dog, the dog then gaits to the end of the line of waiting dogs, so that the judge may see the dog's side movement

Plan your "stop target" on the final leg of your gaiting pattern so that you dog will stop and stack about five or six feet from the judge.

❖ Have your lead gathered up and collar correctly positioned as you release your dog from his examination stack.

❖ As you start, use two or three steps to accelerate smoothly to your dog's proper gaiting speed. Use two or three steps at the end of your gaiting pattern to decelerate, so that you have a smooth stop and walk your dog into position.

❖ Stop a few feet from the judge so that he can see the dog from a reasonable angle and so that you can take a step or two to adjust your dog's stop, if necessary.

❖ Watch your dog's gait and respond *quickly* if you need to restart your gaiting pattern. If your dog's movement *starts* out badly, return to the starting point for that leg, and try again

Final presentation

After the last dog in the class has been examined individually, the judge will evaluate the dogs again as a group. The dogs should be stacked for the final presentation when the last dog in the class is being moved individually. Make sure you know which dog and handler are last in line so that you can move quickly to stack your dog for the final presentation.

In the final group presentation, the judge may walk up and down the line of stacked dogs, comparing fronts and rears.

As in the initial presentation, the dogs are stacked in a line so that the judge can survey the class. At this point, the judge may rearrange the order of the class by having some dogs move to different places in the line-up. If you are asked to move your dog to a different position in the line, move briskly and stack your dog quickly where the judge indicated. If you are interrupted mid-stack because another dog is sent to stand in front of you, take it in stride, move, and quickly stack your dog.

Next, the dogs will move once or twice around the ring together. As soon as the dogs have stopped, they should be stacked again. The judge may repeat the process of rearranging dogs and having them move several times before the winners are chosen.

All the rules for the initial presentation apply to the final presentation: stack your dog quickly, don't crowd the dog ahead of you, and don't keep making minor adjustments to your dog's stack. Your goal is to have a perfectly stacked dog each time the judge glances at him—not a work in progress.

If the judge walks down the line of dogs, obviously examining fronts, make sure your dog's front is perfect: this is not the time to concentrate on your dog's rear legs. Similarly, if the judge walks back up the line looking at rears, don't be so focused on the front that you fail to notice an incorrectly set rear. You should be aware, at all times, of what the judge is looking at—front, rear, or side—and make sure that part of your dog is perfectly stacked.

As the judge moves down the line, the handlers should make sure that their dogs' fronts are correctly set.

If your dog moves a foot *substantially* out of position, quickly reset the foot—do not completely reset your dog. The *only* time you should completely reset your dog is when the stack completely falls apart, and resetting would be faster than trying to fix each thing that has gone wrong. Reset your dog quickly, without disturbing the dogs around you.

Placements

When the judge has made his selections, he will point to his choices, saying or signaling "First," "Second," "Third," and "Fourth." In many cases, the judge may rearrange the class for their final group movement in order of his placements.

The handlers and dogs that are awarded class placements should move quickly to the placement markers by the judge's table to receive their ribbons. The other

The ring placement markers are set along the ring gates near the ring entrance. First place is nearest the steward's table.

handlers should leave the ring quickly so that the handlers in the next class can enter and set their dogs; they should, of course, congratulate the placement winners as they leave the ring.

Summary

Most judges follow the same procedure, or sequence of events, when they judge a class. First, the dogs in a class enter the ring and are stacked, so that the judge may take attendance and form an initial impression of the dogs. The dogs are then moved in a group, which allows the judge to check for lameness and gives the dogs a chance to warm up. Next, the judge examines each dog; he also evaluates movement as the dogs are gaited individually. Finally, the dogs are stacked and then moved as a group, so that the judge can make his decisions and indicate his placements.

The basic ring procedure, therefore, consists of the three basic skills—gaiting, stacking and being examined—linked together with smooth transitions. Being able to transition smoothly from moving to still, so that your dog walks into a stack, will gain you valuable seconds when you set your dog. Being able to transition smoothly from still to moving will ensure that your dog always looks his best when moving in the ring.

<table>
<tr><td>

Chapter

13

</td><td>

Adding Some Polish

</td></tr>
</table>

How do you progress from merely stepping through the mechanics of showing your dog to really "presenting" your dog to the judge? How do you add the little touches to your ring performance that might make the difference between winning and losing? In this chapter you'll learn how to use bait correctly to enhance your presentation of your dog. You'll also learn about "waiting games"—ways to keep your dog on his toes and looking his best while he waits his turn in the ring. Finally, you'll learn about elements of polish and sportsmanship that will take you further down the road to being a seasoned handler.

Using Bait

Bait—food or toy—is a *tool* for enhancing your presentation of your dog. It is *not* a means for controlling an untrained dog. Bait should be used sparingly; small amount of food should go a long way if you're using bait correctly.

❖ Do not throw bait in the ring: even if you pick it up, the slivers left behind are unfair to other dogs. If you place a piece of bait on the ground for your dog to focus on when he is stacked, pick the bait up before your move.

❖ Do *not* use bait *while* you are stacking your dog. If you must bait your dog in order to get his cooperation *while* you are stacking him—as you did when you taught him how to stack—then your dog is not yet ready to show.

After stacking her Siberian Husky, this handler uses bait to enhance her dog's facial expression.

❖ Once your dog is stacked, you may use bait, held in front of your dog, to capture your dog's attention and improve his expression. However, holding the bait too close to your dog's head, or too high or too low, can make him twist his head or move out of position.

The handler uses bait during the judge's exam to keep her Shih Tzu's body properly aligned as the judge examines the dog's rear.

At the end of the individual gaiting pattern, the handler uses bait to help position her Boxer in a perfect stop.

❖ Do *not* give bait to your dog when he is about to be examined. Stack your dog for his exam *without* feeding him bait, so the judge may examine his bite safely.

❖ Bait *may* be used *sparingly* during the examination but only *after* the judge has completed the examination of the head and mouth. If you bait during the exam, hold the bait so that your dog does not stretch or twist toward the bait: this destroys his set and makes it impossible to examine him.

❖ If the judge asks you *not* to bait your dog during the exam, then *stop baiting immediately*.

❖ Do *not* use bait *while* you move. If you carry or wave bait in your right hand while you move, your dog will twist to look at your hand, destroying his movement.

❖ You *may* use bait to help maneuver your dog into a perfect stop, and to hold his attention as the judge studies him. Hold the bait a foot or two in front of your dog and at the correct height to control your dog's head position.

If you carry bait in your right hand when you move, keep it away from your dog so that his movement will not be distorted.

❖ Your bait can also be a reward: when your dog does something well in the ring, reward him with a piece of bait so that he'll keep on working enthusiastically, hoping for more.

Waiting Games

If you are in a large class, there will be time when you are simply waiting your turn: your dog is not being examined or moved. As you wait for your turn to be judged, don't sap your dog's energy and enthusiasm by constant repetition of stacking: dogs, especially young dogs, can quickly become bored with being stacked. The last thing you want is a dog that is so bored and frustrated that he won't cooperate with the judge's exam.

Another reason for keeping your dog happy and occupied while you wait in the ring is that some judges glance at the dogs waiting in line while examining another dog. Your dog should be alert and on his toes whenever the judge looks at him.

An easy way to keep your dog occupied as you wait in the ring is to play games with him. A very simple game is to have your dog catch *small* pieces of bait. Do this *only* if you have already taught your dog to catch little pieces of food and he can catch reliably, so that you don't scatter bait on the ground. Make sure that there is enough space around your dog so that other dogs will not compete for the tossed bait.

If you've taught your dog skills such as "bow," "wave," or "stretch," you can *quietly* ask him to do these in the ring; remember, the goal is to keep your dog amused, not to call attention to your dog.

While waiting to be examined, this Labrador Retriever focuses on his handler, waiting to be tossed a piece of bait.

A favorite small toy or ball can also make the wait in line less boring for your dog. If you use a squeaky toy, be careful not to distract dogs near you, some of which might be toy-crazy and try to lunge for your dog's toy.

Make the most of your environment. If a person or dog outside the ring catches your dog's attention, let him stand and stare. If he focuses on another handler tossing bait to his dog, and stands poised and alert, hoping that he'll get a piece of bait, too, that's great: your dog has created his own game! Be careful, though, that he doesn't lunge for the tossed bait.

Etiquette and Sportsmanship

There are a few guidelines that will make judging go more smoothly and make your ring experience a pleasant one.

❖ Be patient with and courteous to the ring steward when asking questions or when picking up your armband. Don't interrupt the steward when he is trying to do something else—the ring steward has a very complex job, and must juggle many responsibilities at once.

❖ Be ready to enter the ring when your class is called and know which dog you should follow. If the class will be judged in catalog order, try to identify the person you will follow *before* the class is called into the ring.

❖ Don't stack too closely behind the dog in front of you: leave a couple of feet between dogs. Remember that some breeds have long tails that take up space in the line.

❖ When moving in a group, don't crowd the person in front of you. Tailgating interferes with the dog ahead of you and throws off your dog's movement.

For the initial presentation, leave about a body's length between each dog. If the class enters the ring in catalog order, identify the handler you will follow while the previous class is being judged.

❖ Don't refer to your dog by his registered name: the dog is supposed to be anonymous so that he can be judged on his merits. It is permissible, however, to use his callname, as, for example, "Rover, stay!

❖ Keep your dog under control and *always know where his head is*: don't let him sniff or otherwise interfere with another dog.

❖ Don't stare at the judge with a begging or pleading expression.

❖ Don't chat with the judge—reply pleasantly if spoken to but don't start a conversation.

❖ Have your dog stacked, ready for the exam, while the judge watches the dog ahead of you move.

❖ During the exam, control your dog so that the judge can examine it, while staying out of the judge's way.

❖ Don't throw bait on the ground. If you accidentally drop bait, pick it up.

During the exam, the handler must control the dog while staying out of the judge's way.

❖ If you're at the head of the line, before starting the group movement, turn to the handler behind you, smile and ask if he is ready—don't take off until he says "yes." If he doesn't respond, wait for a moment until he appears to be ready, and then begin.

❖ While waiting in line to be judged don't do anything that would interfere with the dog being judged.

❖ Don't chat incessantly with other handlers or spectators—focus on your dog and on the judge. You're in the ring to exhibit your dog, not to socialize or to distract other exhibitors.

❖ If you're showing a bitch in season, avoid unnecessarily close contact with males as you wait outside the ring. Tell the judge that your bitch in season as he begins his examination.

The first dog in line should wait until the other handlers are ready to move before starting.

❖ If your dog relieves himself in the ring, quietly signal the ring steward, who will call for a ring clean-up crew. If your dog stops to urinate or defecate while gaiting, do not try to drag the dog to the side of the ring. Just stop and wait until he is finished; the ring steward will call for cleanup.

❖ Do not allow a male to mark ring gates and tent posts.

❖ Don't play with toys that might distract another exhibitor's dog.

❖ Don't give bait to another exhibitor's dog unless you ask permission.

❖ Make sure that your armband number is not obscured as the judge and steward mark their books.

❖ Accept your ribbon graciously even if you are disappointed—smile and say "Thank you."

❖ Do not make disparaging remarks about other exhibitors or dogs, or about the judge and his judging. If you are upset or angry, leave the ring area as soon as you are allowed to, take a walk, and calm down. Showing dogs is, after all, a sport.

Some of these points are subtle, while others reflect common-sense behavior in the ring. If you're not sure what to do in a given situation, simply think about how you'd like your fellow competitors to treat you and your dog in the ring. For example, you wouldn't want your dog distracted by toys while you try to stack him for his exam, so be careful not to distract other dogs while you play with your dog. In short, treat others in the ring as you would like to be treated.

Summary

When you're in the ring, show discretion in your use of bait. Bait can be a powerful tool if it is not abused. Use bait to enhance your dog's expression when he is stacked, and to keep him alert and focused. You may use bait to steady your dog during the examination *after* the judge has examined the dog's head and bite. However, if the judge asks you not to use bait during the exam, stop immediately.

Keep your dog from becoming bored and listless in the ring. If you're in a large class, play little games with your dog while you wait in line, so that he remains happy and on his toes, always looks his best.

In the ring, basic courtesy and common sense will carry you a long way. Always keep your dog under control: don't let him bother other dogs. Give other exhibitors ample room, both when you're stacking your dog and when you're moving in a group. Don't distract or otherwise interfere with another handler's dog. Whether you win or lose, be gracious to the judge and the other competitors. In short, treat others in the ring as you would like to be treated.

Matches

When your dog has learned his basic showing skills, and when you're confident that *you* know what to do, it's time to test the waters. In this chapter you'll learn about matches, which are a dress rehearsal for your dog's show debut.

Overview

A "match" is a practice show. You cannot earn points toward your dog's championship at a match. A match is far more relaxed and informal than a show, and entry fees at matches are considerably lower than show entry fees.

A match may be open to puppies as young as three months old. Some matches exclude dogs that have earned major points toward their championships, and some matches do not allow professional handlers unless they are handling their own dogs. Champions do not compete in matches.

Sanctioned matches

A "sanctioned match" is a match that is run by an AKC-recognized club under the match rules of the AKC. Sanctioned matches are very similar to shows. The biggest differences between sanctioned matches and shows are:

❖ At an AKC sanctioned match, your puppy cannot earn points toward his championship.

❖ There may be a class for 3-6 month old puppies.

❖ The classes for adults may be limited to Novice and Open.

❖ The judges at the match do not need to be licensed AKC judges.

Puppies as young as 3 months old may be entered in matches.

Matches may be "specialty matches", "group matches" or "all-breed matches." At a specialty match there are limitations on the breeds that can be shown: it is limited to one breed or to a group of breeds with similar characteristics. For example, a Spaniel specialty match would be for Cocker Spaniels, Sussex Spaniels, Field Spaniels, English Springer Spaniels, and so on. A "group match" is limited to a specific group—for example, the Terrier Group or the Hound Group. Finally, an all-breed match (often just called a "match") is open to all breeds. Most matches are all-breed matches.

Fun matches

Any group or organization may hold a "fun match," including private training schools, humane societies, rare breed clubs, and other kennel clubs. Fun matches are often fundraising events for groups or charitable causes. A fun match is not run under AKC rules, and generally has a more relaxed, informal structure than does a sanctioned match.

Because they do not follow the rules of the AKC, the classes and order of judging at fun matches can be quite varied. At very small matches, judging may start at the "group" level rather than at the breed level: that is, they begin by judging all the Sporting puppies together, rather than by first judging each Sporting breed separately. A match like this can be easier on young puppies, since judging doesn't take as long.

Wirehaired Pointing Griffon puppies of very different ages compete against each other at this match: fun match classes might be divided simply into "puppy" and "adult."

Finding and Entering Matches

Finding matches near your home may require a bit of detective work, since they are not always well publicized. There are a number of ways to find matches:

❖ Ask your mentor, class instructor, or other people who show dogs in your area.

❖ Check with your local kennel club—they may be planning a match soon.

❖ Check with your local obedience training club—often obedience and conformation matches are held together.

❖ Check newsletters or Web sites for dog events in your area.

❖ Look for flyers advertising matches, which may be found in local pet stores, veterinary hospitals, the humane society and at handling classes.

❖ If there is an upcoming show in your area, contact the superintendent and ask if a match will be held in conjunction with the show (a sanctioned match may be the evening before a show).

Once you have located a match, check how it should be entered. There are two types of match entry: pre-entry and day-of-match entry. Not all matches offer both types of entry.

❖ Some matches can only be entered prior to the day of the match. The information for making a "pre-entry" will be included in the match announcement.

❖ Some matches will only have day-of-match entries; you just show up and register for the match.

❖ Some matches may have both day-of entry and pre-entry options, possibly with a reduced entry fee for pre-entries. The information for both options will be on the match flyer.

At some matches, entries are accepted on the day of the match at the match registration table.

Matches are usually not tightly scheduled; there is lots of "hurry up and wait" time. You often know when the judging of the breeds in your group will begin, but since you don't know how many dogs will be entered in each breed, or how many breeds will be represented in your group, you need to be available for judging when your group's judging begins.

For example, the match announcement may say:

> Entries 8:00-9:00
> Entry fee: $8/class
> Judging begins at 9:30 for Toy, Terrier, Non-Sporting
> Judging begins at 11:00 for Working, Herding, Sporting and Hound

In this case, the match secretary will accept entries between 8:00 a.m. and 9:00 a.m. on the day of the match. The judging of Toy, Terrier and Non-Sporting breeds begins at 9:30. The Working, Herding, Sporting and Hound breeds must arrive at the match and enter any time before 9:00, but their judging won't begin until 11:00.

Once you've entered the match, you can relax until the time nears for your judging. Check with the ring steward or match secretary *after the entries* close to get an idea of when you should be at your ring—by then, they should have a pretty good idea of how many dogs are at the match, and how long the judging will take.

As your judging time nears, gather your ring equipment—your show lead and collar, and a brush if appropriate—and head to the ring. Wear your armband on your left arm. Watch the classes in the ring before you so you will know where the judge wants the dogs stacked and how he wants them moved. And when it is time for you to enter the ring, go in and practice all the skills—stacking, gaiting, being examined, and making smooth transitions—that you and your dog have been working on!

After each breed in a group is judged, the Best of Breed winners may compete against each other in the group competition.

Using Matches for Training

To make the best use of a match, think of it as a training opportunity rather than a competition. After all, "winning" at a match doesn't mean much. Training to win at a *show* is the object of the game.

This handler uses a piece of food to encourage her Belgian Tervuren puppy to gait happily in the ring. Matches are a great place for "in the ring" training.

Before the match, decide on your goals and *assess your dog's limitations*. Because of the casual nature of matches, it can be a very long time from when you arrive until you are judged. It's possible that the weather may be too much for your puppy—for example, hot and humid— or that it may just be a very long day for him.

Don't push your puppy to his limit. For example, if you have a three-month-old puppy, you may decide to stop showing after breed judging, even if your puppy is eligible to go into the group. Quit while the puppy is still happy, fresh, and eager to participate.

(If you stop early, let the ring stewards know that your puppy's tired and you won't be competing any more that day so they won't delay further judging while waiting for you.)

You should decide on your *goals* for the match. At a fun match, you might even have a judge who will help you meet your goals (at an AKC sanctioned match, however, ring procedure is largely dictated by AKC rules). If you're really lucky at a small fun match, the judge will ask you if there is anything special you want to work on. For example:

❖ Does your dog like to romp and play when he is moving in a group? Be ready with a training plan. Don't let him "get away with it" just because you're in a ring—training him is *exactly* why you're at the match! But remember: harsh corrections are *never* appropriate, in the ring or out.

❖ Is your dog a little unsteady on the examination? Or is there a particular part of the exam, like the bite or the tail, which he doesn't like? Politely ask the judge to do that part of the exam twice, and be ready to train and praise.

❖ Does your dog shy away from the judge when finishing his individual movement? Ask the judge to hold bait in his hand and encourage your dog to come up to the judge, with ears up and tail wagging.

A knowledgeable and helpful match judge can give you help training your dog—and also in learning your role.

At matches, other people can help you train your dog, too. Ask other exhibitors and spectators—strangers to your dog—to examine him while you wait for your turn in the ring. Just be sure not to overdo it; don't wear him out before he goes into the ring. And remember, each "exam" doesn't have to be formal—just being petted by lots of strangers is great socialization and training for your puppy.

Above all, make sure that your dog's match experience is fun, and that he thinks the ring is a wonderful place to be.

A Dry Run for the Handler

Your dog isn't the only one who can use matches as a training ground. You can use matches as a chance to get your show act together, too. For example, a match is an opportunity to figure out what items need to be added to your show checklist, how long it takes you to get ready for a show, and what your pre-ring routine should be.

The match is also a chance to experiment with your dog's show day routine:

❖ Does your dog usually eat in the morning? Some handlers don't feed their dogs breakfast on show days, some feed a tiny breakfast, and some don't change their feeding routine at all (which is the best idea with a young puppy).

❖ If your dog gets car sick, you can experiment with herbs or motion-sickness medications to see how they affect his ring performance: do they make him sluggish in the ring?

❖ Will your dog relieve himself on a leash? If not, you'll need to teach him to do so.

❖ If your dog must be groomed before going into the ring, and is a quiet, well-behaved dog on the grooming table at home, will he be well-behaved on the grooming table at a match?

Match Judges

Anyone can judge at a match. The judge doesn't need to be licensed or to have any proven knowledge of the breeds he is judging. In some cases, match judges are loyal, hardworking club members who are familiar with breed ring procedures and willing to spend a day on their feet, in the sun or rain, putting countless dogs through their paces. In other cases, match judges are may be quite knowledgeable and may have been involved in showing for many years. They may even be licensed AKC judges, or more likely, may be a person who wants to be an AKC judge, and is judging matches in preparation for AKC licensing.

No matter who the judge is, *keep the results of a match in perspective.* Does the judge know your breed's standard? Does he breed or handle your breed? No matter what the judge's opinion of your dog is, be sure to thank the judge, who is a volunteer, as you leave the ring.

Above all, remember the reason you're at the match: it's not to get an opinion about your puppy's merits as a show dog—it's to train your puppy and to train you.

Summary

Matches are an opportunity to have a "dry run" before a show. Sanctioned matches are run under the rules of the AKC, and follow procedures very similar to those of shows. Fun matches are more informal, and may be run by kennel clubs, rare breed clubs, training groups, and other organizations.

Puppies as young as three months old may enter matches. Some matches require pre-entry, while some have day-of-match entries. Information about entries will be found on the match announcement.

A match should be regarded as a training situation for both the dog and the handler, not as a competition. Although informal, matches provide an atmosphere that simulates a dog show. Plan your training goals for the match carefully, keeping in mind that young puppies tire easily.

Picking Your First Show

If all goes well at matches, you'll soon be ready for your first show. In this chapter, you'll learn how to find shows in your area, how to select a show for your debut, and how to decide which class to enter.

Finding a Show

There are several places to find lists of upcoming AKC shows. The most complete and authoritative list is found in each month's *AKC Events Calendar,* which you'll receive as part of your subscription to *The AKC Gazette*. The *AKC Events Calendar* lists shows and other AKC events occurring during the next few months. A calendar of events is also available at the AKC's Web site.

Upcoming shows and matches may also be listed in regional dog event publications, such as the *Match Show Bulletin* (Northeastern and Mid-Atlantic states) and the *Campaign Trail* (California and Nevada). These publications provide information about matches, shows, agility and obedience trials, and training seminars. Many regions also have Internet discussion groups that post announcements of events, such as the "NWDogActivities" list for Oregon and Washington. Ask your handling class instructor or mentor about newsletters and Internet groups in your area.

At AKC shows, superintendents frequently have premium lists available for future shows. Stop by the superintendent's desk to pick up premium lists for shows that you might attend, and to request that your name be placed on the superintendent's mailing list for premium lists. Also, look on the back page of premium lists you pick up: occasionally superintendents print a list of shows they will be running later in the year. Many superintendents also list their upcoming shows on their Web sites.

For long-range planning, you can purchase a 12-month dog show calendar from vendors at dog shows. These calendars are published either by kennel clubs or by dog food companies, and can be either national or regional in coverage. These calendars aren't completely accurate, since event dates are guesses based on the show date the previous year, so you should confirm their information against the *AKC Events Calendar*. The 12-month calendars indicate who the show's superintendent will be, so you can contact the superintendent for premium lists for the shows you are interested in and to confirm the show dates.

Selecting Your First Show

What type of show should you choose for your dog show debut? Consider the following analogy. Suppose that you live in Iowa and that you have been training for the last several months to run in races. For weeks, you run faithfully, increasing your speed, distance, and endurance. You plan your training with the aid of your running mentor, supplemented by ideas gleaned from experience, books, and videos.

Should your first race be the Boston Marathon? Of course not!

It would be silly to travel from Iowa to Massachusetts and enter such a large, perhaps overwhelming, event for your first race. You'd be setting yourself up for a miserable experience. A better tactic would be to pick a smaller race, closer to home, where you could test your new racing skills and where you knew people who could help you if you needed advice or assistance.

A large, crowded show—especially an indoor show in a cavernous building—may not be a good choice as a first show for a puppy.

The same logic applies to picking your first dog show—keep it small, and keep it simple!

Showing your dog isn't just a matter of taking your dog into the ring. It requires lots of logistics—packing equipment for you and your dog, getting to the show on time, finding parking, preparing your dog, finding your ring, and eventually showing your dog. If you aren't properly prepared, your first dog show may be frustrating or even overwhelming.

A few guidelines should govern the choice of your first show:

❖ Pick a show relatively near home. Don't complicate your first show experience with overnight travel or a long drive.

❖ Pick a show at which your mentor, your dog's breeder, your handling class instructor, or experienced friends will be showing. Just having them on the show grounds can boost your confidence.

❖ Pick a relatively small show if possible. Avoid benched shows and large specialty shows.

❖ Unless you already have the show's premium list, pick a show that is *at least six weeks* away so that you have plenty of time to request and receive the premium list, and to enter by the show's entry deadline (usually 2½ weeks before the show). If you already receive premium lists, then pick a show that is at least four weeks away so you have plenty of time to send in your entry.

❖ Indoor shows are generally more difficult for novice dogs because of the crowds and noise. If you have never trained your dog indoors in a large building like a gym or an

In pleasant weather, an outdoor show is a good place to launch your dog's show career.

armory, don't pick an indoor show for your first show. If your training and matches have been outdoors, wait for an outdoor show.

❖ Watch the weather. Nothing can sour a dog (and you) on showing more than being dragged to an outdoor show in humid 95° weather or in bone-chilling rain. If you live in a climate with unpleasant summer or winter weather, wait for an outdoor show in the spring or fall.

Consult with your mentor, your dog's breeder or experienced dog show friends about shows you should target for your debut. Since shows are held at the same sites year after year, they may have suggestions about which shows would be good for a first-timer, and which shows should be avoided until you and your dog have more experience.

For your first few shows, choose shows at which your dog show friends will be present to help your or answer your questions.

If your first show is in a cluster of several shows, *don't* enter all the shows! Entering one or two shows on your first weekend is plenty; you and your dog still have a lot to learn. Remember—finishing your dog's championship isn't a race: there will always be more dog shows to enter in the future. Take your time and have fun.

It's unlikely that the "perfect" show will fall on the weekend you'd like to target for starting your show career. Consider waiting a little longer for a show that is good for a beginner—a short delay can really pay off. Keep in mind all the characteristics of an ideal first show, and try to pick the best conditions for your dog's debut. A careful choice of your first show will make the adventure far more pleasant and will leave you looking forward to your next show weekend.

Which Class Should You Enter?

Once you've picked your first show, your next decision will be which class to enter. There are six regular classes that non-champion dogs may enter, and six regular classes for non-champion bitches:

In the puppy classes, dogs are judged against other dogs of the same age and level of maturity.

❖ *Puppy:* for non-champion dogs at least 6 months old but less than 12 months old on the day of the show (frequently divided into 6-to-9 months old and 9-to-12 months old).

❖ *12-to-18 Month:* for non-champion dogs at least 12 months old but less than 18 months old on the day of the show.

❖ *Novice:* for dogs at least 6 months old which have not yet won a first place in a class (other than Novice or Puppy) nor three first places in Novice, nor earned points toward their championship, prior to the show's closing date for entries.

❖ *Bred-by-Exhibitor:* for non-champion dogs at least 6 months old who are exhibited by their breeder or one of the co-breeders, and who are owned or co-owned by one of the breeders or co-breeders.

❖ *American-Bred Dogs:* for non-champion dogs at least 6 months old who were whelped in the United States.

❖ *Open:* for dogs at least 6 months old.

Given this array of classes, how do you pick which class to enter? There are a few guidelines that should govern your choice.

❖ When possible, enter an age-appropriate class: enter puppies in Puppy class, adolescents in the 12-to-18 month old class, and mature adults in the Open class. Using an age-appropriate class means that your dog will be competing with other dogs at the same level of maturity, and it lets the judge know how mature he should expect your dog to be (although in any class, the judge may ask your dog's age).

❖ The class for dogs that are 12-18 months old is an excellent choice for a dog that is not fully mature, or for a dog whose ring manners aren't quite steady.

❖ The Novice class is rarely used. If your dog is less than 18 months old, then enter him in the Puppy or 12-to-18 month class. If your dog is more than 18 months old, but he still looks immature or his ring behavior isn't quite steady enough for Open, consider entering him in the American-Bred class rather than in Novice.

❖ Dogs that are at least six months old can be entered in the Bred-by-Exhibitor class. However, your dog *cannot* be entered in this class unless he is *co-owned* by one of his breeders, *and* one of his breeders handles him. If *you* did not breed your puppy, then *you* cannot handle him in this class.

Winning points from the Bred-by-Exhibitor class is particularly gratifying, since it is acknowledgement and affirmation of the quality of a breeder's dogs.

❖ The American-Bred class is a good choice if your dog is more than 18 months old but not yet trained well enough for the Open class.

❖ Although any dog can enter Open, dogs in this class are usually fully mature and completely trained for the ring. If an age-appropriate class is available, it is usually a better choice than Open.

In this Winners class, a Standard Poodle puppy has been moved ahead of an adult, indicating that it is under serious consideration by the judge for the points.

When deciding which class to enter, don't fall for the story that judges will only pick Winners Dog or Winners Bitch from the Open class and therefore you *must* enter that class to win championship points. The judge's job is to pick the *best* example of the breed in each Winners class, no matter which class the dog entered. Therefore, you should enter your dog in the class in which you can show him to his greatest advantage.

All things being equal, you should enter your dog in the class most appropriate for his age and level of maturity. If you have questions about which class to enter, consult with your mentor, your dog's breeder, your handling class instructor, or experienced show friends.

Summary

Your first show should *not* be like a blind date; you should have a pretty good idea of what to expect. Select a show that is small, relatively near home, and at which you will know other exhibitors. If you have only practiced outdoors, then pick an outdoor show and wait for suitable weather if necessary. If your targeted show is in a cluster, only enter one or two shows of the cluster: that's plenty in one weekend for an inexperienced dog.

If you already receive premium lists, you can pick a show that is as little as four weeks away—you'll have plenty of time to enter by the show's closing date. If you don't have the premium list yet, then choose a show that is at least six weeks in the future.

Once you've chosen a show, you'll need to select the class that you'll enter. If possible, pick a class that is appropriate to your dog's age, such as a Puppy class. Remember, the first place winner of *any* class—not just Open—can be awarded Winners Dog or Winners Bitch, and therefore earn championship points.

Chapter 16

Premium Lists

A "premium list" (or simply a "premium") isn't really a list at all; it's a pamphlet containing details and entry forms for a dog show or cluster of shows. In this chapter you'll learn about the contents of a premium list, and how to get premium lists for shows in your area.

Getting a Premium List

A premium list is an information booklet about a dog show, printed and distributed by the show superintendent or show secretary. The premium list gives details about the date and location of the show, judges, classes, driving directions, hotels, prizes being offered, and special events. It also contains an entry form for the show.

When shows on consecutive days are at the same location or are near each other, they are referred to as a "cluster" or a "circuit." The information for clustered shows run by the same superintendent may be combined into one multi-show premium list.

If you are not yet on the superintendent's regular mailing list, request the premium list for a particular show from the superintendent or secretary *at least* six weeks prior to the show date. Premium lists are usually available four to six weeks prior to a show. Entries generally close about 2½ weeks prior to the show date (usually on a Wednesday at noon). If you are not sure who the superintendent is for a particular show, check the *AKC Events Calendar*.

To get on a superintendent's mailing list for premium lists, write, call, or e-mail the licensed show superintendents who run shows in your area. Tell the superintendent the breed you show and in which states or region of the country you

At a show's superintendent's desk you'll find premium lists for upcoming shows which will be run by the same superintendent.

will be showing. While some superintendents are regional, other superintendents run shows all over the country. If at some point you plan to attend shows in a different part of the country, you can contact the superintendents and request premium lists for those shows.

If you're at a show, you can often pick up premium lists for future shows run by the same superintendent at the superintendent's desk. Premium lists can also be downloaded from some superintendents' Web sites.

Premium List Contents

Although premium lists differ in format among superintendents, they must all follow the AKC's rules regarding content. Not all premium lists will be exactly like the description or format shown here but they will all contain the information you need about a show.

Overview

There's lots of information in a premium list. Some of it is very important for exhibitors, and some of it (like the names of the people on the Board of Directors of the host club) you can ignore. The useful contents of a premium list can be broken into two groups: information about the AKC competition itself, and information about the logistics of participating in this show.

Important information about the competition includes the things you need to know in order to enter the show:

❖ classes offered at the show

❖ who will judge each breed

❖ entry forms for the show

❖ entry fees for classes

❖ entry limits, if applicable (for example, "entries will be limited to 1700 dogs each day")

❖ entry closing deadline (date *and* time)

❖ prizes and trophies offered

Information about show logistics covers things you need to know that are not directly related to your entry, but are nonetheless important, including:

❖ directions to the show site

❖ information on crate and grooming areas

Event #2001321654

Entries Close at Superintendent's Office at 12:00 Noon, WEDNESDAY, JUNE 20, 2001
after which time entries cannot be accepted, cancelled or substituted, except as provided for in Chapter 11, Section 6 of the Dog Show Rules.

PREMIUM LIST
41st ANNUAL ALL BREED DOG SHOW AND OBEDIENCE TRIAL

(Unbenched)
(Licensed by the American Kennel Club)

SATURDAY, JULY 7, 2001
Rodeo County Fairgrounds
Route 822, Milepost 107
Arroyo Rojo, Texas 75612

All Puppy Classes Divided

THIS SHOW AND OBEDIENCE TRIAL WILL BE JUDGED OUTDOORS

SHOW HOURS
7:00 A.M to 7:00 P.M.

There will be no classes for Japanese Chin at this show

SPECIALITY SHOWS
West Texas Brittany Club, Inc. (& Sweepstakes)
Cavalier King Charles Spaniel Fanciers of Texas, Inc. (& Sweepstakes)

SUPPORTED ENTRIES
Cap Rock Vizsla Club, Inc.
Llano Estacado Bulldog Club, Inc.
Dry Valley Dachsund Club, Inc.

At the discretion of the judge, the following breeds may be judged on a ramp: Clumber Spaniels, Sussex Spaniels, Basset Hounds, Petits Bassets Griffons Vendeens, Staffordshire Bull Terriers & Bulldogs.

Figure: Cover of the Cactus Kennel Club show premium list.

- ❖ local hotel and motel information

- ❖ parking information and reservation forms

- ❖ information about social activities, if any (for example, a BBQ dinner on the Saturday night of a show weekend)

- ❖ information about clinics and services available at the show, such as CERF eye examination, tattooing, microchipping, and semen collection for sperm banks

The first few pages

The first few pages of the premium list contain the most general information about the show. Some of the *most important* information about the show is covered in this part of the premium list, including:

- ❖ the entry closing date and time (often at the top of the front page and repeated on the entry form itself)

- ❖ the name of the host club

- ❖ the location and date of the show

- ❖ the entry limits (if any)

- ❖ whether the judging will be indoors, outdoors, or both

- ❖ whether any breed specialty shows, sweepstakes, or supported entries will be held at this show

- ❖ whether classes for any breed will *not* be offered

- ❖ the name and address of the show superintendent

Be sure to note the date and time entries close. This deadline is when the entry must be *received* at the superintendent's office, not when it must be postmarked.

Note also whether there are entry limits for the show. Many shows limit the number of dogs that will be judged, due to shortages of space or other resources. When there are entry limits, entries close *on the day that the limit is reached* or on the published entry closing date, whichever comes first. If the show you plan to enter has limited entries, send in your entry *as early as possible*.

Occasionally classes for one or more breeds will *not* be offered at an all-breed show. This usually means that there are specialty shows for those breeds in the same area—within 200 miles of the all-breed show—on the same day. For example, if the Manhattan Manchester Terrier Club has a specialty show on the same day as the Brooklyn Kennel Club all-breed show, there will be no classes for Manchester Terriers at the Brooklyn

Kennel Club all-breed show; the Manchester Terriers will be judged at the specialty show.

Judges and classes offered

The next section of the premium list shows names and addresses of the judges, ribbons to be awarded, and:

- ❖ classes offered at the show
- ❖ which breeds, if any, will be judged in divided classes
- ❖ a list of breeds and who will judge them

Check the classes offered at the show. At all shows where championship points can be earned, the regular classes offered for non-champion dogs (and similarly for bitches) *must* include:

- ❖ Puppy Dogs (may be divided in 6-9 months old and 9-12 months old)
- ❖ Dogs, 12-18 Months
- ❖ Novice Dogs
- ❖ Bred-by-Exhibitor Dogs
- ❖ American-Bred Dogs
- ❖ Open Dogs

If the premium list states "Puppy Classes Divided" then the class list will show separate classes for puppies 6-9 months old and puppies 9-12 months old. If your puppy is 6 months old on the day of the show, it can enter the 6-9 Month Puppy class. If your puppy is 9 months old on the day of the show, it must enter the 9-12 Month Puppy class.

The list of judges, or "Judges Panel" is given by group, and then by breed. AKC rules state that no judge may judge more than 175 dogs per day at an all breed show, and that a judge cannot judge the same breed or group at two shows held within 30 days and 200 air miles of each other. Therefore, in a cluster of shows, each breed will have a different judge every day.

Open class divisions

The Open class of some breeds may be judged in divided classes. In this case, the Open entry will be divided into classes by size, coat, color, etc., and each division of the Open class will be judged separately as if it were a distinct class. Not all breeds have the option of class divisions. Whether or not a breed will have divided classes must be indicated in the premium list. If your breed has the option of being judged in a divided Open class, you should check the premium list carefully.

Some premium lists give Open class divisions in the list of judges and their assignments. For example, the premium list may say:

Retrievers (Labrador) ....Miss Crimson
Open Classes Divided, both sexes:
Black; Chocolate; Yellow.

Skye Terriers..Col. Mayo
Open Classes Divided, both sexes:
Drop Ears; Prick Ears.

According to the premium list, Miss Crimson will judge all Labrador Retrievers together except in the Open classes, where the animals will be divided by color: there will be three Open classes for dogs and three Open classes for bitches. Col. Mayo will judge the two ear types of Skye Terriers together in all classes except the Open class. When Open classes are divided, the winner of each Open class will compete in the Winners Class. Thus, for the Labrador Retrievers, there can be as many as three Open Dogs in the Winners Dog class—one of each color.

Alternatively, the premium list may give the breeds that will be judged with divided classes in a table.

For each show, check the list of breeds that will be judged in a divided Open class carefully: just because a breed *may* be divided does not mean it *must* be divided. For example, the table of class divisions for the Cactus Kennel Club does not include Skye Terriers, so at this show, the Open classes of Skye Terriers will *not* be divided by ear type.

This Winners class for Labrador Retrievers includes the winners of the Open Yellow and Open Black classes.

Finally, note that some breeds have both varieties *and* divisions—for example, Dachshunds have three varieties (Longhaired, Smooth, and Wirehaired); each variety can be judged in Open classes divided by size.

Prizes and trophies

This section of the premium list describes the prizes and trophies offered for Best in Show and group placements. Following these, breed prizes (if any) are listed by group and breed; usually a description of the prize and the donor is identified. You don't need to read this section before entering, but it can be fun to see if you might win a crystal trophy, a silver-plated tray, or a dog food gift certificate.

OPEN CLASS DIVISIONS

RETRIEVERS (LABRADOR) Open Classes Divided, both sexes: Black; Chocolate; Yellow.

BASENJIS Open Classes Divided, both sexes: Black & White; Black, Tan & White; Red & White; Brindle & White.

DACHSHUNDS (LONGHAIRED) Open Classes Divided, both sexes: Miniature – 11 lbs. and under and 12 months old or over; Standard over 11 lbs. and 11 lbs. and under if less than 12 months old.

DACHSHUNDS (SMOOTH) Open Classes Divided, both sexes: Miniature – 11 lbs. and under and 12 months old or over; Standard over 11 lbs. and 11 lbs. and under if less than 12 months old.

DACHSHUNDS (WIREHAIRED) Open Classes Divided, both sexes: Miniature – 11 lbs. and under and 12 months old or over; Standard over 11 lbs. and 11 lbs. and under if less than 12 months old.

BOXERS Open Classes Divided, both sexes: Brindle; Fawn.

BULLMASTIFFS Open Classes Divided, both sexes: Brindle; Any Other Allowed Color.

DOBERMAN PINSCHERS Open Classes Divided, both sexes: Black; Any Other Allowed Color.

GREAT DANES Open Classes Divided, both sexes: Black; Blue; Bridle; Fawn; Harlequin; Mantle.

CHINESE CRESTEDS Open Classes Divided, both sexes: Hairless; Powderpuff.

PEKINGESE Open Classes Divided, both sexes: Under 8 lbs. And 12 months old or over; 8 lbs. And Over and under 8 lbs. If less than 12 months old.

POMERANIANS Open Classes Divided, both sexes: Black, Brown & Blue; Red, Orange, Cream & Sable; Any Other Allowed Color.

PUGS Open Classes Divided, both sexes: Black; Fawn.

BOSTON TERRIERS Open Classes Divided, both sexes: Under 15 lbs.; 15 lbs. And Over.

AUSTRALIAN SHEPHERDS Open Classes Divided, both sexes: Black; Blue Merle; Red; Red Merle.

COLLIES (ROUGH) Open Classes Divided, both sexes: Blue Merle; Red; Sable & White; Tri-color; White.

SHETLAND SHEEPDOGS Open Classes Divided, both sexes: Sable & White; Any Other Allowed Color.

Figure: Table of divisions for Open classes listed in the Cactus Kennel Club show's premium list.

If a breed club holds a specialty show with a sweepstakes competition in conjunction with an all-breed show, the details of the sweepstakes competition—judge, classes offered, entry fee, and prizes—are listed in the Breed Prize section of the premium list.

Entry forms

At the end of the premium list you will find one or more copies of the entry form. If the premium list is for a single show, then the entry form will be for that show. If the premium list is for some or all of the shows in a cluster, you will find either:

❖ a different entry form for each show, which will require you to fill in one entry form for each show you enter, or

❖ a combined entry form for the shows, with check-boxes in the top section for indicating which show or shows you are entering. If you enter more than one show, you may use a single entry form if your entry is *identical* on both days; otherwise, you must use a separate entry form for each day.

Entry Fees

Entry fees for the regular classes are frequently printed at the top of the entry form. In many premium lists, the entry fees are also printed elsewhere—usually near the front of the premium. Entry fees for sweepstakes are printed in the Breed Prizes section of the premium list, not on the entry form.

The AKC's "recording fee" is included in the entry fee for a dog's first class. This fee is collected by the AKC to offset the expense of maintaining show records and issuing championship certificates.

Read the entry fee information carefully since the entry fees may vary from show to show, even on the same show weekend. The entry fee description on an entry form might be:

> $20.00 for the first entry of the dog (including $0.50 AKC recording fee) and $15.00 for each additional entry of the same dog. Junior Showmanship Only $15.00 (including $0.50 AKC recording fee) and $15.00 as an additional class.

In this example the cost of entering your class dog in any class is $20.00. If you also enter your dog in an obedience class (as an "additional entry"), the cost of entering the second class is only $15, so your total entry fees for the day would be $35.

To encourage people to enter young dogs, some shows offer reduced entry fees for Puppy or Bred-by-Exhibitor classes:

> $18.00 for the first entry of the dog (including $0.50 AKC recording fee), except for Puppy classes which are $12.00. $12.00 for each additional entry of the same dog. Junior Showmanship Only $12.00 (including $0.50 AKC recording fee) and $5.00 as an additional class.

So, if you entered your 10-month-old puppy in the Novice class, you would pay $18, but if you entered him in the Puppy class, your entry fee would be only $12. Read the premium list carefully and plan your entries accordingly.

Non-Regular Classes and Sweepstakes

Non–regular classes are other special classes in which you cannot earn championship points. Most specialty shows have non-regular classes, and many all-breed shows offer non-regular classes. Veteran classes—classes for dogs and bitches that are, for example, seven years old or older—are often offered as non-regular classes. Other non-regular classes involve entries of multiple dogs, such as "Brace" (dogs are entered in pairs), "Brood Bitch" (an entry consists of a female and two or more of her offspring) and "Stud Dog" (an entry consists of a male and two or more of his offspring).

Many specialty shows—either independent specialty shows or specialty shows within all-breed shows—hold a sweepstakes competition in addition to the regular conformation

SWEEPSTAKES – Cavalier King Charles Spaniels only – Judge: Ms. Xena Fast.

The Cavalier King Charles Spaniel Fanciers of Texas Sweepstakes is open to all Cavalier King Charles Spaniels between the ages of 6 months and under 18 months. All entries in the Sweepstakes must be entered in a regular class at this show. Entries shall be made on the same form as for the Regular Classes, indicating "Sweepstakes" and the age division in the space for "Additional Classes." Entry fee is $15.00 in addition to the regular class entry fee.

Sweepstakes Classifications: Puppy Dogs, 6 mos. & under 9 mos.; Puppy Dogs, 9 mos. & under 12 mos.; Junior Dogs, 12 mos. and under 18 mos. (same classes for bitches).

Prize Money: The money from the entries in the Sweepstakes will be divided as follows: First Prize-40%; Second Prize-30%; Third Prize-20%; Fourth Prize-10%.

Figure: Puppy sweepstakes announcement from the Breed Prizes section of the Cactus Kennel Club show's premium list.

classes. A sweepstakes is a competition among dogs of similar ages. The age categories for the sweepstakes classes are specified in the premium list: usually 6-9 months, 9-12 months, and 12-18 months for dogs. Most clubs require that dogs entered in the sweepstakes must also be entered in the regular competition. Information about the sweepstakes—judges, classes offered, entry fees, and prizes—is given in the Breed Prizes section of the premium list.

The ring procedure in the sweepstakes is exactly the same as the ring procedure in the regular classes. After the sweepstakes classes for dogs and the sweepstakes classes for bitches are judged, however, the first place winner of each class will compete for Best in Sweepstakes and, sometimes, Best of Opposite Sex in Sweepstakes.

Championship points cannot be earned in a sweepstakes competition; you can only earn championship points in the regular classes. However, you can win money and other prizes in a sweepstakes. The entry fees for each sweepstakes class are pooled,, and the club keeps a small portion (10-25 percent) to cover expenses; the remainder is divided among the winners using a sliding scale such as 40 percent for first place, 30 percent for second place, 20 percent for third place and 10 percent for fourth place. The larger the class, the more prize money the winners will receive. The actual percentages used at each show are printed with the sweepstakes information in the Breed Prizes

In Brace class, dogs are judged on their quality, their similarity, and the uniformity of their movement. Each dog is examined individually; they gait together as a brace.

section of the premium list.

A veteran sweepstakes may also be offered with age categories of , for example, 7-9 years old, and 9 or more years old. Retired show dogs are often reunited with their former handlers in veteran sweepstakes, much to the delight of spectators who remembers them from their show days. Prize money is divided up in the same manner as for other sweepstakes.

Everything Else

The rest of the information scattered through the premium list has no regular, predictable place. The printers put the list of motels, directions to the show, parking information, etc. wherever they will fit in the premium list layout, so you'll just have to hunt for the information you need. Check carefully for parking information and for anything else, such as clinics, that might require pre-registration (day parking generally does not require reservation, but overnight parking for motorhomes does). Pay special attention to deadlines and addresses, since these may not be the same as the entry deadline.

The premium list may have little numbers next to the names of the classes and underlined numbers next to the breed names in the list of breed judges. These numbers are used by the superintendent's computer system; you should just ignore them.

Summary

A premium list is the principal source of information about a show. It contains the details of the classes offered, judging panel, entry limit and deadlines, parking information, prizes, sweepstakes, and the show's entry forms. Premium lists are available from the show's superintendent about six weeks before the show; you can also find premium lists at the superintendent's desk at a show.

Study the premium list for a show carefully before you enter. Make sure that classes for your breed will be offered at the show, note whether your breed will be judged indoors or outdoors, and note whether the entry for the show is limited.

Chapter 17

Entering a Dog Show

Once you've picked a show, received its premium list, and decided which class to enter, it's time to make your entry. In this chapter you'll learn how to fill in an AKC entry form, how to submit your entry to the show superintendent, and what to do if you make a mistake on your entry form.

Entering a Show

The deadline for entering an AKC show is approximately 2½ weeks prior to the show. If your entry doesn't reach the superintendent by the entry deadline, it won't be accepted.

There are four ways to enter a dog show:

- ❖ Send a completed paper entry form to the superintendent.

- ❖ Fax a completed paper entry to the superintendent.

- ❖ Use a telephone entry service.

- ❖ Use the Internet.

No matter which method you use, you will need the same information to make your entry. Telephone entry services and Web sites will put some of this information in a database profile of your dog, so you won't have to repeat it for each entry you make. Paper-based entries—mailed or faxed—must be filled out completely each time you make an entry.

There are several different entry forms that you can use for a show, including:

- ❖ the entry form contained in the show's premium list (or a photocopy)

- ❖ an entry form (or photocopy) for any other show, with the show information edited

- ❖ a generic form (no show information in the top section), downloaded from the Web site of a show superintendent or the AKC

OFFICIAL AMERICAN KENNEL CLUB ENTRY FORM

All Breed Dog Show and Obedience Trial   Event #2001321654

CACTUS KENNEL CLUB

(Licensed by the American Kennel Club)

Saturday, July 7, 2001

Rodeo County Fairgrounds   Route 822, Milepost 107   Arroyo Rojo, Texas

MAIL ENTRIES WITH FEES TO: Studie Baker, Supt, PO Box 495, Provo, Utah 93939

MAKE ALL CHECKS payable in US funds to Studie Baker Dog Shows, Inc.

ENTRIES must be received by the Superintendent no later than **NOON, WED. JUNE 20, 2001**

FIRST ENTRY of a dog at this show is $21.00 (including $0.50 AKC recording fee)

Each additional entry of the same dog is $15.00

I ENCLOSE $_____ for entry fees

BREED (A)	VARIETY 1 (B)	SEX (C)

DOG 2 3
SHOW CLASS (D)   CLASS 3 DIVISION Weight, color, etc. (E)

ADDITIONAL CLASSES (F)   OBEDIENCE TRIAL CLASS (G)   JR. SHOWMANSHIP CLASS (H)

NAME OF (See Back) JUNIOR HANDLER (if any) (I)   J.R's AKC NO. (J)

FULL NAME OF DOG (K)

☐ AKC REG NO.
☐ AKC LITTER NO.
☐ I.L.P. NO.
☐ FOREIGN REG. NO. & COUNTRY

Enter number here (L)

DATE OF BIRTH (M)

PLACE OF ☐ U.S.A ☐ Canada ☐ Foreign
BIRTH   Do not print the above in Catalog (N)

BREEDER (O)

SIRE (P)

DAM (Q)

ACTUAL OWNER(S) _____ (R)
4   (S)   (Please Print)

OWNER'S ADDRESS _____

CITY _____ STATE _____ ZIP _____

NAME OF OWNER'S AGENT (IF ANY) AT THE SHOW _____ (T)

I CERTIFY that I am the actual owner of the dog, or that I am the duly authorized agent of the actual owner whose name I have entered above. In consideration of the acceptance of this entry I (we) agree to abide by the rules and regulations of The American Kennel Club in effect at the time of this show or obedience trial, and by any additional rules and regulations appearing in the premium list for this show or obedience trial or both, and further agree to be bound by the "Agreement" printed on the reverse side of this entry form. I (we) certify and represent that the dog entered is not a hazard to persons or other dogs. This entry is submitted for acceptance on the foregoing representation and agreement.

SIGNATURE of owner or his agent
duly authorized to make this entry _____ (U)

TELEPHONE # _____ (V) _____

Figure: AKC entry form with parts labeled.

❖ a generic form printed from a kennel management or pedigree software package, or from a word processing package, using a document template

No matter which form you use, you *must* send both sides of the form to the superintendent for your entry to be valid. So, if you photocopy an entry form, be sure to copy *both sides* of the form. (You don't have to make a 2-sided copy—you can staple the pages together, or photocopy the front and back side-by-side on a single sheet.)

Completing an Entry Form

You can find most of the information you need for filling in your entry form on your dog's AKC registration certificate. You'll write your entry information on the front of the entry form, which has three sections: top, middle, and bottom.

The back of the entry form contains the Agreement and liability waiver. Unless you enter Junior Showmanship, you will not need to write anything on the back of the entry form.

Front top section

The front top section of the entry form contains information identifying the show:

❖ name of the show (*e.g.,* Cactus Kennel Club)

❖ location of the show (*e.g.,* Arroyo Rojo, TX)

❖ date of the show (*e.g.,* July 7, 2001)

If you use the entry form in the show's premium list, you do not need to write anything in the top section of the form. If you use the entry form for another show, cross out the printed name, location, and date, and write in the information for the show that you are entering. If you use a blank AKC form or the entry form in a software package, enter the information for this show on the top of the form.

Front middle section

The middle section of the entry form contains information about your dog and about the class you are entering. In order to fill in the middle section, you will need a copy of your dog's AKC registration certificate. Most of the required information can be copied directly from the AKC registration certificate. Use dark ink to fill in your form, and print or write legibly.

In the figures in this chapter, circled letters identify the boxes on the entry form and the corresponding information on an AKC registration slip. You will *not* find these letters on your registration certificate or an entry form.

The boxes on the entry form are:

A. **Breed.** *Copy this directly from the AKC registration certificate.* If your breed has varieties—for example, "Dachshund [Longhaired]"—write only the breed name "Dachshund" here.

B. **Variety.** If your breed has varieties, write the variety—for example, "Longhaired"—in this box.

C. **Sex.** *Copy this directly from the AKC registration certificate.* You may abbreviate your dog's sex as "M" or "F."

D. **Dog Show Class.** This is the class in which you wish to enter your dog (for example, Open Dogs or 12-18 Month Bitches). The class that you enter here is considered the "first" class for purposes of calculating entry fees. The classes normally offered at a show for dogs are:

❖ Puppy (may be divided into 6-9 month old and 9-12 month old classes)

❖ 12-to-18 Month Dogs

❖ Novice Dogs

❖ Bred-by -Exhibitor Dogs

❖ American-Bred Dogs

❖ Open Dogs

The same classes are offered for bitches, *e.g.* Open Bitches.

Not all shows divide the puppy class into 6-9 months and 9-12 months, so check the premium list. If you don't have the premium list for the show, assume that the puppy classes are divided.

E. **Class Division.** Not all breeds have divisions for the Open class. Check the premium list. For example, if you are entering Open Dogs in Labrador Retrievers, and the premium list says that Labrador Open classes will be divided into black, yellow and chocolate, write "black", "yellow," or "chocolate" in this space. If you are entering an undivided class (for example, American-Bred Bitches), you can leave the division box blank. If you do not know whether the classes are being divided at this show, assume they will be divided and provide the division information for your dog.

F. **Additional classes.** This is the space for entering non-regular classes or sweepstakes. For example, if a sweepstakes for your breed is offered at this show, write "Sweeps 9-12 months" in this space. Remember that the entry fee for sweepstakes is listed under breed prizes in the premium list, and is not the same as the entry fee for the regular classes.

G. **Obedience trial class.** If you are entering an obedience trial class in addition to a conformation class, write the obedience class name here.

AMERICAN KENNEL CLUB

(K) FREEDOM'S FUZZYFOOT FREDERICK
NAME

(A) CAVALIER KING CHARLES SPAN
BREED

BLENHEIM
COLOR

(P) CH FREEDOM'S WASN'T FUZZY WUZZY
SIRE   TN123123/01 (1-97)

(Q) CH FREEDOM'S FUZZY WUZZY WANNABE
DAM   TN213456/03 (6-98)

(O) MARTY PIETRANGELO & SIMON KLEE
BREEDER

(R) JOHN WOODS & MARTY PIETRANGELO
18 HANGING TREE LANE
POSSUM TROT, TX 79823

OWNER

(L) TN892099/01
NUMBER

(C) MALE
SEX

(M) APR 19 2000
DATE OF BIRTH

JUN 28 2000
CERTIFICATE ISSUED

IF A DATE APPEARS AFTER THE NAME AND
NUMBER OF THE SIRE AND DAM, IT INDICATES
THE ISSUE OF THE STUD BOOK REGISTER IN
WHICH THE SIRE OR DAM IS PUBLISHED.

THIS CERTIFICATE ISSUED
WITH THE RIGHT TO COR-
RECT OR REVOKE BY THE
AMERICAN KENNEL CLUB

See Transfer Instructions
on Back of Certificate

REGISTRATION CERTIFICATE

Figure: AKC registration certificate with parts labeled.

H. **Junior Showmanship Class**. If you are entering Junior Showmanship, write the class here. Check the schedule of entry fees for the Junior Showmanship fee.

I. **Name of Junior Handler**. If you are entering Junior Showmanship, write the name of the Junior Handler here.

J. **Junior's AKC Number**. If you are entering Junior Showmanship, write the junior handler's AKC number here. (This is the AKC number of the junior handler, not of the dog!) Every junior handler who participates in the AKC's Junior Showmanship program must be registered with the AKC.

K. **Full Name of Dog**. *Copy this directly from the AKC registration certificate.* If your dog has earned any AKC titles, such as Companion Dog (CD) or Junior Hunter (JH), you should include the abbreviations for these titles. You will find the dog's full name, without titles, on the AKC registration certificate.

L. **Registration Number**. *Copy this directly from the AKC registration certificate.*

❖ If the dog has a regular individual registration certificate and number, check the "AKC REG NO" box. (Note: AKC registration can be either "full" or "limited." Dogs with limited AKC registration cannot enter conformation classes.)

❖ If your dog has an I.L.P. (Indefinite Listing Privilege) number, check this box. (Note: Dogs with I.L.P registration *cannot* enter conformation classes.)

❖ If your dog has a foreign registration, check this box and fill in both the registration number and the country.

M. **Date of Birth.** *Copy this directly from the AKC registration certificate.*

N. **Place of Birth.** Check the appropriate box.

O. **Breeder.** *Copy this directly from the AKC registration certificate.* There may be more than one breeder; include all names. You may use initials rather than first names if you need to save space, *e.g.,* "M. Pietrangelo & S. Klee" rather than "Marty Pietrangelo & Simon Klee".

P. **Sire.** *Copy this directly from the AKC registration certificate.* If the sire has earned additional AKC titles since the litter was registered you may include them.

Q. **Dam.** *Copy this directly from the AKC registration certificate.* If the dam has earned additional AKC titles since the litter was registered you may include them.

R. **Actual Owner(s).** *Copy this directly from the AKC registration certificate.* The only exception occurs if you have just acquired the dog and haven't gotten your new registration certificate from the AKC. However, if you have filed the paperwork for the new registration certificate with the AKC, then you are the owner.

S. **Owner's Address.** *Use the address to which you wish your entry conformation mailed.* In most cases, this will be your current mailing address.

T. **Name of Owner's Agent (if any).** If you will use a professional handler (called an "agent") at the show, put his or her name here. If you plan to use a handler at the show, but you don't yet know who, you may leave this line blank. If you put a handler's name here, that person will be listed in the show catalog as your dog's handler.

Front bottom section

U. **Signature.** This should be the signature of one of the owners, co-owners, or anyone the owner has given permission to make this entry.

V. **Telephone Number.** Put your daytime phone number here. The superintendents will use this number if they need to contact you about your entry (for example, if you forgot to fill in the dog's AKC number). Some superintendents also ask for e-mail addresses, if available.

You might not need to put information in every blank on the entry form. It's a good idea to draw a line in blanks you leave empty so that the superintendent will know the omission was intentional.

Back of the form

Once you've read the back of the entry form, you can ignore it unless:

❖ you are entering Junior Showmanship, in which case you need to fill in the Junior Showmanship information, or

❖ you are faxing in the entry and the superintendent has put a space for your credit card number and signature on the back of the form.

Remember, every entry form you submit to a superintendent—by fax or by mail—*must* include both the front and back of the form. If you're using a photocopied entry form, just copy the front and the back on two separate pages. This is also the easiest way to fax both sides of the entry form to the superintendent.

An Example

In the following example, a completed entry form—for a regular class and a sweepstakes class—is shown based on the AKC registration certificate given above.

The dog in this example is 14 months old on the day of the show. His owners enter him in the 12-18 Month Dog class. The entry information has been copied directly from his AKC registration certificate, with two exceptions:

❖ His sire has earned the NA (Novice Agility Dog) and TD (Tracking Dog) titles since he was registered, so his owners include these AKC titles in the sire's name (Box P), and

❖ His owners have moved since he was registered, so they use their current mailing address on the entry form (Box S).

In addition, there is a sweepstakes for Cavalier King Charles Spaniels at this show, so his owners enter him in the sweepstakes class for 12-18 month old males (additional classes, Box F).

The first entry for a dog at this show is $21.00, and the fee for sweepstakes (found in the Breed Prizes section of the premium list) is $15.00. Thus, their total entry fee is $36.00 for this show.

Submitting Your Entry

When your entry form is filled out correctly, the next step is to get the entry to the superintendent before the show's entry deadline. If you use a paper entry form, make a photocopy of your completed entry form if possible; if you use an online entry service, print out a copy of your entry information.

Using a paper entry form

❖ If you're at a show and the superintendent is the same as the one you need to send your entry to, you can drop off your entry forms and fees at the superintendent's table at the show.

❖ You can use regular mail, which may be a dangerous gamble if the entry deadline is less than a week away. Express Mail or Priority Mail may be able to meet the deadline. Remember, however, that Express Mail and Priority Mail do not offer guaranteed delivery dates and times.

OFFICIAL AMERICAN KENNEL CLUB ENTRY FORM

All Breed Dog Show and Obedience Trial   Event #2001321654

CACTUS KENNEL CLUB

(Licensed by the American Kennel Club)

Saturday, July 7, 2001

Rodeo County Fairgrounds   Route 822, Milepost 107   Arroyo Rojo, Texas

MAIL ENTRIES WITH FEES TO: Studie Baker, Supt, PO Box 495, Provo, Utah 93939

MAKE ALL CHECKS payable in US funds to Studie Baker Dog Shows, Inc.

ENTRIES must be received by the Superintendent no later than **NOON, WED. JUNE 20, 2001**

FIRST ENTRY of a dog at this show is $21.00 (including $0.50 AKC recording fee)

Each additional entry of the same dog is $15.00

I ENCLOSE $ 36.-- for entry fees

BREED Cav King Chas Span	VARIETY 1 ___	SEX M	

DOG 2 3 SHOW CLASS 12-18 mo. Dogs   CLASS 3 DIVISION Weight, color, etc. ___

ADDITIONAL CLASSES Sweeps 12-18 mo. Dogs   OBEDIENCE TRIAL CLASS ___   JR. SHOWMANSHIP CLASS ___

NAME OF (See Back) JUNIOR HANDLER (if any) ___   J.R's AKC NO. ___

FULL NAME OF DOG Freedom's Fuzzyfoot Frederick

(X) AKC REG NO. ☐ AKC LITTER NO. ☐ I.L.P. NO. ☐ FOREIGN REG. NO. & COUNTRY   Enter number here TN892099/01

DATE OF BIRTH April 19, 2000

PLACE OF (X) U.S.A. ☐ Canada ☐ Foreign BIRTH Do not print the above in Catalog.

BREEDER Marty Pietrangelo & Simon Klee

SIRE Ch. Freedom's Wasn't Fuzzy Wuzzy, TD NA

DAM Ch. Freedom's Fuzzy Wuzzy Wannabe

ACTUAL OWNER(S) 4 John Woods & Marty Pietrangelo
(Please Print)

OWNER'S ADDRESS 2810 Dogwood Court

CITY Palomino   STATE TX   ZIP 79735

NAME OF OWNER'S AGENT (IF ANY) AT THE SHOW ___

SIGNATURE of owner or his agent duly authorized to make this entry John P. Woods

TELEPHONE # (512) 555-1268

Figure: Example of a completed entry form for a regular class and a sweepstakes class.

❖ You can use a private courier service such as Federal Express, DHL or UPS. When you use a private courier, make sure that you select the level of service that will deliver your entries by *the date and time* specified on the premium list. If your package is delivered at 4:00 p.m. and entries closed at noon, you're out of luck. Also, when you use a private delivery service, you must use the street address of the superintendent; entries cannot be delivered to a post office box.

If you are entering more than one show run by the same superintendent, or if you are entering multiple dogs in a single show, you may put all the entry forms in one envelope and write a single check covering all of the entry fees.

Other ways to enter

There are other ways to enter dog shows:

❖ **Fax**. You can enter shows via fax to the superintendent, paying for your entries with a credit card. There is a service charge of $3-$5 per dog per show for faxed entries. So, if you enter your dog in each show of a four-day weekend, you will pay $12-$20 in fax service charges on top of your entry fees. In this case, it may be less expensive to use a courier service for overnight delivery.

❖ **A telephone entry service**. Several of these services are advertised in the *AKC Events Calendar*. The entry service creates a file for your dog with most of the information needed for an entry (name, AKC number, sire, dam, breeders, etc.) An entry is placed by calling the service *before entries close* and telling them which show and which class you wish to enter. The entry fee and service charge ($3-$5 per entry) are charged to a credit card.

❖ **The Internet**. Many of the large superintendents will accept entries for their shows over the Internet, right up to the day and time of entry closing. Some will also accept entries for other superintendents, but the cutoff for these entries is usually 24 or 48 hours prior to the show's closing date. Payment for the entry is made by credit card; there is a service charge ($3-$5) for each entry.

Errors in Your Entry

Occasionally you will discover that you made an error in your entry. The only errors that really matter are:

❖ making a mistake in the dog's AKC number

❖ entering the dog in the wrong class (*e.g.*, entering a 10 month old puppy in the 6-9 month old puppy class)

❖ entering the dog in the wrong breed or variety

If you realize that you have made one of these mistakes in your entry, contact the superintendent for instructions. Other mistakes—misspelled names, incorrect addresses, missing dog titles—do not need to be corrected.

Withdrawing Your Entry

Occasionally, you may change your mind about showing your dog in a show you have already entered. If the show's entries have closed, you're out of luck; you cannot withdraw your entry, so if you don't go to the show, your dog will be counted as "absent." If, however, entries have not yet closed, you may notify the superintendent *in writing* (by mail or by fax) that you wish to withdraw your entry. The request to withdraw your entry must be received by the superintendent *before entries close*. Your entry fee, perhaps minus a service charge, will be refunded. In your written request to the superintendent, state:

- ❖ the name and date of the show

- ❖ the breed and AKC number of the dog

- ❖ the class entered

- ❖ your name, address and telephone number

- ❖ that you wish to withdraw your entry

You do not need to tell the superintendent the reason that you are withdrawing your entry.

Summary

The deadline for entering a show is approximately 2½ weeks before the show. You can enter a show using a paper entry form, fax, an entry service, or by using the Internet. In any case, the information you need to make your entry is the same.

A show's entry form is included in the show's premium list. If you don't have the entry form for the show, you can use a generic form or an entry form for another show. Write the show's name, date, and location on the top of the entry form.

Most of the information that you will need to fill in an AKC entry blank can be found on your dog's AKC registration slip. Check the premium list for entry fees and, if applicable, for the details of sweepstakes competition.

If you make an *important* error in your entry, contact the superintendent to correct it as soon as possible. If you decide to withdraw your entry, the superintendent must receive your written request for withdrawal before the show's entry deadline is reached.

Chapter 18

Entry Confirmations and Judging Schedules

During the week prior to the show, you should receive a confirmation of your entry and a schedule of judging in the mail. In this chapter you will learn how to read and check your entry confirmation, how to read a judging schedule, and how to estimate when your dog will be in the ring.

Your Entry Confirmation

Entry confirmations vary among superintendents in the amount of detail they provide. At a minimum, your entry confirmation will state the show and class in which your dog is entered, his catalog (armband) number, his breed, and either his name, his AKC number, or both. In some cases, your entry confirmation slip will also double as your admission ticket to the show.

Cactus Kennel Club Rodeo County Fairgrounds				Saturday, July 7, 2001		
Arroyo Rojo, Texas Please Bring This Acknowledgement to the Show Site						
Freedom's Fuzzyfoot Frederick				Cavalier King Charles Spaniel		
Class	No.	Time	Ring	Day	Entry/Breakdown	Judge
Dog 12-18mo	17	11:15A	9	Sa	16/4-5-(6-1)	K. Smith
OWNER:	John Woods & Marty Pietrangelo 2810 Dogwood Court Palomino, TX 79735					

Figure: Example of a detailed entry confirmation.

Some superintendents provide detailed entry confirmations while other superintendents' confirmations are very simple. For example, the detailed entry confirmation illustrated above lists the show's name, date, and location; the dog's name and breed; his catalog (armband) number and the class in which he is entered; and details of the show logistics, including ring number, number of dogs entered in the breed, judging time and the judge's name.

In contrast, a very simple entry confirmation may only report, for example, the show's name and date, the dog's AKC number, his name, his breed, and the class in which he is entered. For information on the judging time, ring number, and entry breakdown, you must check the judging program that comes with your entry confirmation.

There are four items that you should check, if possible, for accuracy as soon as you receive your entry confirmation:

❖ the name of the show

❖ the AKC number, if given, and/or the dog's name

❖ the class entered

❖ the breed or variety

| Cactus Kennel Club |
| Saturday – July 7, 2001 |
| |
| TN 89209901 |
| Freedom's Fuzzyfoot Frederick |
| Dog 12-18 mo |
| |
| Cavalier King Charles Span |
| CTLG # ('S): 17 |

Figure: Example of a simple entry confirmation.

The last item may seem silly, but a German Shorthaired Pointer (GSP) can become a German Shepherd Dog (GSD) if the superintendent misreads a sloppily written entry form.

If any of these items is incorrect, contact the superintendent. This is when having a photocopy of your entry may be useful; you can check the entry to find out whether the mistake was made by the superintendent or by you. In either case, contact the superintendent to see if the error can be corrected. Other errors, such as the incorrect spelling of your name or the name of the sire, don't need to be corrected.

If the show, your dog's breed, his AKC number (or name), and the class entered are correct, then turn to the judging program.

The Judging Program

The judging program (sometimes called the judging schedule) is a multi-page pamphlet which lists when and where each breed will be judged and whether there have been any changes in judges since the premium list was issued. The judging program has three major parts: the breed index, the ring schedule, and announcements of judge changes. The judging program may also contain directions to the show, information about parking, and a map of the ring layout.

The breed index

The first section of the judging program that you should check is the breed index. The index lists, in alphabetical order, the number of dogs entered in each breed, the ring in which they will be judged, and the approximate time they will be judged.

In this example, there are 16 Cavalier King Charles Spaniels entered in the show. They will be judged in Ring 9, beginning at 11:15 a.m. Long Coat and Smooth Coat Chihuahuas will also be judged in Ring 9 at 11:15; they will be judged in the same "set" or block of judging time as the Cavalier King Charles Spaniels and, perhaps, other breeds.

Entry	Breed	Ring	Time
:	:	:	:
:	:	:	:
17	Bullmastiffs	13	12:45
5	Cairn Terriers	7	1:00
16	Cavalier King Charles Spaniels	9	11:15
10	Chihuahuas (Long Coat)	9	11:15
2	Chihuahuas (Smooth Coat)	9	11:15
23	Chinese Cresteds	9	8:00
:	:	:	:
:	:	:	:

Figure: Example of an index of breeds.

The ring schedule

Once you have found your ring number in the breed index, turn to the ring-by-ring schedule of judging for the day. Exhibitors of Cavalier King Charles Spaniels would, for example, turn to the judging schedule for Ring 9.

The ring schedule is divided into sets, during which several breeds are judged. The set structure has several functions: it gives some flexibility to the judging schedule, and it allows exhibitors to calculate approximately when they will be in the ring. At the end of each set, the judge may take a break if time permits. Each set, however, must begin on time if the show is to stay on schedule.

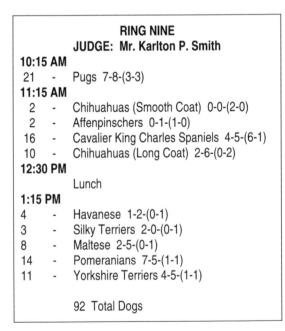

RING NINE
JUDGE: Mr. Karlton P. Smith

10:15 AM
21 - Pugs 7-8-(3-3)
11:15 AM
2 - Chihuahuas (Smooth Coat) 0-0-(2-0)
2 - Affenpinschers 0-1-(1-0)
16 - Cavalier King Charles Spaniels 4-5-(6-1)
10 - Chihuahuas (Long Coat) 2-6-(0-2)
12:30 PM
Lunch
1:15 PM
4 - Havanese 1-2-(0-1)
3 - Silky Terriers 2-0-(0-1)
8 - Maltese 2-5-(0-1)
14 - Pomeranians 7-5-(1-1)
11 - Yorkshire Terriers 4-5-(1-1)

92 Total Dogs

Figure: Example of a ring schedule.

In Ring 9, Mr. Smith begins his judging at 10:15 with 21 Pugs. The rough rule of thumb is that 25 dogs can be judged in an hour (2½ minutes per dog, or about six dogs every 15 minutes). The 21 Pugs, if all are present, should take a little less than an hour to judge. The schedule allows 60 minutes for judging Pugs, so there may be a bit of time for photos immediately after the Pugs are judged. Mr. Smith should begin his next set at 11:15.

In the set that begins at 11:15, there are four dogs (two Chihuahuas and two Affenpinschers) to be judged before the Cavalier King Charles Spaniels. If all four dogs are present, this should take about 10 minutes (four dogs at 2½ minutes per dog). Therefore, *at the latest*, the judging of Cavalier King Charles Spaniels will begin at 11:25. However, if any of the Smooth Coated Chihuahuas or Affenpinschers are absent, the judging of the Cavaliers would begin earlier (but not before 11:15). It is always a good idea to assume that there will be some absent dogs ahead of you in the set, and to be at the ring early. In this case, Cavaliers should be checked in and ready for judging at 11:15, when the set begins.

If none of the Cavalier King Charles Spaniels is absent, it will take about 40 minutes to judge them (16 dogs at 2½ minutes per dog). Finally, there are 20 dogs to be judged before the Long Coated Chihuahuas (2 Smooth Coated Chihuahuas, 2 Affenpinschers, and 16 Cavalier King Charles Spaniels), so the Long Coated Chihuahuas will be judged a little after noon (12:05, or 11:15 plus 50 minutes) *at the latest*; they will be judged earlier if any dogs entered in the preceding breeds are absent.

The judging schedule may be posted on the ring number pole.

Thus, in this set there are 30 dogs entered, which should require about 75 minutes of judging time. If any dogs are absent, the judging should take less time. The schedule allows 75 minutes for the set (from 11:15 until 12:30), followed by the judge's lunch break.

The entry breakdown

Another important piece of information included in the ring schedule is the "breakdown" of the breed entry. The numbers following the breed name tell you how many class (non-champion) dogs and bitches are entered, and how many special (champion) dogs and bitches are entered. The class dogs and bitches are listed first, and the special dogs and bitches are noted inside the parentheses. For the Cavalier King Charles Spaniels, the breakdown is listed in the ring schedule as "4-5-(6-1)" which means:

- ❖ 4 class dogs
- ❖ 5 class bitches
- ❖ 6 dog specials
- ❖ 1 bitch special

This breakdown accounts for the 16 Cavalier King Charles Spaniels entered. For the Smooth Coat Chihuahuas, the breakdown is 0-0-(2-0): there are no class dogs or bitches, two dog specials, and no bitch specials. Therefore, you know before the show that the Best of Variety Smooth Coated Chihuahua will be a male, and there will be no Best of Opposite Sex.

Judge changes

The last important thing to look for in the judging program is an announcement of changes of judges, if any. The location and format of the judge change announcements varies among superintendents. Scan the judging program carefully to see if there are any changes to the panel of judges.

There are 2893 dogs entered in this show with a total entry of 3293 in 145 different Breeds or Varieties, including 117 obedience entries.

In accordance with Chapter 7, Section 13, of "Rules Applying to Dog Shows" due to the large entry and with American Kennel Club approval the following changes apply:

Breed	Original Judge	New Judge
Scottish Deerhounds	Ms. Belle N. Jerzey	Mr. Raleigh von Tanner
Papillons	Ms. Fancy Moore	Mr. Willy B. Ballerstedt
Cavalier King Charles Spaniels	Dr. Sarah B. Ballerstedt	Mr. Karlton P. Smith
Pomeranians	Dr. Sarah B. Ballerstedt	Mr. Karlton P. Smith
Silky Terriers	Dr. Sarah B. Ballerstedt	Mr. Karlton P. Smith

Figure: Example of a judge change announcement.

Why would judging assignments change after the premium list is published?

❖ A judge will not be at the show at all—perhaps because he is ill or has cancelled for other personal reasons. In this case, his entire judging assignment will be transferred to one or more other judges.

❖ The entry in the breeds assigned to the judge may exceed the daily judging limit. At an all-breed show, the AKC allows judges to judge up to 175 dogs per day. If the number of dogs entered in the breeds assigned to a single judge exceeds 175 dogs, then some of the breeds must be transferred to another judge.

If there has been a judge change for your breed, and if you do not wish to exhibit to the new judge, you may withdraw your entry and your entry fee will be refunded. Your entry withdrawal request *must be received* by the superintendent, in writing or by fax, at least half an hour before *the day's judging* begins—not half an hour

DUE TO A CHANGE OF JUDGE, PLEASE WITHDRAW THE FOLLOWING ENTRY:

CACTUS KENNEL CLUB
SATURDAY, JULY 7, 2001
Arroyo, Rojo, Texas

CAVALIER KING CHARLES SPANIEL
DOG, 12-18 MONTHS OLD
FREEDOM'S FUZZYFOOT FREDERICK
AKC # TN892099/01

John P. Woods
(512) 555-1268

Figure: Example of a written request for withdrawal of an entry.

before your class is judged.

The written withdrawal of an entry must state the show and date, the dog's AKC number, name, and breed, the class entered, and the reason for the entry withdrawal. The superintendent often has forms at his desk for you to fill in, so you don't have to write out a withdrawal request from scratch.

The request to withdraw your entry can be mailed or faxed to the superintendent prior to the day of the show. On the day of the show, it must be turned in at the superintendent's desk at least half an hour prior to the start of the day's judging. Even if your breed is not judged until the afternoon, you *must* request your withdrawal before *any* dogs are judged that day.

Summary

In the week prior to the show, the show superintendent or show secretary will mail you a confirmation of your dog's entry and a judging schedule for the show. Check the entry confirmation for accuracy, and if there is an error in your dog's AKC number, breed, or class entered, contact the superintendent.

You should look at the judging schedule to estimate when your breed will be judged. Most judges will judge 25 dogs in an hour, which works out to about 2½ minutes per dog. As you estimate when your breed will be judged, be sure to allow for absent dogs in your calculation, and get to ringside with plenty of time before you enter the ring.

You should also check the judging schedule for announcements of changes in judging assignments. If there has been a change in the judge for your breed, you may withdraw your entry and receive a refund of your entry fee. The superintendent must receive your written request for entry withdrawal at least half an hour before any classes are judged, which usually means the superintendent must have your request by 7:30 or 8:00 a.m. on the day of the show.

Chapter 19

Before the Show: Timelines and Planning

Good advance planning is essential to having a pleasant and successful day at a dog show. In this chapter you'll learn about the timelines governing your preparation for a dog show, and about the planning you'll need to do. You'll also learn about traveling with your dog, and about what to wear in the show ring.

Timing is Everything!

Dog shows run on strict schedules, not only on show day but also during the weeks before the show, so you must know what you need to do and when you need to do it. From the time you decide to enter a show, the activities leading up to the show can span as few as 2½ weeks to as many as 6 weeks, depending on whether you have the show's premium list and on how you submit your entry to the superintendent.

2½ to 6 weeks before the show

Once you have selected the show you want to enter, you should get its premium list. You can find lists of shows in the *AKC Events Calendar*, in dog show calendars, and on the Web sites of the AKC and show superintendents. Contact the show's superintendent four to six weeks prior to the show and request a premium list.

The deadline for entering most shows is approximately 2½ weeks prior to the show. If you use regular mail to submit your entry, mail your entry at least one week before the entries close. If you submit your entry by fax, Internet, courier service, or telephone entry service, you can wait until a day or two before entries close to submit your entry.

Some shows limit the number of dogs that can enter. Entry limits, if applicable, are printed in the premium list—usually on the cover and on the entry form. If a show has a limited entry, then entries close on the show's closing date or on the day that the entry limit is reached, whichever comes first. If the show has a limited entry, submit your entry to the superintendent as soon as possible.

Last, but not least, think about where you will spend the night if you travel a long distance to the show or if you have a very early ring time. If you plan to stay on the show grounds in a motorhome, you need to reserve an overnight parking space; the parking information and reservation form should be in the premium list. If you plan to stay in a motel, make your reservations early, since motels that accept dogs fill quickly. A list of motels that accept well-behaved dogs should be in the premium list.

To decide whether or not to spend the night on or near the show grounds, ask yourself, "If I have an early judging time can I cope with traveling to the show that morning?" Suppose, for example, that your judging time is 8:00 a.m. If the show site is three hours from your home, and if it takes two hours to groom your dog at the show site, you would need to leave home no later than 3:00 a.m. Even such an early departure doesn't allow any time for unloading, setting up a grooming area, finding your ring, picking up your armband, or exercising your dog when you get to the show! If, on the other hand, you live an hour from the show grounds and have a breed that requires no show-site grooming, then you could leave home at 6:00 a.m. and have plenty of time at the show prior to judging.

Think about your worst-case timing scenario, and plan accordingly. If you think you *might* want to travel the day before the show, make reservations for an overnight stay as soon as your entry is submitted. A precautionary motel reservation for the night before the show can usually be canceled if you luck into a judging time that's relatively late in the day.

One week before the show

Approximately one week before the show, your entry confirmation and judging schedule will arrive in the mail. If you have not received anything three days prior to the show, contact the superintendent to confirm that your entry was received, that your dog is correctly entered, and to find out when your breed will be judged.

Check your dog's entry confirmation for errors as soon as you receive it. If the show, the AKC number, the breed, the sex, or the class entered is incorrect, contact the superintendent immediately. Other errors, such as misspelling or missing titles, do not need to be corrected.

Next, figure out your schedule for the show day. To do this, you will need to know:

❖ what time you will show (estimated from the judging schedule)

❖ how long it will take to get to the show (allow plenty of time for traffic jams, bad weather, and finding the show grounds)

❖ how long it will take to park, unload, and set up your grooming area (if any)

❖ how long it will take to groom your dog prior to showing (if necessary)

Add up your travel time, unloading/set-up time, and grooming time. Remember to allow plenty of time in your schedule for loading last-minute gear into your car before you leave. Then *add at least an extra hour* for finding the ring, exercising your dog, buying a catalog, checking in at the ring and picking up your armband. Now you know what time you must leave home—and if you can't do it *safely* on the day of the show, you should travel the night before.

During the week prior to the dog show, you should gather up your equipment, make checklists, and organize as much as possible. Plastic storage bins with lids make packing and loading gear much easier, especially if each bin is labeled with its contents.

The week before the show is also the time to make sure that your car is in good condition—tires in good shape, oil at the correct level, and so on. Breaking down when you have a dog with you is difficult to cope

If you set up a crating or grooming area, you'll need a dolly to carry your equipment from the unloading zone or parking lot.

with, especially if your car has to be towed. If you have a cell phone, make sure the battery is charged, and if you belong to AAA or another auto club, be sure you have your card with you.

Finally, the week before the show, decide what you will wear when you show your dog and take it to the cleaners if necessary.

In summary, the week before the show you should:

❖ check your entry confirmation for errors

❖ plan your travel time to the show based on your judging time

❖ make checklists and gather up equipment

❖ make sure your car is in good condition

❖ get your show clothes in order

The day before the show

At this point, you should be nearly ready for the show: your gear should be organized, your major grooming should be done, and your paperwork—entry confirmation, judging schedule, and directions to the show—should be in a safe place. So, on the day before the show, you should:

❖ load gear and non-perishable items into your car

❖ check maps, confirm your route, and pack your paperwork

If you will travel on the day before the show, then you should also:

❖ load perishable items such as bait, medicines, and food

❖ double-check that you have your map, entry confirmation, motel reservation confirmation number, and judging schedule

Show day

If you travel to the show the night before, then on show day, you need to arrive at the show grounds with plenty of time to:

❖ park, unload, and if necessary, set up a grooming area

❖ find your ring, pick up your armband, and if possible, watch your judge to see how he uses his ring

❖ allow your dog to relieve himself

Arriving at the show an hour before you are scheduled to enter the ring is usually adequate unless your breed requires grooming at the show site. If your breed is groomed at the show site, allow time to unload your equipment, set up a grooming area and groom your dog.

If you travel to the show on show day, then in addition to the above, you will need allow time to:

❖ load perishable items

❖ double-check that you have your directions to the show, entry confirmation, and judging schedule

Allow *plenty* of time to travel to the show, allowing for heavy traffic, bad weather, and getting lost at least once. It's better to get to the show earlier than you planned than to arrive after your breed has been judged!

Checklists and Packing

Lots of factors will influence your decision about the gear that you take to a show. Factors to be considered include:

❖ Is the show indoors or outdoors?

❖ What's the weather forecast?

❖ Are you going to the show as a day trip or will you spend the night at a motel or on the show grounds?

❖ Does your breed require show-site grooming? Will electricity be available?

❖ Will you eat at restaurants, buy food and drinks from show vendors, or bring provisions from home?

The following items should be taken by everyone to every show:

❖ plenty of fresh water from home for the dogs

❖ medications needed by dogs or people

❖ a first aid kit for dogs and people

❖ plastic bags for cleaning up after your dog

❖ show collar, lead, and bait

❖ entry confirmations and directions to the show site

Consult with experienced dog show friends about what you should take to shows. Your own packing list will evolve as you attend shows and discover what you do and don't need. And remember: it is important to reevaluate your checklists periodically and remove the things that you *never* use at shows!

One of the simplest ways to pack for shows is to use plastic containers; these are easily stacked, can be secured in your vehicle, and can be quickly loaded and unloaded. Since some items are used only at shows and not at home (for example, stakes and tie-downs for an awning, or space blankets, clips, and shade cloth), these containers can be kept packed at all times. "Packing" for the show can simply mean loading the container.

Equipment can be stored in plastic containers, which are easy to secure in your vehicle and carry to your grooming or crating area.

For other items such as grooming tools are used in between shows, designate plastic containers the items. Keep a checklist of the contents with the container so you won't have to guess what to pack before each show. Label the containers clearly so you can identify their contents at a glance.

Finally, do a trial run of packing your vehicle well before the show. Don't wait until the day before the show to discover that you don't have room for important items!

Travel Safety

Dogs should be crated or restrained *whenever* they are in a vehicle. Even dogs that travel calmly under normal circumstances—dogs who have good "car manners"—can become wildly excited when they arrive at a show and see all the other dogs.

Crates should be secured in your vehicle with bungee cords or by some other means, so that they will not shift or roll as you drive.

You must devise a way for securing equipment in your vehicle. Crates should be anchored so that they cannot roll over or shift while you are driving. Make sure that your crate—wire or plastic—will protect your dog if you are in an accident, and that the door will not pop open.

Dollies, awnings, and grooming boxes that can fly through the vehicle when you make an abrupt stop can be dangerous, and should be secured so that they cannot move and injure dogs or people. Bungee cords, nylon straps, and load nets can be used to secure loads inside your vehicle. Bumper-mounted racks can carry ex-pens, wire crates, and dollies.

Be sure that your crated dogs have plenty of fresh air; do not pack your vehicle so tightly that the flow of air to the crates is blocked off. A battery-powered or 12-volt fan can help circulate air to the rear of your car, which is especially important in the summer to ensure that cool air from the air conditioner reaches dogs in the back of your vehicle.

In the summer, make sure your crates are protected from sun coming through the car windows. A sheet draped over the crate top and sides makes an effective sunscreen; be careful, however, not to block off the flow of cool air to your dog.

Think carefully about what could happen to your dogs if you are in an accident and cannot take care of them. Your dogs should be microchipped or tattooed so they can be identified if they escape from your vehicle. If your dog is wearing a collar, emergency workers will have a safe way of handling him if necessary. If you don't want your dog to wear a collar when he travels, hang a collar and lead on the crate door so that your dog can be removed safely from his crate if necessary.

Draping your car with silver reflective "space blankets" is a good way to create shade for your dogs. The space blankets are anchored to the car with large spring clips.

Finally, make sure emergency instructions regarding your dogs can be found easily by emergency workers. The instructions should include whom to call, a guarantee of payment of veterinary and boarding expenses, and information about your dog's medical conditions or drug allergies (if any). Put clearly labeled instructions in a plastic bag or an envelope on the crate door. If your dog needs prescription medications, consider including a carefully labeled three-day supply of the medicine in the emergency instruction bag.

Instructions about caring for your dog in an emergency should be easy to spot; leads (and collars) should hang on the crate doors.

These emergency preparations may sound excessive, but remember the adage that the emergency you prepare for is the one least likely to happen!

Staying at a Motel

There may be occasions when you will stay at a motel with your dog. Most premium lists have the names, addresses, and phone numbers of motels near the show site that will accept dogs. Many travel books list the pet policies of motels. There are also guidebooks for travelling with dogs which list dog-friendly accommodations.

Policies regarding dogs at motels vary. Some motels will only allow dogs in smoking rooms, while others may restrict dogs to "unrenovated" rooms. Some motels may charge an extra fee for pets or require a pet deposit, refundable when the room is inspected and found clean and free of damage upon checkout. If you stay at a motel that requires a pre-checkout inspection, *call the front desk at least an hour before you check out to request room inspection*. If there are several "dog rooms" to be inspected, you may have a long wait before you can check out, and you don't want to be late getting to the show.

At the motel, be a considerate guest by following a few simple rules:

❖ Always clean up after your dog on the motel grounds.

❖ If you groom your dog in the motel room, put sheets or a tarp on the floor to catch the hair. Clean up after you finish grooming.

❖ If you bathe your dog in the bathtub, do not let hair clog the drain. Clean the tub afterwards.

❖ Put a blanket, sheet, or tarp on the floor underneath your crates.

❖ Carry carpet cleaner, paper towels, and old towels so you can clean up any accidents.

❖ Bring a sheet to cover the bedspread if your dog will sleep on the bed.

❖ *Never* leave a dog loose and unattended in a motel room. If you must leave your dog in the room, put the dog in a crate. Turn on the TV to keep your dog company, and to muffle noises from the outside that might make your dog bark.

❖ If your dog will not be quiet when left crated in a motel room, then *take the dog with you.*

A barking dog should *never* be left in a motel room—he will make the other guests and the management angry and may get you thrown out of the motel.

Show Attire

The object of the game in dog showing is to present a polished professional picture to the judge. The appearance of the handler is an important element of the overall presentation.

The traditional attire for competition in the breed ring is "office professional": men wear ties and jackets, and women wear suits, dresses, or comparable business attire. Pay attention to what most exhibitors and judges are wearing at the dog shows you visit as an observer, and to take your cue from the tasteful attire you observe.

"Business professional" attire is appropriate for the show ring. Pockets in the jacket or skirt are a must.

Men should wear a coat and tie when showing, unless the judge indicates that they may remove their coats.

The structure of the clothing you wear should enhance your ability to show your dog. Select your clothing for easy movement when you run, bend, and kneel. Note, however, that some clothing may *interfere* with your ability to show your dog. For example, a very full skirt may billow around a moving dog, making it impossible for the dog to gait. An open, flapping jacket may smack a dog in the face as you bend over him. An untacked necktie may dangle in a dog's face when he is being stacked.

Consider the colors you will wear when showing your dog. The color of your clothing should complement your dog's color while giving some contrast: for example, blue or green are better choices than yellow when showing a Golden Retriever, while yellow or other pastels and primary colors work well with dark dogs. A solid black outfit may be very stylish but if your dog is black, he will blend with your clothes and "disappear" in the ring.

Unless the handler's clothes contrast with the dog's coat, the dog will "disappear." In this case, the judge will find it much easier to evaluate the topline of the Basset Hound on the left than on the right.

Your show clothes should have pockets on the right side—bait is usually kept in your right pocket. You should be able to slip your hand quickly and easily into your bait pocket. If necessary, you may need a pocket that can accommodate a brush, or need a waistband into which you can tuck your brush's handle. And of course, remove keys and loose change from your pockets before you enter the ring.

Jewelry should not interfere with your ability to stack and present your dog.

Some jewelry is fine—many people wear pins, tie tacks, rings, bracelets, and necklaces in the ring. However, you should avoid jewelry that makes excessive noise when you move, such as a set of bangle bracelets, or dangling jewelry that could snag on your dog's coat or interfere with your ability to stack your dog.

Choose your shoes carefully. Slick leather soles can be dangerous on both cement and grass. High heels are awkward for running, but can be worn by exhibitors of toy breeds. Loose loafers can fly off the feet of exhibitors as they move their dogs around the ring. Handlers often wear sneakers so that they can move safely. Choose shoes that give you good traction and which are comfortable enough to wear all day.

Finally, outdoor shows may present additional challenges. In rainy weather it is acceptable to wear a raincoat or rainsuit while showing your dog, but never carry an umbrella into the ring. In hot weather gentlemen should wear a jacket and tie unless the judge indicates that men may remove their jackets.

Summary

If you don't plan well for a dog show, it can be a frustrating and unrewarding experience. Be aware of the chain of events that occur before a show and are cognizant of deadlines.

Ask dog show friends about their pre-show routines: what chores do they tackle a week before the show, and what do they leave to the last minute? Make *lists* of the equipment you need to take to a show—don't try to pack on a hit-or-miss basis.

If you stay at a motel, make your reservations well in advance, and be a courteous hotel guest. Clean up after your dog on the hotel grounds, clean up after grooming, and don't leave a barking or loose dog in a motel room!

Give some thought to the safety of your dogs, both on the road and at the show. Make sure their crates and all other gear are secured in your car, and that they will get plenty of fresh air. At rest stops and the show, create shade for them if necessary in the summer, or make sure they stay warm in the winter. And, in case of an accident, make sure emergency workers will be able to deal with your dogs safely.

There's a lot to consider, but after a few shows, the planning, timelines, and checklists for a successful show experience will become a natural part of your pre-show routine.

Chapter 20

Before You Enter the Ring

No matter how carefully you plan everything leading up to a dog show, failure to effectively plan your show-day schedule can sabotage your efforts. In this chapter you'll learn about the things you need to do at the show before you enter the ring.

Arriving at the Show

There are several things you will need to do at the show before you set foot in the ring. You should arrive at the show grounds with plenty of time to:

- ❖ park

- ❖ unload, and set up a grooming area, if needed for your breed

- ❖ exercise your dog

- ❖ groom your dog if necessary

- ❖ find your ring

- ❖ pick up your armband

- ❖ watch your judge to see how he uses his ring

- ❖ buy a catalog if you wish

- ❖ warm up your dog for the ring

In general, arriving at the show *an hour before you enter the ring* is sufficient unless your breed requires grooming at the show, in which case you should allow time to unload your equipment, set up a grooming area, and groom your dog. In addition, as you plan your travel time to the show, you should allow plenty of time for a traffic jam at the parking lot (especially if you arrive in the hour before the day's judging begins, when most exhibitors arrive), heavy traffic, bad weather, detours, and getting lost. If the show is on a weekday rather than a weekend, allow for commuter traffic in your travel plans.

Parking and Unloading

The logistics for parking, unloading gear, and setting up a grooming area are different for every dog show. In general, indoor shows require parking in a "loading zone" near the show building, hauling your gear into the building, and then moving your car to the parking lot. The process is simpler at an outdoor show: you frequently set up your grooming area beside your vehicle or under a large grooming tent that is accessible to vehicles for unloading. Don't leave your vehicle in an unloading area any longer than absolutely necessary; it's not fair to other exhibitors, and your vehicle might be towed away.

Parking

Parking conditions vary greatly among show sites. For example, if the show is held at a county fairground, there should be plenty of parking at the site. On the other hand, if the show is held in a high school gymnasium, you may end up parking on the street several blocks away from the show. If possible, ask someone who has shown at the site before about the parking conditions. Information about parking may be included in the premium list for the show, especially if reservations are being taken for parking near the show rings. Parking information may also be included in the judging schedule that you receive with your entry confirmation. Other times, you will just have to wing it at the show!

Finally, you may be charged a small fee to park. Some shows divide the parking so you have a choice: you can pay to park near the show rings, or you can park for free in a distant lot. Other shows offer "reserved day parking": pre-paid parking spaces near the show rings which you reserve by mail prior to the show (similar to reserving overnight parking before the show). Check the premium list for parking information when you make your entry.

Parking conditions can influence a number of your show day strategies:

❖ Will you have easy access to your vehicle, or will you need to tote all the gear you will need for the day into the show site? If you will have to haul a lot of gear a long way, do you have a dolly to carry your crate and other gear?

❖ What will you do with your dog when he isn't it the ring? Do you plan to leave your dog crated in your vehicle (*only if the weather is appropriate*)? Do you plan to set up a grooming or crating area at the show? Or do you plan to simply keep your dog with you on a lead at all times at the show?

As you walk around the show prior to judging, be careful not to exhaust your dog.

Grooming and crating areas

At indoor shows, grooming and crating areas are usually clearly marked by tape, signs, or floor markings. Some shows have areas reserved for professional handlers, while others do not. Some shows offer "reserved grooming areas" for a small fee; check the premium list. If a specialty show is being held in conjunction with an all-breed show, a grooming area may be reserved near the specialty show ring for the breed involved. If there is a map of the show layout in the judging schedule, grooming and crating areas will be marked.

An "ex-pen," or exercise pen can be used to hold several dogs.

Space is limited at indoor shows, so don't bring more gear than you need. If you use an extension cord, bring duct tape to the show: some shows require that electrical cords be taped down. Keep your grooming or crating area neat and confined—don't block the aisles or the access of other people to their crating areas.

Never leave an unattended dog in a noose on a grooming table!

Unless you need electricity, grooming may be easier at outdoor shows. Depending on the weather and the parking conditions, you may simply set up your grooming area beside your car. Some shows provide large grooming tents near the show rings, under which you can set up a grooming area. As at indoor shows, keep your grooming area compact and clean.

You may be able to drive up to the grooming tent and unload your equipment. If so, unload your equipment quickly and move your car to the designated parking areas so that other exhibitors can unload their equipment.

Getting Oriented

Once you have unloaded your gear and, if necessary, set up your grooming and crating area, it's time to begin your show chores.

At an outdoor show, you may decide to groom your dog by your car.

A large grooming tent provides a sheltered, communal grooming area.

Your first task is to get oriented at the show. Wandering around as you locate your ring, the superintendent's desk, and the catalog sales table gives your dog a good opportunity to get used to the sights and sounds of the show site. If you have a dog that's skittish during the exam, this is a good time to stack him near a ring and to ask a stranger to "play judge" by doing a quick exam.

Find your ring and check the footing

Early in your exploration of the show you should locate your ring. Ring numbers are posted at each ring, usually on a pole that can be spotted from a distance. There may be a map of the ring locations included in your judging schedule, but it's a good idea to find your ring in case the show superintendent was not able to lay out rings as planned.

Once you have found your ring, look at it carefully. If it is an indoor ring, check whether the matting is securely taped down, or whether there are loose edges, bumps, or wrinkles that might trip you. Check the slickness of the flooring beside the mat (remember, the mat is for the dog—if you have a medium or large breed, you'll probably be running off the mat). Watch the dogs in the ring: are dogs the same size as yours slipping on the mats? If so, you may wish to set your dog at a *slight* angle, so that his feet push slightly across the ribs of the mat. You may also use a spray on his feet to give him better traction.

If the ring is outdoors, look at the ground for bumps or hollows that might cause you to stumble as you move around the ring. Check for muddy spots or wet patches. If a tent or canopy covers a portion of the ring, locate tent legs, ropes or tent stakes that might trip you as you move with your dog.

Finally, if the show is outdoors, and the weather is either rainy or hot and sunny, check the availability of nearby canopies or shade trees. You will need to find a protected place near your ring to wait without drenching or melting your dog.

Observe your judge

When you have found your ring, it's time to observe your judge if possible. Check the judging schedule to see if the person in the ring is your judge. (Frequently, more than one judge will use a ring during the day.) If not, then check the judging schedule to see if your judge is in another ring; sometimes judges will spend part of their day in one ring, and the rest of their day in another. If you can't find your judge when you do your first walk around the show, arrive at your ring when your judging set starts so that you can see your judge in action.

Take time to watch your judge and learn about his ring procedure as he judges other breeds.

When you locate your judge, watch him for a few minutes to get a general idea of his ring procedures. Look for the following:

❖ Does he want the dogs to be in catalog order? (Do you know where you want to be in the line-up if he does not require catalog order?)

❖ Where does he want the dogs set for their initial group presentation?

❖ Where does he want the dogs set up for the exam?

❖ What gaiting pattern does he use for dogs the same size as yours: a triangle? an out-and-back?

❖ Is the judge a "glancer?" That is, when performing the individual exam and observing the movement for each dog, does he concentrate only on that dog, or does he glance at the other dogs as they wait in line?

❖ If the entry is large, how does the judge sort out his choices? Does he keep everyone in their initial order and just point out his placements during the final group go-around? Or, does he rearrange dogs after the individual exam and then have them move as a class before indicating his placements?

You probably won't get answers to all these questions by watching your judge for a few minutes, but you will learn a good bit about his ring procedure.

Finally, don't panic if your breed is the first one the judge sees that day—if so, you won't have a chance to observe your judge, but neither will anyone else. In this case, just listen carefully to the judge's directions and watch what the other exhibitors do. If you can't hear what the judge says, follow the example of the exhibitors ahead of you.

The superintendent's desk

If you contacted the superintendent after you received your entry confirmation to correct an *important* error (AKC number, dog's sex, or the class entered), stop by the superintendent's desk and confirm that the correction was processed and that the judge's book is correct.

Some superintendents have forms at their desks for making other entry corrections and updates (errors in spelling, addresses, owners, etc). Superintendents keep information about your dog in a computer database indexed by your dog's AKC number; they don't input information such as sire, owner, etc., with each individual show entry. If you need to change anything in your dog's "file," fill out a form at the superintendent's desk if possible. You can also pick up premium lists for upcoming shows at the superintendent's desk.

Stop at the superintendent's desk to pick up premium lists and to update the information about your dog in their database, if necessary.

Catalogs

Catalogs are sold at the host kennel club's table, which is usually set up near the superintendent's desk or the announcer's table. If the show is part of a cluster of shows, the catalogs for all the shows may be combined into a single volume.

At the front of the catalog you will find the judging schedule for the show, which is identical to the one you received in the mail. Next, you will find the listings for the individual breeds, organized by group and then, within each group, organized alphabetically by breed. Within each breed, the entries for each class are given, first for dogs and then for bitches. After the Open Bitch class, the entrants for Best of Breed Competition are listed.

Take a look at the entries for your breed before judging begins. If you don't purchase a catalog, you may look at the "desk copy" at the superintendent's desk, or, *briefly*, at the catalog being used by you ring's steward. Note how many classes there are for each sex in your breed (some classes may not have entries), and how many dogs there are in your class.

Watch the Time!

It is imperative that you keep track of time when you are at a show! From the judging schedule, you know what time you need to be at your ring, allowing ample time for picking up your armband and watching the judge before you enter the ring. Also, remember that dogs absent from the breeds and classes ahead of you will affect your schedule. Judges may not start judging a set *before* the time listed in the judging schedule, but absentees can accelerate the judging *within* a set.

Ringside Chores

Arrive at your ring with plenty of time to let your dog become accustomed to his new surroundings: the noise, the jostling and bumping of several dogs in a crowded space, flapping ring canopies, and the public address system. You must strike a balance; don't arrive ringside so late that you must dash frantically to get into the ring, but don't arrive ringside so early that your dog stands around becoming bored and restless. As you attend more shows, you will get a better sense of how much time to allow for your preparations ringside, and how much time your dog needs to spend ringside before he's settled, focused, and ready to show.

Checking in

As the time approaches for the judging of your set, you must check in with the ring steward. When you check in, you should know your dog's armband number and the class in which he is entered.

Wait patiently by the steward's table until the steward is ready to check you in. *Don't interrupt the steward*—he has several jobs to juggle at once (checking in exhibitors, calling classes into the ring, organizing the class ribbons and trophies, marking his book, and handing out armband numbers). When the steward is ready to give you your armband number, quickly provide the information he needs: "Dalmatian, Open Bitch, number 14." Do *not* identify your dog by name. If you don't remember your armband number, ask to see the steward's catalog so that you can look up your dog's number or point to your dog's entry. When you get your armband, also pick up a couple of rubber bands to secure it, and *move away from the steward's table* so that other exhibitors can check in.

When you check in and pick up your armband, identify your dog by his number, *not* his registered name.

Wearing your armband

Armbands are worn on the upper *left* arm—the arm with which you hold your lead. The armband is held in place by a rubber band slid over and up your arm like a bracelet. To keep the armband from slipping down your arm as you move, tear a notch in each side of the armband for the rubber band; the notches will hold your number in place.

Plastic armband holders, such as those used by obedience competitors, are more trouble than they are worth for the breed ring. The only reason to use a plastic armband holder in the breed ring is if your arm is so large that you cannot comfortably wear a rubber band.

Tear notches in your armband to hold the rubber band; this prevents the armband from slipping down your arm as you move.

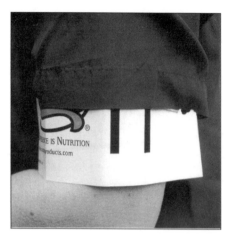

If you have short sleeves, wear the armband high on your arm so that the sleeve does not creep over your armband and obscure the number.

Alternatively, if you have large arms, simply remember to bring your own supply of large rubber bands to the show. Gentlemen should make sure that they can comfortably wear a rubber band *over* their jacket sleeves.

Take special care if you wear short sleeves when you show. The short sleeve can easily slip out from underneath your armband, obscuring the number. If you wear short sleeves, make sure that you wear your armband high enough to prevent your sleeve from covering the number.

How many classes?

Another thing to check *quickly* when you pick up your armband is which classes are represented in your breed that day. If you have not already looked at a catalog, take a *quick* look at the steward's catalog. If the entry is small, not all classes will have exhibitors. Classes are always judged in the same order; empty classes are skipped. Classes for dogs are judged first in the order:

- ❖ Puppy, 6-9 months

- ❖ Puppy, 9-12 months

- ❖ 12-18 months

- ❖ Novice

- ❖ Bred-by-Exhibitor

- ❖ American-Bred

- ❖ Open

❖ Winners (Winners Dog and Reserve Winners Dog)

These are followed by the classes for bitches in the same order and then by the Best of Breed competition.

Catalog order or not?

The last thing to check *quickly* in the steward's catalog as you pick up your armband is how many animals there are in your class, and what armband number is ahead of you. If the judge wants his class to enter the ring in catalog order, you need to know which armband number to follow. As you check in with the steward and pick up your armband, you may ask the steward if the judge is asking for catalog order or not.

Try to spot the person wearing the armband number that you will follow into the ring. Remember, however, that there may be absentees, so only look for the number ahead of you that has been picked up from the steward.

If the judge does *not* want his class in catalog order, decide where you want to be in the class. If the class has only two or three dogs, do you want to be first, second, or last? If the class is large, do you want to be one of the first competitors in line, or somewhere in the middle of the class, or at the end? Your decision will depend on a number of factors. Do you want to follow someone else so that you can copy what he does? When moving in a group, is your dog better off at the head of the line or with a dog ahead of him? How long does it take to set your dog? The first dog in line needs to be set very quickly, while dogs farther down the line have more time for stacking before the judge's eyes reach them.

Warming up

Unless you've warmed him up, don't expect your dog to sparkle the instant he sets foot in the ring.

As the classes before yours are judged, start warming your dog up for the ring. Play a few of your quiet "silly ring games" with your dog so that he wakes up and begins to focus his attention on you. Move to an uncrowded area near your ring (but close enough that you can watch the classes being judged) and stack your dog once or twice; if you think it would be helpful for your dog, ask a bystander to do a quick exam, or simply to pet your dog as he stands in his stack. If possible, gait your dog for a few paces—but don't try to gait your dog in the crowded area around the ring's entrance!

As you warm up your dog up, you'll have to strike a balance: *don't* wear your dog out with repeated stacking and gaiting. If you do too much when you warm your dog up, he'll be tired by the time you enter the ring. The purpose of the warm-up is to get your dog pumped up, alert, and ready to enter the ring and show.

Summary

Careful advanced planning for the show day itself can pay big dividends in terms of your success at the show. No matter how hard you've worked before the show, failure to plan your show-day schedule can sabotage all your efforts. The good news is that planning is pretty simple.

Arrive at the show at least an hour before you're scheduled to enter the ring, and more if you must groom your dog at the show site. Allow plenty of time to unload gear, set up a grooming or crating area at the show, if necessary, and park your car.

There are several things you should do at the show before judging: find your ring, watch your judge, perhaps buy a catalog, and check in with the ring steward. When you pick up your armband, check the catalog, and note how many dogs are entered in your class, which dog you follow in catalog order, and which class is ahead of your class.

Finally, your dog needs time to walk around and become used to the show conditions as well, so that when he's in the ring he can focus on you and *not* on everything going on around him.

Chapter 21

Showtime!

This is it: all your training and preparation for the ring will come into play shortly as you and your dog enter the ring. You've groomed your dog and trained him, you've watched your judge during the classes ahead of you, and you've learned the rules of the game. It's showtime!

Entering the Ring

When the class before yours is being judged, make sure you're near the ring entrance, but not blocking it. After the awards have been given to that class, the ring steward will call your class into the ring. Most stewards will announce the class name—for example, "Open Bitches"—and then read out the armband numbers in the class. The steward may also announce "catalog order" or "any order" before calling out the armband numbers. If the steward does not specify "any order" then assume that the class should enter and line up in catalog order, which is the most common practice.

When the steward calls your class into the ring, enter quickly *after* all the members of the previous class have left the ring. Don't create a bottleneck—and risk dog fights—at the ring entrance by trying to enter while the previous class is exiting. Go directly to the place where you will stack your dog for the initial presentation and set your dog.

If the steward calls for the class in catalog order, try to enter the ring in catalog order if possible: if the catalog lists your dog second in the class, then try to be the second handler to enter the ring. If there is a traffic jam at the ring entrance and you can't follow the dog ahead of you into the ring, simply enter the ring as soon as you can, and move directly to your position in the line-up to set your dog. If the person in line ahead of you hasn't entered the ring when you enter, stack your dog, leaving space for the late dog in front of you. If you don't leave enough space, you will have to move and reset your dog when the dog ahead of you claims his space.

If the class is *not* called in catalog order, try to *enter* the ring in the order you'd like to be in the class. Of course, this isn't always possible—for example, two exhibitors may want the "second in line" position: the one that enters the ring second gets that position. The order in which you *enter* the ring is the order in which you line up your dogs for the initial presentation. If you want the second position but entered the ring third or fourth in line, *do not* cut in front of the second person; he got there first.

Not getting the position you want in the line-up is *not* a disaster; you'll do just as well *near* the position you wanted. Remember, in catalog order you don't get *any* choice about where you line up, so you and your dog should be able to cope with any place in line!

In the Ring

Once the class has entered the ring, everything should go like clockwork. The judge has a tight schedule to maintain, and exhibitors who delay his class through inattention or carelessness will frustrate him. Judges will, of course, give a little slack to novice handlers, but they do expect you to know what your job is and to attempt to do it as well as you can.

Watching the judge as he works through the classes ahead of yours will boost your confidence that you know what your judge wants and that you can do it well.

Initial presentation

When you enter the ring, go immediately to the side of the ring indicated by the steward (or that the previous class used for its initial stack) and set up your dog for the initial presentation. As the class enters the ring and stacks, the judge will check armband numbers against his judging book, verifying that the correct dogs are in the ring and marking any that are absent. Thus, your armband should be visible to the judge as you enter and stack your dog. Hold your dog in his stack until all the dogs have entered the ring, and the judge has verified the armband numbers and had a good look at the dogs in their initial presentation.

Rules for the initial stack are:

❖ Don't crowd the dog ahead of you: leave a couple of feet between the end of his tail and your dog's nose.

❖ Stack your dog directly behind the dog ahead of you: not closer to the center of the ring, not further away from the ring center, and not on an angle.

❖ Don't keep tweaking your dog's stack: set him once and hold him in position.

All breeds are stacked on the ground during the group presentations—even the breeds that are examined on a table.

❖ If he moves a foot, quickly reset it.

❖ If the dog moves out of his stack completely, don't try to repair it—put him back in his place and quickly restack him from the beginning.

❖ When your dog is stacked, keep one eye on him and one on the judge; don't stare at the judge, pleading for him to look at your dog.

If the class is very small and the judge can check armband numbers as the class enters, he may decide not to have the handlers stack their dogs, but simply have the dogs move once or twice around the ring together before setting up for the individual examination.

Initial group movement

The judge will next ask the handlers to move the dogs together as a class. Even if you are in a class of one you will gait your dog around the ring so the judge can check for lameness. Gather up your lead quickly and be prepared to move out. The dogs will move around to the side of the ring where the judge will do his individual exam. The first person in line is told where to lead the line and stop. Common instructions are, "Take them around to there (judge points to a location)," or "Take them around one time (you come back to the same place you start)," or "Take them around two times ending up there (judge points to a location)."

Rules for moving in a group are:

❖ If you are first in line, ask the person behind you if he is ready before you take off. Simply glance back and ask, "Ready?" If you don't get an answer, just pause until the person behind you seems ready to go, and then start.

❖ If you are first in line and the judge's instructions aren't clear—either how many times to go around, or where to stop—*ask* him for clarification before you start.

❖ When starting, do not crowd the person moving ahead of you; wait briefly before you start.

❖ Do not tailgate the dog move ahead of you, and do not crash into the dog or person ahead of you at the end of the group movement.

When moving in a group, space the dogs closely enough that the judge can observe two or more at once, but don't let them bunch together.

Individual exam and movement

Next comes the individual exam and movement: the handler stacks his dog for the judge's exam; the dog gaits using the pattern requested by the judge; and finally the dog moves around the ring to the end of the line.

Rules for the individual exam and movement are:

❖ Don't keep tweaking your dog's stack; set him once and hold him in position.

❖ Follow the judge's instructions for the mouth exam: some judges will ask you to show your dog's bite to them, and others will open your dog's mouth themselves.

❖ Do not feed your dog bait right before the judge tries to examine his head and mouth.

❖ If you bait your dog after the head and mouth are examined, hold the bait so that your dog does not bounce, slouch or stretch to eat it; this will distort your dog's stack and make it difficult for the judge to examine him.

❖ Don't impede the exam: keep out of the judge's way while keeping your dog under control.

❖ If the dog moves a foot during the exam, you should quickly and quietly reset it as the judge moves back to take his final look.

❖ If your dog starts his movement badly— for example, galloping or pacing— remember the "1/3 — 2/3 rule": you can restart your dog within the first 1/3 of the pattern. If, on the other hand, your dog starts to gallop when you're more than 1/3 of the way into the pattern, you need to get him under control *there*, rather than returning to the judge and restarting him.

❖ Plan your dog's stop about five or six feet in front of the judge; take a step or two if necessary to correct your dog's position, but don't mill around.

Whenever your dog is in the ring and can be seen by the judge, he should be looking his best.

Final presentation and group movement

As the last dog finishes his individual gaiting pattern, the other dogs in the class should stack in a line for their final presentation. The first dog at the head of the line is stacked where the individual examination stack was done; this may or may not be along the same side of the ring as the initial presentation stack.

The rules for the initial stack and group movement apply to the final presentation and group movement:

In the final group presentation, set your dog and hold the stack: don't fidget or try to call the judge's attention to your dog's strengths by stroking or pointing to a particular area.

❖ Stack your dog quickly. Don't fidget with his stack.

❖ If your dog moves, quickly restack him.

❖ Allow ample space between moving dogs. Move your dog at the correct speed.

❖ Keep one eye on the judge and one eye on your dog.

❖ Have your dog looking his best at all times.

Never stop working at showing your dog until the judge has made *and indicated* his decisions. Even after re-ordering the dogs in the class, some judges will change their minds during the final lap of group movement. Never stop working!

The sort

If you are in a very large class, the judge *may* divide the dogs into those that he will keep for further judging and those who are no longer contenders for placements. The "sort" is usually done by separating the dogs into two groups, sending some dogs to another side of the ring. Sometimes the judge will do a sort during the individual exam; more often, he will wait until he has studied the dogs stacked as a group, *after* the individual examinations and movement are complete.

The judge may evaluate the dogs in pairs or small groups. Here, the dogs are stacked facing the judge so he can compare their fronts.

Keep working at presenting your dog well as the judge goes down the line making his sort—he might make a last minute decision to keep your dog in competition based on your current stack. When the sort is finished, handlers that are dismissed from further judging will hear a statement such as, "Thank you for showing today," or "I am going to continue working with these dogs (gesturing toward the 'keepers'), thank you." Leave the ring quickly and quietly.

If you are still in the ring, *keep on working*. Remember the old adage, "It ain't over 'til it's over," and continue to work at showing your dog. Every stack and every move counts even more now. Your job is to have your dog looking as good as possible all the time you are in the ring, and especially when you are under consideration for a placement ribbon.

The judge will continue working with the dogs, repeating the stacking and gaiting process individually, in pairs, and in groups as necessary. He may ask for the dogs to be stacked facing toward him, so that he can compare all the fronts in the group, or walk behind them to compare rears. *Keep on working*. The judge may shuffle the order of dogs in the class several times. Don't assume that the current order is the final order and stop working. If your dog isn't gaiting, he should be stacked, unless instructed otherwise by the judge.

Class awards

When the judge has chosen his class placements, he will indicate them to the competitors. Pay close attention: some judges point to their selected animals very clearly, and some are more casual in their gestures. Some judges will sort their dogs into their final order before the last group go-'round, and some won't; don't assume that the order of the dogs in the final group go-'round is it—*keep on working* until the judge has indicated his placements.

Once the judge has designated the first through fourth place winners, the winners should move quickly to the placement ring markers, which are near the judge's table and the ring entrance. Non-placers should exit the ring quickly, remembering to congratulate the winners as they leave.

Before awarding the ribbons, the judge and steward mark their books. Make sure that your armband is clearly visible to the judge.

As the placement winners stand at their markers, the judge and the ring steward will record the placements in their books. Make sure that your armband number is visible to the judge and to the steward.

Finally, the judge will come down the line, handing a ribbon to each placer. Smile, take the ribbon, thank the judge, and leave the ring—the judge has a schedule to keep! If you want to talk to the judge, wait until he has a break in his judging schedule.

After your class has been judged and you have left the ring—with or without a ribbon in hand—you should move away from the ring entrance so that the next class can enter.

If you won first or second place in your class, you must stay ringside for Winners class. If you won third or fourth place, or if you did not place, you are through for the day and may leave the ring area if you wish.

Winners Class

The Winners class for dogs is judged immediately after the last dog class is judged; Winners class for bitches is judged after the last bitch class is judged. If there is more than one class with entries, *the first and second place winners in each class must be available ringside* for judging in the Winners class.

If there is only one class with entries that day—say, only entries in the Open Dog class— then the winner of the Open class is also Winners Dog, and the dog awarded second place in the Open class is Reserve Winners Dog. In this case, the judge will award Winners Dog and Reserve Winners Dog when he makes the Open class awards; there will not be a separate Winners class.

When the awards for the last class with entries are made—assuming there is more than one class—the first place winners from each class should re-enter the ring and go to the side of the ring where the initial stack was made in each class. The dogs are stacked in reverse class order, with the winner of the Open (or last) class at the head of the line, and the winner of the 6-9 month puppy class at the end.

In Winners class, the dogs are stacked in *reverse* class order, with the winner of the Open class at the head of the line.

The judging procedure for Winners class is completely unpredictable. The judge may run it exactly like a regular class. Or, having just judged the classes, the judge may already have a clear idea of which animal will be his Winners Dog or Winners Bitch, and may simply point to his choice during the initial presentation. If the race is tight between two or more competitors, the judge may put the dogs through their paces repeatedly, stacking and gaiting individually and in pairs. Anything can happen, *so keep on working* until Winners Dog or Winners Bitch has been awarded.

As the Winners Dog moves to the placement markers to receive his ribbon, *the second place dog*, if any, from the class that yielded Winners Dog should enter the ring and immediately take up the place vacated by Winners Dog. For example, if Winners Dog came from the Open class, then as Winners Dog is receiving his ribbon, the second place Open dog should enter the ring, go to the head of the line (the place for the Open Dog), and stack.

The judge will next make his choice for the Reserve Winners Dog. The judging is likely to be brief—the judge has already had a second look at all the dogs in the ring but one. When the Reserve Winners Dog is selected, he should move to the placement markers to receive his ribbon, and the other dogs should leave the ring. Judging for the Reserve Winners Bitch proceeds in exactly the same way.

All the class dogs, except Winners Dog and Winners Bitch, may leave the ring area if they wish. Winners Dog and Winners Bitch must stay ringside for Best of Breed judging.

Best of Breed

After the judging of the Winners Bitch class, the Best of Breed class is judged. The breed champions enter the ring first, followed by Winners Dog and then by Winners Bitch.

Best of Breed class proceeds along the lines of the other classes: initial presentation and group movement, individual exam and movement, and then group presentation and movement again while the judge makes his selections.

The judge may decide *not* to repeat the individual exam and gaiting for Winners Dog and Winners Bitch—this is the third time they've been in the ring. The judge may simply have them wait to the side, and then move them together when making his selection for Best of Winners.

Three awards are made in the Best of Breed class:

- ❖ Best of Breed
- ❖ Best of Winners
- ❖ Best of Opposite Sex

Either Winners Dog or Winners Bitch will be Best of Winners—whichever one the judge thinks is the better animal. It is possible for the Winners Dog or Winners Bitch to receive multiple awards from this class: for example, if Winners Bitch is awarded Best of Breed, she is automatically Best of Winners.

The awards in this class are indicated in the order: Best of Breed, Best of Winners, Best of Opposite Sex. The judge may rearrange the class so that the first three animals in line reflect his choices. Or, he may simply gesture to his selections saying, "Breed," "Winners," and "Opposite," as he points to his choices.

Dogs receiving awards should move to the placement markers; Best of Winners stands *between* Best of Breed and Best of Opposite Sex. The other exhibitors should leave the ring, congratulating the winners on their way out. The judge and steward will mark their books, and the judge will present the ribbons.

Photos

Occasionally, you'll want to document your milestone successes with a professional photo. Having a photo taken is completely optional. Ask your mentor or other dog show friends how much show photos usually cost so that you won't be surprised when the photo and the bill are mailed to you!

Photos are taken *at the judge's discretion,* usually at the end of the judging set if the judge's schedule permits. Sometimes, however, a judge's schedule will be so tight that the judge will delay photos until the end of the morning or even the end of the day—remember, the judge must keep to a strict schedule if the show is to remain on track.

If you would like to have a photo taken, tell the steward after Best of Breed has been judged. The steward may already know when the judge will be available for photos; if not, the steward will check with the judge and let you know. You may have a substantial wait until photo time—if so, then take your dog back to his crate or ex-pen to rest. You don't want your photo spoiled by a tired, droopy dog.

When it's time for your photo, hand your ribbons, and, possibly, trophy or prize, to the judge, who will hold them in the photo.

When the judge breaks for photos, there will be probably several people waiting. Have your ribbons ready. Since several pictures must be taken in a very brief time, move quickly when it is your turn. As you move into place, tell the photographer what your award was (for example, "Winners Bitch and a major" or "Winners Dog, Opposite, and a new champion!") so that he can adjust his sign. Hand your ribbons to the judge. Make sure that the photographer can see your armband number so he can identify your photo and send you the photo.

Tell the photographer which awards you won so that he can adjust his sign. Listen carefully if he gives you suggestions for stacking your dog for the photo, and warn him if your dog is crazy about thrown toys.

Stack your dog quickly where the photographer tells you. The photographer may have you adjust your dog's stack by moving a foot, or by holding the head higher or lower. Listen to the photographer—he's telling you *exactly* what he sees through his lens. The judge might also have suggestions about how to stack your dog—heed the judge's advice.

The photographer may also tell *you* where to look. If not, then look down at your dog's head. Do *not* stare into the camera!

The photographer will often squeak or toss a toy to get your dog's attention. If your dog goes berserk around toys, warn the photographer and hold on tightly. Two photos may be taken to ensure that you have a good shot.

When the photos have been taken, reclaim your ribbons from the judge, thank him for taking time to do the photos (after all, photo sessions come out of his break time), and move quickly out of the way so that the next dog can have a turn.

Summary

When you're in the ring, it's time to *present* your dog to the judge. You've learned all the basic skills you need to show your dog—stacking, gaiting, and standing for the examination—and you've learned how these skills are linked together into the standard show procedure.

It may seem as though there are lots of rules to follow in the show ring—where to stack, when to move, what to say—but almost everything that happens in the ring is dictated by common sense or good sportsmanship. Don't crowd the dogs ahead of you, follow the judge's instructions, and treat the other competitors in the manner in which you wish to be treated.

Never stop working when you're in the ring with your dog. You never know what's running through a judge's mind, and if you stop trying to present your dog to the judge, the judge may no longer have reason to consider your dog for a placement. If you're in the ring, show your dog!

Chapter 22

Counting Championship Points

The real "prize" for non-champion animals at AKC conformation shows are the points earned towards an AKC championship. Championship points are won by the Winners Dog (the best non-champion male) and the Winners Bitch (the best non-champion female). In this chapter you'll learn how to count points toward your dog's championship.

Earning a Championship

In order to earn a championship, a dog must earn at least 15 points at specialty or all-breed dog shows. Winners Dog and Winners Bitch are the only dogs who earn points; they can earn from one to five points at a show. The more dogs or bitches there are in competition at a show, the more points can be won. Wins of three or more points are *major wins* ("majors"); wins of one or two points are *minor wins*. To earn a championship, a dog's 15-point total must include at least two majors, awarded by two different judges.

The Point Schedule

At each show, the number of points earned by Winners Dog and Winners Bitch in each breed is determined by:

- ❖ the breed of the dog

- ❖ the number of males and the number of females of that breed in competition that day

- ❖ the geographic location of the show

The basic idea behind the point schedule is that the more popular (or numerous) a breed, the more males (or females) it takes to win points. For example, in New York it may take an entry of 98 Labrador Retriever females to earn five points, but only seven Smooth Fox Terrier females to earn five points.

Breed popularity also varies geographically across the United States. For example, the 98 Labrador Retriever females needed for five points in New York may drop to 33 Labrador Retriever females in Louisiana, and 12 Labrador Retriever females in Alaska.

To cope fairly with this geographic variation, the AKC divides the US and Puerto Rico into 12 Regional Divisions.

Each year, the AKC calculates the point schedule for each Division, based on a number of factors. The result is the annual "Schedule of Points," by breed, for each of the

Division	States
Division 1	CT, ME, MA, NH, NY, RI, VT
Division 2	DE, NJ, OH, PA
Division 3	KY, MD, NC, TN, VA, WV, DC
Division 4	AL, AR, FL, GA, LA, MS, SC
Division 5	MI, IL, IN
Division 6	IA, KS, MN, MO, NB, WI
Division 7	AZ, NM, OK, TX
Division 8	CO, ID, MT, NV, ND, OR, SD, UT, WA, WY
Division 9	CA
Division 10	AK
Division 11	HI
Division 12	PR

Figure: Geographic Divisions in the AKC Point Schedule.

12 divisions. The Schedule of Points is valid for one year, from May to the next May[1].

The point schedule is published annually by the AKC in the April issue of the *Events Calendar*. The point schedule is also available at the AKC Web site. For every show, the relevant point schedule is printed in the show catalog, either at the front or on each breed's page.

BREED	1 POINT		2 POINTS		3 POINTS		4 POINTS		5 POINTS	
	Dogs	Bitches	Dogs	Bitches	Dogs	Bitches	Dogs	Bitches	Dogs	Bitches
:	:	:	:	:	:	:	:	:	:	:
:	:	:	:	:	:	:	:	:	:	:
Collies (Rough)	2	2	7	9	12	15	16	19	24	25
Collies (Smooth)	2	2	3	4	4	7	5	8	6	10
German Shepherd Dogs	2	3	10	13	17	22	22	27	31	37
Old English Sheepdogs	2	2	4	5	7	8	8	11	11	16
Pulik	2	2	3	3	4	5	5	7	6	10
Shetland Sheepdogs	2	3	9	9	15	16	19	22	27	34
:	:	:	:	:	:	:	:	:	:	:
:	:	:	:	:	:	:	:	:	:	:

Figure: Example of a division's annual point schedule for the Herding group.

---

[1] The point schedules shown in this chapter are only representative of AKC point schedules and do not reflect current point values.

Interpreting the point schedule

What does the point schedule mean? The point schedule gives the *minimum* number of males or females that must be *in competition* that day in order for a show to be worth a given number of points.

Look again at a point schedule for German Shepherd Dogs:

BREED	1 POINT		2 POINTS		3 POINTS		4 POINTS		5 POINTS	
	Dogs	Bitches	Dogs	Bitches	Dogs	Bitches	Dogs	Bitches	Dogs	Bitches
German Shepherd Dogs	2	3	10	13	17	22	22	27	31	37

Figure: Example of a point schedule for German Shepherd Dogs.

According to this schedule, you need:

- ❖ *at least* two non-champion GSD males competing that day for the show to be worth one point for the Winners Dog

- ❖ *at least* 10 non-champion GSD males for the show to be worth two points

- ❖ *at least* 17 non-champion GSD males for the show to be worth three points and therefore be a "major" show for the males

For the females there must be:

- ❖ *at least* three non-champion females in competition that day for the show to be worth one point for the Winners Bitch

- ❖ *at least* 13 non-champion females for the show to be worth two points

- ❖ *at least* 22 non-champion females for the show to be worth three points

In order to earn at least one point, every breed requires that there be at least two males or two females in competition: Winners Dog can't earn a point from Winners class unless he defeats at least one other male; Winners Bitch must defeat at least one other female. In some popular breeds, the minimum entry required for earning one point may be much larger.

The number of points won by Winners Dog and by Winners Bitch at a show will not always be the same. For example, there may be a very lopsided entry, with many more of one sex entered than of the other. Or, there may be almost equal numbers of each sex entered, but different points earned by Winners Dog and Winners Bitch because the point schedules for males and females are almost always unequal.

Counting Animals in Competition

The first task in calculating how many points Winners Dog and Winners Bitch can earn at a show is to figure out how many males and how many females should be counted in the point calculations. The *entry* of males and females at the show—that is, the males and females listed in the catalog—doesn't matter: you need to figure out how many of each sex are *in competition* for points that day. Do not count any animals that are:

❖ entered but absent

❖ excused by the judge

❖ disqualified by the judge

❖ have their award withheld

An absent male (or female) is one that was entered, but was not checked in with the ring steward, and is not shown. The dog may be on the show grounds, but if, for any reason, the handler decides not to show the dog and doesn't check in with the steward and pick up the armband, the dog is considered absent. Once a dog or bitch is checked in with the ring steward, it *must* be shown unless excused by the judge.

Once in the ring, a dog or bitch may be excused by the judge for a variety of reasons: it may be lame that day, become ill in the ring, have stitches or be wearing a bandage, or behave badly enough to prevent it from being judged. In any of these cases, the judge will excuse the animal from competition that day. Being excused is a temporary ban from the ring; it applies only for that show.

Being disqualified is more serious than being excused: a disqualification goes on an animal's permanent record with the AKC. Most commonly, an animal will be disqualified from judging if it has a "disqualifying fault" such as being too large or too small (for example, a Pekingese weighing more than 14 pounds, or a Basset Hound more than 15 inches tall), having color mismarking (for example, a Poodle with a coat of two or more colors, or a white German Shepherd Dog, or an Samoyed with blue eyes), or having fewer than two descended testes for a male of any breed. Disqualifying faults for each breed are given in the breed's standard.

Having an award withheld is a rare occurrence. When a judge withholds a dog's award, he is saying that the dog is of such poor quality that he cannot even consider the dog in the competition, and that other dogs should not get credit for defeating it. The dog is said to be "lacking in merit." Being deemed "lacking in merit" applies only to that show.

Count the absent, excused, and disqualified animals and the animals whose awards were withheld. Subtract these from the entered animals listed in the catalog. The remaining animals are the animals in competition at the show.

Finally, to complete the count of animals in competition, divide the animals in competition into four groups:

- ❖ class (non-champion) males

- ❖ class (non-champion) females

- ❖ special (champion) males

- ❖ special (champion) females

"Class" animals are dogs and bitches entered in the Puppy, 12-to-18 Month, Novice, American-Bred, Bred-by-Exhibitor, or Open classes. "Special" animals are entered in the Best of Breed competition. A dog that finishes his championship, but has already been entered in upcoming shows as a class animal, may be moved up to the Best of Breed competition by making a written request to the superintendent. If a male or a female is moved up to the Best of Breed competition, then that animal is counted as a special male or female rather than as a class animal.

Example. At the Colony Kennel Club show, there is an entry of 19 Golden Retrievers: 7 class males, 8 class females, 3 male specials and 1 female special. One class male and one male special are absent. One class female is excused for lameness. How many animals may be counted in the point calculation?

- ❖ One class male is absent, so there are 6 class males in competition (7 entered – 1 absent).

- ❖ One class female is excused, so there are 7 class females in competition (8 entered – 1 excused).

- ❖ One male special is absent, leaving 2 male specials in competition (3 entered – 1 absent).

- ❖ There is one female special in competition.

Thus the animals counted in the point calculations are: 6 class males, 7 class females, 2 male specials and 1 female special.

Earning Points

Only the Winners Dog and Winners Bitch earn points toward their championships. They win points from Winners class, based on how many class dogs or bitches were in competition. Then, in Best of Breed class, they have the chance to win "bonus" points if they are awarded either Best of Opposite Sex or Best of Breed.

Winners Dog and Winners Bitch

Points are awarded in the Winners classes to the Winners Dog and the Winners Bitch based on the number of *class male*s and *class female*s in competition that day. The number of specials doesn't matter in calculating points awarded from the Winners classes.

The calculation of points earned from the Winners classes is pretty simple:

❖ The Winners Dog counts all the *class males* in competition that day to determine the points he wins from Winners class.

❖ The Winners Bitch counts all the *class females* in competition that day to determine the points she wins from Winners class.

So, if you've counted the class dogs and class bitches in competition that day correctly—remembering not to include absent, excused, or disqualified animals, or animals whose awards were withheld—you can figure out the points earned from Winners class by Winners Dog and Winners Bitch.

Example. At a show in Missouri, there are 3 class male Miniature Poodles and 6 class female Miniature Poodles in competition. How many points do Winners Dog and Winners Bitch earn from Winners class?

	1		2		3		4		5	
Points	D	B	D	B	D	B	D	B	D	B
Poodles (Miniature)	2	2	3	5	4	7	6	8	7	11

The Winners Dog earned 2 points (because there were 3 class males in competition), and the Winners Bitch earned 2 points (because there were 6 class females in competition).

Best of Opposite Sex from the classes

Winners Dog and Winners Bitch earn points in Winners classes. They also have the opportunity to earn more points: Winners Dog and Winners Bitch go on to compete in the Best of Breed class. If they are awarded either Best of Opposite Sex or Best of Breed, they *might* earn additional points. Whether or not they do earn additional points, however, will depend on the point schedule and how many specials they defeat.

If Winners Dog or Winners Bitch is also awarded Best of Opposite Sex, then all the animals *of its sex*—class and special—are counted toward points. So, for example, if Winners Dog is also named Best of Opposite Sex—that is, he is the best male being shown that day—he counts *all the males* in competition, both class and special, towards championship points, since he defeated them all. The addition of the male specials *may* be enough to earn more points for the Winners Dog, or it may not.

Example. At a show in Minnesota, the St. Bernards in competition that day consisted of:

- ❖ 4 class males
- ❖ 5 class females
- ❖ 1 specials male
- ❖ 1 specials female

The schedule of Points for St. Bernards in Division 6 that year was:

	1 pt		2 pts		3 pts		4 pts		5 pts	
	D	B	D	B	D	B	D	B	D	B
St. Bernards	2	2	3	4	5	6	6	8	9	13

Winners Bitch was also awarded Best of Opposite Sex. How many points did she earn?

There were 5 class females, so by being awarded Winners Bitch, she earned 2 points (there must be at least 4 females to have 2 points, and at least 6 to earn 3 points).

Next, because she was also awarded Best of Opposite Sex, add the number of *female* specials she defeated to get the total number of females: 5 class females + 1 female special = 6 females in competition. In this case, 6 females is worth 3 points, so the Winners Bitch earned a major by winning Best of Opposite Sex.

So, if Winners Dog is also awarded Best of Opposite Sex, count all the class males in competition and all the male specials in competition; the total determines how many points the dog earns. Exactly the same logic works for Winners Bitch when she is awarded Best of Opposite Sex: count all the class females and all the female specials in competition.

Best of Breed from the classes

Winners Dog (or Winners Bitch) counts the specials of his (or her) *own* sex when awarded Best of Opposite Sex; the judge has said they are the best animal *of that sex* in competition that day. If Winners Dog or Winners Bitch is awarded Best of Breed, he (or she) counts *all* the specials of *both* sexes: the judge has said that Winners Dog (or Winners Bitch) is the best animal *of either sex* competing that day.

So again it's pretty simple. If Winners Dog is also awarded Best of Breed, count all the class males in competition, the male specials *and* all the female specials in competition; the total determines how many points the Winners Dog earns. Exactly the same logic works for Winners Bitch when she is awarded Best of Breed; count all the class females, all the female specials, and all the male specials in competition to figure out how many points she has earned.

Example. At a show in Texas, the following Rottweilers are in competition:

- ❖ 10 class males
- ❖ 14 class females
- ❖ 11 male specials
- ❖ 6 female specials

The point schedule that year for Rottweilers in Texas (Division 7) is:

Rottweilers					
Point Scale for Dogs	3 = 1 pt	9 = 2 pts	16 = 3 pts	21 = 4 pts	29 = 5 pts
Point Scale for Females	3 = 1 pt	10 = 2 pts	17 = 3 pts	22 = 4 pts	32 = 5 pts

If the Winners Dog is also awarded Best of Breed, how many points does he earn?

The Winners Dog counts all the class males, the male specials, and the female specials: 10 + 11 + 6 = 27 animals. According to the point scale for males, by winning Best of Breed the Winners Dog earned 4 points—being awarded Best of Breed earned him 2 more points in addition to the 2 points he earned in Winners class.

Best of Winners: "sharing the points"

During the Best of Breed competition, either the Winners Dog or the Winners Bitch will be awarded Best of Winners; the judge compares the Winners Dog and Winners Bitch, and decides which one is better. What happens to the points?

Suppose that the Winners Bitch earned two points from her Winners class, and that Winners Dog earned one point from his Winners class. Then, during Best of Breed judging, the Winners Dog was declared Best of Winners. Then it seems logical that he should earn as many points as the Winners Bitch; it would be unfair if he beat her, but earned fewer points. And that's exactly what happens: Best of Winners receives as many points as Winners Dog or Winners Bitch earned, whichever is greater. This is often called "sharing," "spreading," or "splitting" the points.

So, the steps in calculating the points that could be earned by Best of Winners are:

- ❖ Calculate the points earned by Winners Dog and by Winners Bitch from their respective Winners classes.

- ❖ Add any bonus points Winners Dog and/or Winners Bitch earned by being awarded Best of Breed or Best of Opposite Sex.

- ❖ When Best of Winners is awarded, balance the points between Winners Dog and Winners Bitch (including bonuses earned for BOB or BOS) by "sharing the points."

Example. At a recent show in Oklahoma, the point schedule for Boxers was:

	1 POINT		2 POINTS		3 POINTS		4 POINTS		5 POINTS	
	D	B	D	B	D	B	D	B	D	B
Boxers	2	3	10	12	17	22	22	29	31	41

The Boxers in competition were:

- ❖ 11 class males
- ❖ 13 class females
- ❖ 1 male special
- ❖ 2 female specials

Best of Breed and Best of Opposite Sex were awarded to specials. Winners Dog was awarded Best of Winners. How many points did he earn?

Winners Dog and Winners Bitch each earned two points from Winners Class. Because Winners Bitch did not earn more points than did Winners Dog, he did not earn any additional points for Best of Winners.

Example. Suppose, after Best of Breed and Best of Opposite Sex awards are made, Winners Dog has earned 2 points and Winners Bitch has earned 3 points.

Next, the judge awards Best of Winners to the Winners Dog. The Winners Bitch earned 3 points, and he defeated her, so the Winners Dog earns 3 points for the day by being awarded Best of Winners.

On the other hand, suppose the judge awards Best of Winners to the Winners Bitch. Since she has already earned more points (3 points) than the Winners Dog (2 points), she does not get any extra points for being named Best of Winners.

Counting Points: A Review

The basic rules for counting points are straightforward: count class dogs and bitches separately, and calculate points earned *in the right order*: Winners Dog, Winners Bitch, Best of Opposite Sex, Best of Breed, and finally Best of Winners.

Counting animals in competition

Count the number of dogs and the number of bitches that are in competition at that show.

- ❖ Do not count animals that are absent, disqualified, excused, or have their awards withheld.

❖ Count dogs and bitches separately.

❖ Count class (non-champion) and special (champion) animals separately.

You should have four numbers: the number of non-champion males, the number of non-champion females, the number of champion males, and the number of champion females.

You can get an *approximate* count of animals in competition before judging begins by reading the judging schedule or catalog. However, you must wait until judging is finished to make a final count of animals in competition that day since you need to know if any of the entered animals are absent, excused, disqualified, or have awards withheld.

Counting points

First, calculate the points earned by Winners Dog in Winners class. The Winners Dog earns points based on the number of *class males* in competition at that show.

Next, calculate the points earned by Winners Bitch in Winners class. The Winners Bitch earns points based on the number of *class females* in competition at that show.

If Winners Dog is awarded Best of Opposite Sex, count the *class males* and the *male specials* for his points. Compare the *total number of males* to the point schedule for males to calculate how many points he earns as Best of Opposite Sex.

If Winners Bitch is awarded Best of Opposite Sex, count the *class females* and the *female specials* toward her points. Compare the *total number of females* to the point schedule for females to calculate how many points she earns as Best of Opposite Sex.

If Winners Dog is awarded Best of Breed, count the *class males*, the *male specials,* and the *female specials* toward his points. This *total number of class males plus specials of both sexes* is compared to the point schedule for *males* to calculate how many points he earns as Best of Breed.

If Winners Bitch is awarded Best of Breed, count the *class females*, the *male special,s* and the *female specials* toward her points. This *total number of class females plus specials of both sexes* is compared to the point schedule for *females* to calculate how many points she earns as Best of Breed.

During the Best of Breed competition, either the Winners Dog or the Winners Bitch will be awarded Best of Winners, which may earn him or her more points:

❖ After awards are made for Best of Opposite Sex and Best of Breed, calculate how many points Winners Dog earned that day.

❖ After awards are made for Best of Opposite Sex and Best of Breed, calculate how many points Winners Bitch earned that day.

❖ The animal awarded Best of Winners then earns same number of points as Winners Dog or Winners Bitch, whichever is greater.

Example. Look at the following point schedule for Airedale Terriers in Tennessee.

	1 POINT		2 POINTS		3 POINTS		4 POINTS		5 POINTS	
	D	B	D	B	D	B	D	B	D	B
Airedale Terriers	2	2	4	5	7	8	8	12	11	15

The animals in competition are: 4 class males, 6 class females, 1 special male, and 1 special female.

Suppose that Winners Bitch is awarded Best of Breed. She earned 2 points for being Winners Bitch (6 class females in competition). When she is awarded Best of Breed, she also counts the 1 special male and the 1 special female she defeated, for a total of 8 animals defeated (6 class females + 1 male special + 1 female special). According to the point schedule *for bitches*, 8 animals is worth 3 points, so Winners Bitch has earned an extra point for being awarded Best of Breed: she gets 3 points at this show.

Note: because Winners Bitch was Best of Breed, she is automatically Best of Winners, too.

Example. At a show in Tennessee, the entry for Basset Hounds is 7-10-(2-3). Two of the class females move up to Best of Breed competition. One class male is absent. No dogs are disqualified or excused, and the judge makes all the customary awards. If the Winners Bitch is Best of Breed, how many points does she earn?

	1 POINT		2 POINTS		3 POINTS		4 POINTS		5 POINTS	
	D	B	D	B	D	B	D	B	D	B
Basset Hounds	2	2	4	5	7	9	10	17	16	32

The animals in competition are:

- ❖ 6 class males (7 entered – 1 absent)
- ❖ 8 class females (10 entered – 2 move ups)
- ❖ 2 male specials
- ❖ 5 female specials (3 entered + 2 move ups)

The Winners Bitch counts the class females and *all* the specials. According to the point schedule for females, she earns 3 points: she has converted a minor win (2 points for defeating 8 class females as Winners Bitch) to a major win (3 points).

Summary

For dogs "in the classes" the real prize at a show are the points they can earned toward a bench championship. To earn a championship, a dog must be awarded points by at least three judges. The dog must also earn at least two "majors" (wins of three, four or five points), awarded by two different judges.

Every year, the AKC publishes a "Schedule of Points." The schedule is valid for one year, from May to the next May. The schedule is broken into 12 Divisions, and gives the point value for the show—from one to five points—by breed, based on the number of dogs and bitches in each breed in competition that day.

Counting the points earned at a given show requires following a few simple rules. First, for each breed or variety, count the animals in competition at the show. Next, calculate the points earned by Winners Dog and Winners Bitch from Winners class, based on the number of class dogs and class bitches in competition that day. If Winners Dog or Winners Bitch is also awarded Best of Opposite Sex or Best of Breed, calculate any additional points they might earn. Finally, calculate the extra points, if any, earned by Best of Winners.

At first, counting points may seem a bit confusing, but if you approach it systematically and remember a few simple rules, you will soon find it easy to understand.

Chapter 23

Minoring Out and Finding Majors

After you begin earning points toward your dog's championship, you'll need to learn some of the more advanced strategies associated with achieving this goal. In this chapter, you'll learn about major and minor points, "minoring out," and searching for majors.

Major Points and Minor Points

"Minor" points are wins of one or two points. "Major" points, or "majors," are wins of three, four, or five points. A dog must defeat more dogs to win major points than minor points, so it is harder to earn major points than minor points. In order to earn a championship, a dog (or bitch) must earn at least 15 championship points, including two major wins. Most dogs earn a combination of minor and major points.

The 15 championship points:

❖ must be awarded by *at least* three different judges. (You can't find just one judge who likes your dog and show only to that judge!)

❖ must include at least two major wins awarded by *different* judges. (These judges may also award your dog minor points.)

Under these rules, dozens of different point combinations are possible:

❖ A dog can win 9 single points and two 3-point majors, for a total of 15 points including two majors. This is the slowest way to earn a championship.

❖ A dog can earn three 5-point majors for a total of 15 points, including the compulsory two majors. This is the most spectacular way to earn a championship.

❖ A dog can earn 8 minor points (in some combination of 1 and 2 point wins), a 3-point major and a 4-point major. This yields a total of 15 championship points including two majors.

❖ A dog can earn 5 minor points (say, as 2 points, 1 point, 2 points) and two 5-point majors for a total of 15 championship points, including two majors.

There are many other point combinations which yield the required 15 points with at least two majors. As long as the dog has earned at least 15 points, awarded by at least three judges—including at least two majors awarded by at least two different judges—the dog has earned his bench championship.

Example. A male Chihuahua has earned 5 minor points. He has also earned a 3 point major awarded by Judge Ron Kessel. Judge Kessel is judging at the Fig Leaf Kennel Club show, and the Chihuahua's owners enter that show.

At the show, Judge Kessel awards Winners Dog to the Chihuahua, and the dog earns 4 points. He now has 5 minor points, a 3 point major and a 4 point major, for a total of 12 points including two majors.

However, the Chihuahua still must earn another major: even though he has already won 2 majors, *the same judge awarded the majors*. The second major can count toward his point total, but he still needs another major, awarded by a different judge, to finish his championship.

A dog or bitch may finish a championship with *more* than 15 points; the rules just say that the dog needs *at least* 15 points.

Example. A female Cocker Spaniel has earned 8 minor points from 4 different judges. She has also earned a 4-point major awarded by Judge Catherine Creswick, so she has a total of 12 points including 1 major. She needs a 3-point major, awarded by someone other than Judge Creswick, to finish her championship.

At the Ballyhoo Kennel Club show, Judge James Howard awards her a 5-point major. She now has 17 points awarded by six different judges, including two majors awarded by different judges. She is now a champion.

"Minoring Out"

A dog must win at least two majors for his championship. Since the smallest major is three points, at least six of the 15 points must be major points. In turn, this means that only 9 minor points will actually count towards a championship. A dog with, say, 13 minor points still needs to earn at least 6 major points to be a champion—he will finish his championship with at least 19 points.

Because a dog needs to earn at least 6 of its 15 points as major points, a dog that has earned 9 or more minor points is called *"minored out:"* that is, earning more minor points will not get him any closer to his championship.

"Insurance" points versus greed

If only nine points count toward a championship, should you try to win extra minor points for your dog?

Sometimes you will gain extra minor points unintentionally: for example, if your dog has eight minor points and you win two points at a show, you'll have 10 minor points. That's fine, since you've now got an "insurance point" just in case you or the AKC counted points incorrectly. But you shouldn't continue *trying* to win minor points—you've got plenty.

If you have nine minor points, you might decide to try to win another minor point or two as insurance points against counting or record-keeping errors. That's probably a good idea, and is considered within the bounds of good sportsmanship.

On the other hand, if you have more than 10 minor points—if your dog is truly "minored out"—*do not continue to compete for minor points.* Dogs that finish their championships with a large number of minor points are not "better" than dogs that finish with nine or 10 minor points. By continuing to compete for minor points, you are simply keeping other dogs from earning their minor points, while not gaining anything useful for yourself.

Showing a dog that is minored out at minor point shows, although permitted under AKC rules, is considered bad sportsmanship by the dog showing community. The only exception is if there is the possibility of converting a minor win to a major by winning Best of Breed, Best of Opposite Sex, or Best of Winners; in this case, showing a minored-out dog is acceptable.

Searching for Majors

If your dog is minored out, you'll need to choose your remaining shows carefully, instead of entering every show that comes along. You should only show your dog at shows in which:

❖ he (or she) earn win a major by being awarded Winners Dog (or Winners Bitch)

❖ he (or she) can earn a major by winning Best of Breed, Best of Opposite Sex or Best of Winners

Unfortunately, you won't know whether a show *could be* a major until after you have entered it and have seen the entry breakdown in the judging schedule.

Sometimes you can get a good idea ahead of time about whether a show will have majors by its recent history. If the show has rarely had majors in the past, you may decide not to enter rather than gamble your entry fee. If the show usually attracts enough dogs to be a major in at least one sex, then it is probably a good gamble to enter it. Check with other people who show your breed or who subscribe to the *AKC Awards* magazine about whether a particular show is likely to be a major.

The entry breakdown

Once you've gambled on entering a show as you search for majors, the next step is to study the entry breakdown that is included with your entry confirmation (or posted on the superintendent's Web site).

The entry breakdown, together with the point schedule for the show, will indicate whether there is the *possibility* of earning a major at the show, either by winning Winners Dog or Winners Bitch, or by converting a minor win to a major by earning an award in Best of Breed competition.

However, the entry breakdown only tells you the *maximum* number of dogs that may be competing; it cannot tell you about absent, excused, or disqualified dogs, dogs whose awards are withheld, or dogs that have been moved up from the classes to the Best of Breed competition. All these factors will affect your final count of animals and, therefore, the points available at the show.

What you *can* tell from an entry breakdown is whether the show has *absolutely no* chance of being a major. If the entry is so small that even winning Best of Breed from the classes is only worth one or two points, then you cannot earn a major at the show.

Building and Breaking Majors

Sometimes exhibitors will cooperate to "build majors"—several people who need majors will agree to enter the same shows to try to make a big enough entry for a major. Building a major is perfectly legal and within the bounds of good sportsmanship, since everyone who enters has a chance to win the major (including people who weren't part of the group working to build the major). In fact, in some relatively rare breeds, building a major is often the only way to get a large enough entry for a major.

Building a major requires cooperation among exhibitors, so this is where your history of good—or bad—sportsmanship come into play. If, for example, you continued to show a minored out dog at small shows, taking minor points away from other exhibitors, those exhibitors probably won't want to help you build majors for your dog!

Another situation arises when a competitor "breaks" a major, either by withdrawing a dog or bitch from competition, or by moving a class dog that has finished his championship up to Best of Breed class.

Suppose that it takes nine bitches to make a major in your breed, and that the entry for this Saturday's show is exactly nine class bitches. If any bitch is absent, then the major will break; there will be fewer than nine bitches in class competition, so Winners Bitch will not earn a major from Winners class.

Of course, there are legitimate reasons for being absent and breaking a major—you could have a family emergency, have car trouble, or your bitch could be ill or lame. But breaking a major without good reason is considered bad sportsmanship.

Example. You have a Cairn Terrier bitch with 9 minor points and a 4 point major. You have entered her in a show with the following point schedule:

	1 POINT		2 POINTS		3 POINTS		4 POINTS		5 POINTS	
	D	B	D	B	D	B	D	B	D	B
Cairn Terriers	2	2	4	5	7	9	10	17	16	32

If the entry is 6-6-(3-1), could your bitch finish her championship at this show?

If every entered animal competes, and there are no move-ups to Best of Breed competition, then:

Winners Dog could earn

♦ 2 points from Winners Class (6 class males), or

♦ 3 points by winning Best of Opposite Sex (6 class males + 3 male specials = 9 males) or

♦ 4 points by winning Best of Breed (6 class males + 3 male specials + 1 special female = 10 animals).

Winners Bitch could earn

♦ 2 points from Winners Class (6 class females), or

♦ 2 points by winning Best of Opposite Sex (6 class females + 1 female special = 7 females) or

♦ 3 points by winning Best of Breed (6 class females + 3 male specials + 1 female special = 10 animals).

So your bitch could win a major and finish her championship if:

♦ she wins Best of Breed (for 3 points), or

♦ Winners Dog is awarded Best of Opposite Sex (for 3 points) and she is awarded Best of Winners (so she gets the same 3 points that he earned).

Note that, if Winners Dog is awarded Best of Breed (for 4 points) your female *cannot* win a major, because Winners Dog, as Best of Breed, is also Best of Winners.

Points Are Invisible

Keep track of the points that your dog earns! Points are invisible; you are not given any evidence at the show of points you earn. The judge does not say, "Congratulations—you won three points today." It is your responsibility to count points at the show and to keep track of how many points your dog has earned.

Keep all the ribbons you win from a show at which you earn points, since they (and a photo) are your only proof of your win if you have a discrepancy with the AKC. If you win a major, it is a good idea to buy a catalog and mark it completely, documenting your win. Periodically, check with the AKC via its Web site or telephone information system to make sure that their point records match yours. If not, then you need to be able to prove that you won any disputed points.

Summary

Once you begin to win points toward your dog's championship, you need to start thinking a bit more strategically about when and where to enter your dog. If your dog is minored out, you'll need to search for shows that are either outright majors from Winners class, or which can be converted to majors by earning Best of Breed, Best of Opposite Sex, or Best of Winners.

Be a good sport. If your dog is minored out, then don't show him unless he has a chance of winning a major—you're just taking points from another exhibitor. Study the entry breakdown and determine if your dog could earn a major at the show.

Don't break majors without good reason. If the show you've entered is a major, and you intend to break it, either by not attending or by moving your finished dog up to Best of Breed competition, it is courteous to let other competitors know in advance, when possible, that the major will break. They might not need minor points and you could save them an unnecessary drive to a show. Your good sportsmanship will stand you in good stead with your competitors in the future, when they may return the favor or help you build a major.

<table>
<tr><td>Chapter
24</td><td># Keeping Dog Show Records</td></tr>
</table>

Keeping good records is an important part of showing dogs. From the very beginning, you'll need to keep track of what happens at each show you enter. When your dog earns points, you'll need to keep accurate records, especially of major wins and of the names of the judges who awarded them. In this chapter you'll learn about show catalogs and how to mark them, how to check to the judge's book for show results, and how to keep a show logbook for your dog.

The Catalog

A show catalog is a book containing information about the show and about all the dogs entered in the show. A catalog may contain information for a single show, or if two or more shows are clustered together, a combined catalog may be printed for the show cluster. The AKC requires that a catalog—single or combined—be published for every show held under its auspices.

At the front of a show's catalog, you'll find most of the information that was printed in the show's premium list. You'll also find a copy of the judging schedule that was sent with each entry confirmation, and, possibly, a copy of the schedule of points in effect at the show.

The majority of the catalog consists of information about the dogs entered in the show. The information about each dog is taken either from the show entry form or from the superintendent's database, if the dog has entered shows run by this superintendent in the past.

The information about the dogs is organized by group, and then, within each group, alphabetically by breed. In some catalogs, the point schedule for each breed is printed on the breed's pages, while in

The table for catalog sales is usually near the show's entrance or by the superintendent's desk.

other catalogs, the combined point schedule for all breeds is printed near the front of the catalog. Within each breed, information about each entered dog is given under the class in which the dog is entered. The classes are arranged in the order in which they are judged: classes for dogs, classes for bitches, and then Best of Breed.

The AKC stipulates that the catalog must provide the following information for each dog:

- ❖ catalog (armband) number

- ❖ dog's registered name

- ❖ dog's AKC registration number and date of birth

- ❖ dog's breeder(s), sire and dam

- ❖ name and address of owner(s) (The owner's address may be printed in an index of exhibitors at the back of the catalog, or on the breed page.)

In the example shown for Miniature Schnauzers at the Cactus Kennel Club Show, the point schedule is given at the top of the page. It is followed by the classes for dogs: at this show, there are only entries in Bred-by-Exhibitor and Open Dogs. Next are the classes for bitches: there are six females entered in four classes. Finally, the two Miniature Schnauzers entered in the Best of Breed competition are listed.

In the individual listings for Best of Breed, the sex of the entry—dog or bitch—is listed after the owner's name and address.

If the dog's entry form listed a professional handler or "agent," this person will be identified at the end of the dog's listing.

Marking a catalog

A correctly marked catalog—one in which you have written the results of the day's judging—can be an important part of your dog show records. If a catalog is marked correctly, the reader can tell *exactly* what happened at the show.

For example, from the marked catalog for this show, you can see that during the judging of class dogs:

- ❖ #5 won the Bred-by-Exhibitor class.

- ❖ In the Open Dog class, #9 placed first ("1" is written by his name) and #7 was second ("2" is written by his name).

- ❖ Winners Dog class therefore consisted of #5 and #9: the judge awarded Winners Dog to #9 ("WD" is written by his name) and awarded Reserve Winners Dog to #5 ("RWD" is written by his name).

MINIATURE SCHNAUZERS

Mr. Harold Vollmann   Ring 4; 1:15 pm

Miniature Schnauzers	1 POINT		2 POINTS		3 POINTS		4 POINTS		5 POINTS	
	D	B	D	B	D	B	D	B	D	B
	2	2	4	6	7	9	9	13	13	21

MINIATURE SCHNAUZERS, Bred by Exhibitor, Dogs

5   *RWD 1*   **Batman's The Riddler, RM163456/01**. 11/10/99. Breeder: Mark and Sylvia Stark. By Ch. Batman's Boy Robin – Ch. Batman's First Love. Owner: **Mark and Sylvia Stark**. 1234 67th Avenue, San Antonio, TX.

MINIATURE SCHNAUZERS, Open, Dogs

7   *2*   **Clayton's Lone Ranger, RM175792/13**. 12/13/99. Breeder: Angela Morrison. By: Ch. Hi Ho Silver – Ch. San Diego Sand Dollar. Owner: **Shelly Gordon**. 89254 Townes Lane, New Braunfels, TX.

9   *WD 1*   *BW*   **Batman's The Joker, RM163456/02**. 11/10/99. Breeder: Mark and Sylvia Stark. By Ch. Batman's Boy Robin – Batman's First Love. Owner: **John Bridges**. 3702 Ridley Way, Shertz, TX.

Winners Dog *9*   **Reserve** *5*   **Points** *1*   **Dogs** *3*

MINIATURE SCHNAUZERS, Puppy, Bitches, 6 Months and under 9 Months

8   *1*   **Sniggle's Luv Bunny, RM184235/02**. 1/5/01. Breeder: Carla Lippman. By: Ch. Mister Rogers– Ch. Sniggle's Green Jean. Owner: **Jason McCoy and Mary Ellen Gwaltney-McCoy**. 5637 Western Way, Roundrock, TX.

MINIATURE SCHNAUZERS, Puppy, Bitches, 9 Months and under 12 Months

10   *1*   **Kirk's Warp Factor Four, RM182635/03**. 8/5/00. Breeder: Eugenia Simoni. By: Ch. Kirk's Beam Me Up Scotty-Ch. Vadar's Princess Leila. **Owner: Lucas Fitzgerald** P.O. Box 911, Buda, TX.

MINIATURE SCHNAUZERS, Bred By Exhibitor, Bitches

12   *RWB 1*   **Gala's Arctic Fox, RM162837/04**. 6/1/00. Breeder: Barbara Jennings. By: Ch. Rodman's Prime Suspect-Ch. Gala's Society Belle. Owner: **Thomas and Barbara Jennings**. 4652 Monticello Blvd, Richardson, TX.

14   *AB*   **Wilson's Little Woman, RM167665/05**. 4/27/00. Breeder: Sam Jackson, Kate Wilson and Joshua Feldman. By: Ch. Kerregy's Minute Man-Ch. Wilson's Louisa May. Owner: **Kate and Susan Wilson**, 8464 West Brookside Lane, Houston, TX.

MINIATURE SCHNAUZERS, Open, Bitches

16   *2*   **Batman's Cat Woman, RM163456/05**. 11/10/99. Breeder: Mark and Sylvia Stark. By Ch. Batman's Boy Robin – Batman's First Love. Owner: **Elizabeth and Paul Grosvenor**. 7711 Apple Way, Cedar Lake, TX

18   *WB 1*   *BoS*   **Tahoe's Emerald Bay, RM154623/03**. 11/6/99. Breeder: Elaine Herald. By Ch. Jedediah Smith – Ch. Tahoe's Double Diamond. Owner: **Daphne Silverton**, 17925 Bartley Court, Artesia, NM.

Winners Bitch *18*   **Reserve** *12*   **Points** *1*   **Bitches** *5*

MINIATURE SCHNAUZERS, Best of Breed

21   *BoB*   **Ch. Daly's Maker's Mark, RM123452/03**. 5/13/98. Breeder: Donna Bach & Joseph Lucas. By: Ch. Holling's Crowd Appeal – Ch. Daly's Circuit Judge. Owner: **Albert Lincoln**, 665 Timber Road, Bastrop, TX. Dog.

24   **Ch. Tahoe's Ruff Cut Diamond, RM136893/02**. 2/27/98. Breeder: Elaine Herald. By: Ch. Zane's Midnight Sun-Ch. Tahoe's Casino Lass. Owner: **Elaine Herald**, 556 Pine Way, King City, CA. Bitch. (Agent: W. Fulsom)

Best of Breed *21*   **Best of Winners** *9 (2 pts)*   **Best of Opposite Sex** *18 (2 pts)*

Figure: Example of a marked catalog page.

❖ There were three dogs in competition, and so Winners Dog earned one point from Winners class.

The catalog for bitches is marked in exactly the same way. From this catalog you can see that:

❖ #14 was absent ("AB" by her name).

❖ Winners Bitch class included #8, #10, #12, and #18 (all the class winners).

❖ #18 was Winners Bitch ("WB" by her name) and #12 was Reserve Winners Bitch ("RWB" by her name).

❖ There were five bitches in competition (six entered – one absent), so Winners Bitch earned one point from Winners Class.

You can now figure out what happened in the Best of Breed class:

❖ There were four animals in the class: #21 (dog special), #24 (bitch special), #18 (Winners Bitch), and #9 (Winners Dog).

❖ The dog special, #21, was awarded Best of Breed ("BOB" by his name).

❖ The judge thought #18, Winners Bitch, was better than the bitch special, so he awarded Best of Opposite Sex to #18 ("BOS" by her name).

❖ The judge awarded Best of Winners to #9, the Winners Dog ("BW" by his name).

Notice that by defeating the bitch special, Winners Bitch could count *six* bitches in competition—five class bitches plus one bitch special—so she earned two points instead of one. And because Winners Dog was named Best of Winners, he got two points also.

You probably won't buy a catalog for every show that you enter. However, you should consider buying and marking the catalog for any show at which your dog wins points, and you should *certainly* buy and mark the catalog when your dog earns a major. If, at some time, there is a discrepancy between your count of your dog's points and the AKC's records, a marked catalog, your ribbons and a photo are your first line of defense in validating the points your dog has earned.

A fully marked catalog, completed ringside while judging is fresh in your mind, is an important component of your show records.

The judge's book

To verify your catalog markings, your can compare your notes against the "judge's book," which is the official record of the day's judging.

For every breed he judges that day, the judge has a set of forms—an original and three copies—in which to record his actions; these forms are called the judge's book. When judging is completed, the original goes to the AKC, the superintendent and the judge each keep a copy for their own records, and the last copy is made available at the superintendent's desk for people to read.

In the judge's book, only class and armband numbers identify the dogs—not names. As the class enters the ring, the judge checks attendance, comparing armband numbers to his judge's book and noting absent dogs. If any dogs are excused or disqualified, the judge records it in his book. When the judge has made his placements in the class, and the placement winners stand by the markers, the steward will remind the winners to show their armbands to the judge so that he can mark his book and then award the ribbons

The judge records absent, excused and disqualified dogs, and all awards, in her judge's book.

Copies of the judges' books are posted at the superintendent's desk for public view.

At the end of each set, or sometimes after two or more sets, the judge's book is turned in to the superintendent's desk. A short while later, one of the copies of the judge's book will be made available at the superintendent's desk for exhibitors to examine and compare against their own catalog marking.

If your dog was Winners Dog or Winners Bitch, be sure to check the judge's book at the superintendent's table to confirm that the class results were recorded accurately, since occasionally an error occurs. If you believe that an error has been made, tell the superintendent and show him your ribbons; he will investigate your claim. It is much easier to correct an error on the day of the show, when the judge and ring steward are readily available, than after the show.

Cactus Kennel Club	(2001321654)		07, 07, 2001
NAME OF KENNEL CLUB	(EVENT#)		**DAY, MONTH DATE, YEAR**
BREED or VARIETY	Miniature Schnauzers		**JUDGE** H. Vollman

(CLASS)	DOGS	(CLASS)	DOGS	(CLASS)	DOGS	(CLASS)	DOGS	(CLASS)	DOGS	(CLASS)	DOGS
BBE		**OPEN**									
Catalog#	Award	Catalog#	Award	Catalog#	Award	Catalog#	Award	Catalog#	Award	Catalog#	Award
5	1	7	2								
		9	1								

WINNERS WITHHELD ____   RESERVE WITHHELD ____

PLEASE ENTER CATALOG NUMBER IF AWARDED

I certify that in my opinion, the **WINNER** [9] and **RESERVE** [5] are deserving of championship points on this day.

(CLASS)	BITCHES	(CLASS)	BITCHES	(CLASS)	BITCHES	(CLASS)	BITCHES	(CLASS)	BITCHES	(CLASS)	BITCHES
PUPPY 6-9		**PUPPY 9-12**		**BBE**		**OPEN**					
Catalog#	Award	Catalog#	Award	Catalog#	Award	Catalog#	Award	Catalog#	Award	Catalog#	Award
8	1	10	1	12	1	16	2				
				14	AB	18	1				

WINNERS WITHHELD ____   RESERVE WITHHELD ____

PLEASE ENTER CATALOG NUMBER IF AWARDED

I certify that in my opinion, the **WINNER** [18] and **RESERVE** [12] are deserving of championship points on this day.

BEST OF BREED COMPETITON

21	24						

Best of Breed   Best of Winners   Best of Op Sex

21   9   18

Figure: Example of a marked judge's book.

Show: Cactus Kennel Club   **Date:** July 7, 2001

Location: Arroyo Rojo, TX   **Distance/ driving time:** 150 mi, about 3 hrs

Judge: Harold Vollman

Class entered: BBE   **Placement:** 1, RWB   **Points earned:** --

Winners Dog: Batman's the Joker   **Winners Bitch:** Tahoe's Emerald Bay

Reserve WD: Batman's the Riddler   **Reserve WB:** Foxy

Best of Winners: WD-Joker

Best of Breed: Daly's Makers Mark   **Best of Opposite:** WB--Emmy

In Competition		Point Schedule	1 pt	2 pts	3 pts	4 pts	5 pts
Class Dogs:	3	Dogs:	2	4	7	9	13
Class Bitches:	5	Bitches:	2	6	9	13	21
Dog Specials:	1						
Bitch Specials:	1						

Notes: Vollman likes square dogs and very feminine bitches

NO SHADE!!! Bring canopy for grooming area

Turn into show grounds after the Texaco station on right.

Figure: Example of an entry in a dog's show record book.

Your Show Record Book

You should buy and mark a catalog each time your dog earns a major, and possibly each time he earns minor points as well. But you should keep records—less detailed, to be sure—of *every* show your dog enters in a logbook or journal.

After a while, shows may begin to blur in your memory, so it's good to have some notes about each show. A good way to keep show notes is in a dog show record book, which you can buy from a show supply vendor or dog equipment catalog. As you get more experience at shows, you may begin to recognize the names of judges in the premium list, so having good show notes may help you decide whether or not to enter under the judge again. Your notes should indicate whether or not a show was a major (useful information when you are hunting for majors in the future). You should also note important things about the show conditions and travel to the show site, to help you in your planning and packing for the next show at that site.

Checking Your Dog's Point Total

During your dog's show career, it is a good idea to check your point count periodically against the AKC's to make sure there are no discrepancies. Contact the AKC by telephone or Internet to check your dog's point total. When you contact the AKC, you'll need to have your dog's AKC number handy.

If your records differ from those of the AKC, gather your data and contact the AKC. You'll need your ribbons to establish the awards that your dog received; photos and a fully marked catalog are also useful in establishing your case.

Summary

Keeping accurate dog show records is important. Every year, there are over two million entries for AKC dog shows, and although the AKC's record keeping systems are amazingly efficient, errors do occur. Remember: points are invisible. It is your responsibility to keep track of the points that your dog earns, and to ensure that your records match those of the AKC.

Keep a show record book, or journal, of your dog's show career. If your dog wins points at a show, keep the ribbons and check the judge's book to make sure it was correctly marked. Consider buying a catalog and marking it; you should *always* buy a catalog and mark it if your dog wins a major, in case there are any clerical errors after the show.

Chapter 25

A Well-Balanced Dog

Conformation isn't the only type of competition you can enjoy with your dog. There are many other sports you and your dog can play together—before, during, and after his breed-ring career. In this chapter you'll learn about other dog sports, the titles your dog can earn, and how to start training your dog for these activities.

A Well-Balanced Dog

A saying in the dog sport world is "A well-balanced dog has titles at both ends." A breed champion—a dog that comes close to meeting the physical ideal for the breed as expressed in the breed standard—may use the title "Champion" before his name. A dog that demonstrates his intelligence and athletic abilities in other sports, such as obedience, agility, or hunting, may use titles showing those achievements *after* his name. A dog that can do it all—who has "brains and beauty"—will be a well-balanced dog with titles at both ends of his name.

The AKC offers competition in a number of dog sports other than conformation. Some sports are relatively unknown to the general public, while others, such as agility (obstacle course) competition, are frequently televised and are great crowd-pleasers.

Sports for All Breeds

Some dog sports offered by the AKC are open to all breeds that the AKC recognizes. These sports—obedience, agility, and tracking—are not based on the original purpose or function of any particular breed.

Obedience trials

In obedience trials, dogs perform a set of standard exercises that test their ability to work closely with their handlers and follow instructions. The format of the exercises is the same at every obedience trial. There are three levels of obedience competition: Novice, Open and Utility. At the Novice level, dogs must demonstrate their ability to heel (both on and off lead), come to their handlers when called, and stay, both sitting or lying down in a line of dogs, while their handlers stand in a line on the other side of the ring. Dogs that pass the Novice class three times earn the "Companion Dog" (CD) title.

At the higher levels, the exercises become more difficult. At the Open level, jumping and retrieving are added to the tests. Dogs must also stay with a group of other dogs while their handlers go out of sight. Dogs that pass the Open class three times earn the "Companion Dog Excellent" (CDX) title.

The handler tosses a dumbbell over the jump. The dog goes over the jump, gets the dumbbell, and returns over the jump to his handler.

In the Utility class, which is the highest level of competition, scent discrimination and working at a distance from the handler using only hand signals are added to the tests. Dogs that pass the Utility class three times earn the "Utility Dog," or UD, title. Dogs with both the CDX and UD titles can continue to compete, earning a Utility Dog Excellent (UDX) title or accumulating points towards an Obedience Trial Championship, designated by "OTCH" in front of the dog's name.

Tracking tests

In tracking tests, dogs demonstrate their scenting ability by following a path walked by a person acting as tracklayer. In the first level of competition, the track is walked in a field and is 30 minutes to 2 hours old when the dog follows it. The track has four or five turns, and is 440-500 yards long. The dog must closely follow the footsteps of the tracklayer and locate an article at the end of the track, while the handler follows the dog at the end

In a TDX tracking test, the dog follows a path walked several hours earlier by a tracklayer. The handler follows at the end of a 40-foot tracking lead.

of a 40-ft. lead attached to the dog's tracking harness. The handler may not say anything to the dog that will help him follow the track; he must do it by himself, scenting the route. Dogs that pass this test earn the "Tracking Dog" (TD) title.

Dogs that pass the TD test are eligible to participate in two more types of tracking tests. In the Tracking Dog Excellent (TDX) test, the track is longer, older and more complicated. The Variable Surface Tracking (VST) test takes

EVENT	TITLE	ABBREVIATION
Obedience	Companion Dog	CD
	Companion Dog Excellent	CDX
	Utility Dog	UD
	Utility Dog Excellent	UDX
	National Obedience Champion	NOC
	Obedience Trial Champion	OTCH *
Agility	Novice Agility	NA
	Open Agility	OA
	Agility Excellent	AX
	Master Agility Excellent	MX
	Novice Jumpers with Weaves	NAJ
	Open Jumpers with Weaves	OAJ
	Excellent Jumpers with Weaves	AXJ
	Master Excellent Jumpers with Weaves	MXJ
	Master Agility Champion	MACH *
Tracking	Tracking Dog	TD
	Tracking Dog Excellent	TDX
	Variable Surface Tracker	VST
	Champion Tracker	CT *

* Prefix title: abbreviation goes before the dog's name

Figure: AKC obedience, agility and tracking titles.

place in an urban setting: the track will cover a number of different surfaces, such as concrete, grass, dirt, and asphalt, and may go up stairs and between buildings. A dog that earns all three tracking titles—TD, TDX, and VST—is a Champion Tracker and uses the title "CT" in front of his name.

Agility trials

Agility is the newest and fastest-growing sport offered by the AKC. In agility competitions, dogs run obstacle courses of jumps, teeter-totters, tunnels, and weave poles. Dogs are judged on their speed and their ability to negotiate the obstacles in the correct order without knocking down any jumps or making other mistakes.

Every agility trial has many different courses, each designed

In an agility trial, dogs negotiate an obstacle course that includes jumps and tunnels.

TITLE	ABBREVIATION	REQUIREMENT
Versatile Companion Dog 1	VCD1	CD, NA, NAJ, TD
Versatile Companion Dog 2	VCD2	CDX, OA, OAJ, TD
Versatile Companion Dog 3	VCD3	UD, AX, AXJ, TDX
Versatile Companion Dog 4	VCD4	UDX, MX, MXJ, VST

Figure: Requirements for the Versatile Companion Dog titles.

specifically for that day by the judges. Competitors do not see the courses until the day of the trial.

The three levels of agility are Novice, Open, and Excellent. As a dog progresses through the levels, the courses become increasingly long and complex, and dogs are given less time to complete the courses without penalty. Dogs competing at the Excellent level may also earn points towards an agility championship, designated by the title "MACH" in front of the dog's name.

Versatile Companion Dog titles

Dogs that earn titles in each of the three sports open to all breeds—obedience, tracking, and agility—are designated "Versatile Companion Dogs." A dog that earns the lowest level title in each sport is awarded the VCD1 title, and as a dog earn more advanced titles in obedience, agility, and tracking, the level of the his VCD titles increase.

Performance Events

In addition to obedience trials, tracking tests and agility trials, which are open to all breeds, there are some sports that are based on the original purpose of certain breeds. These sports are known as "Performance Events" since they assess the ability of the dog to perform the functions for which he was bred. Competition in each of these sports is limited to a few breeds.

Hunting tests

Hunting tests are designed to test the ability of the dog to hunt in the style appropriate for the breed: pointing, flushing, or retrieving. The hunting tests have three levels: Junior, Senior, and Master. In hunting tests for pointing breeds (e.g., English Setters, German Shorthaired Pointers, Irish Setters, Brittanys, and Weimaraners), the dogs must find birds and indicate them by pointing, and, at the more advanced levels, retrieve a bird after it has been flushed and shot. In hunting tests for retrieving breeds (e.g., Golden Retrievers, Labrador Retrievers, Irish Water Spaniels, and Standard Poodles) dogs are judged on their ability to watch ("mark") birds as they fall after being shot, and to retrieve the birds on land and in water.

Earthdog tests

Earthdog events are competitions for dogs bred to follow their prey into tunnels, or "go to ground." Earthdog tests have four levels: Introduction, Junior, Senior, and Master, with increasingly complex "dens" that the dog must negotiate to find their quarry (caged adult rats). Eligible breeds include the Dachshund and many of the terriers, such as the Scottish Terrier, the Border Terrier, and the Bedlington Terrier.

Lure coursing

In lure coursing, dogs that hunt by sight—the "sight hounds"—are given a chance to demonstrate their hunting abilities. Eligible breeds include Afghan Hounds, Rhodesian Ridgebacks, Irish Wolfhounds, Basenjis, and Whippets. Lure coursing competitions have three levels: Junior, Senior, and Master. A lure course consists of a braided fishing line threaded through a series of pulleys staked to the ground in a very large field; the lure (a plastic bag) is tied to the line, and a motor whips the lure through a zig-zagging course at speeds up to 40 miles per hour. Dogs are judged on their speed and their ability to follow the lure closely.

These handlers are releasing their Rhodesian Ridgebacks at the starting line of a lure course. Dogs run in pairs and are identified by colored jackets.

Herding tests and trials

In herding trials, dogs have the opportunity to demonstrate their ability to herd groups of livestock (ducks, sheep, goats, or cattle) over courses that increase in difficulty as a dog progresses through the levels of competition: Started, Intermediate and Excellent. Breeds in the Herding Group are eligible to compete in herding tests and trials; Samoyeds and Rottweilers may also compete in herding tests and trials.

Training the Well-Balanced Dog

Getting started in other dog sports is exactly the same as getting started in conformation competition. You must learn the rules of the sport, you must train your dog, and you must learn what is expected of you during the competition.

The resources you'll use are similar to those you're using to learn how to show your dog in the breed ring. When you have selected a sport, look for clubs or classes in your area, such as a dog-training club or an agility club. Visit the classes, and decide whether the class meets your needs and those of your dog. Go to competitions and observe what goes on. As at dog shows, most competitors will be willing to answer questions, but don't try to talk to them right before they compete, or as they are working with their dogs.

The Internet contains a wealth of information about the different dog sports. Visit the AKC's Web site for an overview of the different competitions, and to locate clubs in your area. There are also excellent books and videos for all dog sports.

Dogs *can* be trained for the conformation ring and other sports at the same time! In fact, training for more than one sport will help keep your dog from becoming bored with a single activity. Remember, though, that young puppies tire easily, so don't overwhelm them with long and complicated training sessions. As in training for the breed ring, several brief sessions during the day, each a few minutes long, work well for a puppy. Make all the training sessions upbeat, happy, and full of praise and reward, never punishment.

Tracking, which relies on a dog's ability to follow a scent trail, is a wonderful sport for young puppies.

Summary

There are many dog sports in which you and your dog can compete. Some events, such as obedience trials, agility trials and tracking tests, are open to all breeds recognized by the AKC. Other sports, such as hunting and herding tests, which are based on the ability of the dog to perform his breed's original function, are limited to a few breeds.

Dogs can be trained for, and compete in, several sports at once. In any sport, make sure that you understand the rules, and that you have adequate instruction in training your dog for the sport. Clubs, such as obedience, agility, and herding clubs, often offer classes for beginners.

If you use common sense when training your dog, and find the resources that you need to help you learn and enjoy the competitions, you'll have fun with your well-balanced dog for many years.

A-Z Glossary

A-Framing: an unnatural stance in which the dog's front feet are too far ahead of the shoulders and the rear legs are pulled too far back. Also called "hobby-horsing."

Agent: a person authorized by the owner of a dog to enter and/or show the dog, usually applied to the person who handles the dog in the show ring for the owner.

AKC: The American Kennel Club.

Angulation: the angles of the skeleton. "Front angulation" refers to the angles of the front legs and shoulders. "Rear angulation" refers to the angles of the rear legs and hips.

Armband: the numbered card worn on the handler's left arm; the number corresponds to the dog's number in the show catalog.

Bait: *(noun)* food or toys used to increase the alertness of the dog in the show ring; *(verb)* to "perk up" the performance of the dog or to capture the dog's attention with bait.

Balance: symmetry in structure, allowing the dog to perform efficiently, moving in a smooth, even fashion.

Bandy-legged: a faulty rear in which the natural stance is wide and the legs bend or rotate outward, away from the centerline of the body.

Benched show: a show at which the dogs are on display during show "benching" hours in an exhibit area (the benching area). Dogs are required to be in their assigned places in the benching area when not competing in the rings.

Best of Breed: the dog or bitch judged to be the best example of its breed shown that day. The Best of Breed winner is eligible to compete against other Best of Breed winners in the Group competition. *Abbreviation: BOB.*

Best of Opposite Sex: the dog or bitch who is considered the best example of the opposite sex to the dog or bitch awarded Best of Breed. If a male is awarded Best of Breed, then Best of Opposite Sex is awarded to a female, and vice versa. *Abbreviation: BOS.*

Best of Winners: The dog judged as the better of Winners Dog and Winners Bitch. *Abbreviation: BOW.*

Bitch: a female canine.

Bite: the position of the upper and lower teeth of the dog when the jaws are closed. The bite is frequently defined in the breed standard. Bite types include level, scissors, overshot and undershot.

Breaking a major: failing to show a dog whose absence turns a possible three-point (major) win to a two-point win. For example, "John's dog wasn't shown, so the major broke."

Breed: a distinct type of dog defined by specific characteristics and parentage. Also used as shorthand for "Best of Breed," as in, for example, "The Golden Retriever from Texas won the Breed."

Breed standard: The official description of a breed, giving details of the physical and, in some cases, temperamental attributes of that breed. The breed standards describe the *ideal* specimen of each breed, and are the basis of judging at dog shows. They are published in *The Complete Dog Book*.

Breeder: (also "Breeder of Record") the person who owns or leases a female when she is bred. Also used to refer to the person who bred your puppy, as in "My breeder is coming to the show."

Catalog: a book published by the show-sponsoring kennel club, which contains information about the club, and the show and for each dog entered, its name, date of birth, sire and dam, sex, breeders and owners.

Catalog order: dogs lined up for judging in the same numerical sequence as their names/numbers appear in the catalogue.

Champion: a title awarded by AKC, indicating that a dog has earned his bench (conformation) championship through competition at AKC dog shows. The title appears in front of the dog's registered name. *Abbreviation: Ch.*

Circuit: three or more shows held over the span of several days, within easy driving distance of one another.

Class Division: a dog show class that is divided by a specified characteristic such as weight, age or color. For example, the Labrador Retriever Open class may be divided into three classes by coat color (black, chocolate, and yellow).

Class dog: a dog that has not yet earned his conformation championship.

Classes: the divisions for entry in a dog show. Usually these are Puppy; 12-18 Months; Bred-by-Exhibitor; American-Bred; Open; and Best of Breed.

Centerline: a spatial reference used by the judge when examining the gait of a dog, envisioned as a straight line on the ground extending from the nose to the tail. Thus, the phrase, "At a fast trot the feet of the dog converge toward the centerline," means that a dog's feet move more narrowly, under his body, (*i.e.* closer to the centerline), rather than under his shoulders and hips, when he moves quickly.

Close-coupled: a dog with a short back, referring particularly to a short distance between the last rib and the hind legs.

Closing date: the date specified by a kennel club by which entries for their show must be received.

Cluster: three or more dog shows held on consecutive days at or near the same site.

Complete Dog Book, The: a book published by the AKC containing all breed standards.

Condition: *(noun)* the general health of an animal as evidenced by its condition. *(verb)* to exercise a dog in order to improve or maintain his physical condition.

Courtesy turn: a movement in which the handler moves the dog in a small circle in front of the judge before beginning an individual gaiting pattern.

Cow-hocked: a faulty rear in which the hocks turn in and the toes turn out.

Crabbing: a faulty gait in which the dog moves with its body at an angle to its line of travel. Also called "sidewinding."

Crossing over: a faulty gait in which the legs crisscross. Sometimes called "knitting and purling" or "weaving."

Dam: the female parent of a dog.

Dentition: the number and types of adult teeth. For example, a breed standard may use the phrase, "Full dentition is greatly to be desired."

Depth of chest: a measure of the volume of chest cavity, often described by how close the sternum is to the elbow. For example, "This dog lacks depth of chest," means that the bottom front portion of the chest is above the dog's elbow.

Disqualifying fault: a condition specified in a breed standard which does not permit the dog to compete in AKC conformation competition. For example, blue eyes are a disqualifying fault for the Samoyed. Dogs with disqualifying faults may compete in obedience, tracking, agility and other events.

Diving: an unnatural stance in which the dog's front feet are placed too far under the body, so that the dog appears to be falling forward, or diving.

Division: *(1)* the 12 geographic regions defined for the championship point schedule published by the AKC; *(2)* a split of a dog show class by color, size, age, etc.

Dock: to surgically remove a portion of the tail.

Dog: a male canine.

Down in the pastern: a faulty construction of the wrist in which the angle is greater than is specified for the breed.

Drive: the power and thrust of a dog's hindquarters.

East west: a faulty front construction in which the front feet of the dog point outward, away from the centerline of the dog's body.

Elbowing out: elbows not held closely to the body, so that space is visible between the elbows and chest. Sometimes called "out at the elbows" or "flying elbows."

Exhibitor: a person showing a dog at a show.

Fancier: a devotee of a given breed.

Fancy: (also "The Fancy") the entire body of people (fanciers) involved in showing dogs.

Feathering: hair that is longer than the surrounding coat.

Finished: a dog that has met all the requirements to for a conformation championship. For example, "He's finished," means that the dog has earned his championship.

Flews: the upper lip of the dog, covering the side and front of the mouth.

Free bait: (also "Free Baiting") using bait to have a dog come to a show stance, as opposed to placing the legs by hand in a formal or hard stack.

Free stack: the presentation of a standing dog without the handler setting each foot individually.

Fun match: an informal match which mimics a dog show but is not sanctioned under the rules of the American Kennel Club.

Futurity: a competition, run by national breed clubs, in which breeders showcase their breeding programs by exhibiting select puppies from litters they have nominated for the competition. Futurity rules are created by individual breed clubs and vary from breed to breed. Not all breeds recognized by the AKC have a Futurity competition.

Gait: the pattern of footsteps, which have a distinct timing, speed, placement and rhythm.

Gaiting: moving the dog in a trot in the show ring. For example, "The handler is gaiting the Saluki around the ring for the judge."

Gaiting pattern: a defined pattern of movement in the show ring, specified by the judge, and used during the individual movement portion of judging.

Groom: the cleaning, trimming and preparation of a dog to meet the specified appearance for its breed and general hygienic condition.

Group: the seven divisions of dog breeds, based largely on original function of the breeds. Group competition is the second round of judging at a dog show. The Groups are: Sporting; Hound; Working; Terrier; Toy; Non-Sporting; and Herding.

Hackney gait: a high stepping, reaching gait in which the front legs move straight forward in front of the body, and the foot bends at the wrist.

Handler: the person who presents a dog in the show ring.

Handling class: a class in which the students are taught how to present a dog in the show ring.

Hand-stack: (also "Hard-stack") to place a dog's legs in a show stance as opposed to letting the dog stand freely.

Hocking in: a faulty rear construction in which the hocks point inward toward the center of the body.

Hocking out: a faulty rear construction in which the hocks point outward, giving the appearance of being bowlegged.

ILP: ("Indefinite Listing Privilege") a designation given by the AKC to a dog that appears to be of a recognized breed but whose parents are unknown or of unregistrable stock. Dogs with ILP numbers may not be shown in conformation competition, but may be show in obedience, agility, tracking and other events.

Judge's Award of Merit: (also "Award of Merit") an honorary award usually given only at Specialty shows, presented to dogs who are not chosen for Best of Breed or Best of Opposite Sex to Best of Breed but are of very high quality. *Abbreviation: JAM or AOM.*

Judge's book: the official document in which the judge records the results of his judging at each show. When completed, this book is given to the show's superintendent and once constitutes the official record of the show's results.

Knuckle over: a serious fault of the front legs in which the carpal (wrist) joints hyperextend, causing a forward flexing of the wrist.

Layback: the angle of the shoulder blade as viewed from the side.

Lead: a leash. In the conformation ring, a dog is show on a "show lead."

Level bite: a bite in which the upper and lower teeth meet exactly, rather than overlapping.

Licensed kennel club: an organization that meets the criterion for a kennel club as defined by the American Kennel Club, and is therefore licensed to run events under the auspices of the American Kennel Club.

Major/minor win: refers to the number of championship points won at a dog show for defeating a given number of dogs of the same breed. Minor wins consist of one or two points; major wins are wins of three, four, or five points.

Match show: an informal competition restricted to non-champion dogs in which championship points cannot be earned. Match shows give the dog and handler an opportunity to practice for shows in which points can be earned.

Minored out: a dog with nine or more minor points toward his championship.

Moving close: a gait in which the dog's legs converge too closely toward the centerline of the body.

Moving up: to change the class in which a dog is entered to Best of Breed class when the owner believes the dog has met the requirements to be a champion, but the American Kennel Club has not yet officially confirmed the championship. Sometimes called "bumping up."

National Club: an organization of enthusiasts for a particular breed, which supports events, provides information about that breed, and defines the breed's standard.

National Specialty: (also "Nationals" or "the National") the annual show held by the national club for its breed. For example, "Last year the National was held in California."

Non-regular class: a class from which championship points cannot be won. An example of a non-regular class is the Veterans class. The eligibility for a non-regular class entry is defined by the club holding the show.

Off-side: the side of a dog that is away from the judge's view (usually the dog's right side).

Out at the shoulders: shoulder blades loosely attached to the body, giving the appearance of angular, jutting shoulders.

Over-reach: a faulty gait caused by greater angulation in the rear than in the front. When moving, the reach of the rear legs is so great that the rear feet move to one side of the forefeet in order to avoid colliding.

Overshot: a bite in which the top front teeth protrude beyond the lower front teeth.

Pace: a gait in which the legs on the same side of the body move forward at the same time, causing a rolling motion.

Paddling: a faulty gait caused by pinched shoulders and elbows causing the dog to swing the front feet in an outward arc.

Pads: the hard underside of the foot.

Parent club: the national club for a breed.

Pedigree: the written record of a dog's ancestry, containing multiple generations.

Performance event: competitions that test the ability of a dog to perform the function for which the breed was developed. Performance events include herding tests and trials, field trials, lure coursing events, hunting tests, and earthdog events.

Placement: an award of first, second, third or fourth place in a dog show class or in Group competition.

Point schedule: the AKC's tabulation of the number of dogs that must be in competition at a show in a particular geographic division for Winners Dog or Winners Bitch to earn from one to five points toward their championship. This schedule is published annually and remains in effect from May 15 of one year to May 15 of the following year. Twelve geographic divisions are defined, covering the United States and Puerto Rico.

Pounding: a faulty gait in which the length of stride of the forelegs is shorter than that of the rear legs.

Premium list: a brochure issued by a kennel club (or show superintendent) in which information about a show is given. Information includes the date and place of the show, judges, classes being offered, entry forms, and trophies offered.

Professional handler: a person hired by the owner of a dog to show the dog and, in some cases, to board, groom, and transport the dog to a show.

Pull: *(1)* to withdraw an entry of a dog to fail to attend the show, (*e.g.,* "I pulled my entry for next Saturday's show."); *(2)* to select dogs for further judging, dismissing the rest of the class (*e.g.,* "The judge pulled six dogs from a class of dogs.")

Ramp: a low table or platform on which some heavy, short breeds, such as the Bulldog and the Basset Hound, are stacked for the judge's examination. The name comes from the ramp the dog walks up to get on the table.

Reach: the length of the stride of the forelegs.

Regular class: a class from which the winners may progress to the Winners class and earn championship points (Puppy, 12-18 Month, Novice, Bred-by-Exhibitor, American-Bred, Open).

Roaching: (also "Roached") a pronounced arching or rounding of the back.

Rough coat: a thick or full coat; the term is often used in contrast with "smooth coat." For example, the two varieties of Collie are "smooth coated" and "rough coated."

Rough shoulder: rolls of skin where the neck meets the shoulder, usually caused by a faulty attachment of the shoulder to the body.

Sanctioned: an event that is held under the rules and regulations of the American Kennel Club, such as a sanctioned show or sanctioned match.

Scissors bite: a bite in which the inner side of the upper incisors touches the outer side of the lower incisors.

Set: (*verb*) to position a dog in a formal stacked position; (*noun*) a block of time in a judge's schedule, as published in the judging program, during which specified breeds will be judged.

Sharing points: increasing the number of points earned by Winners Dog or Winners Bitch as a result of being awarded Best of Winners. Sometimes called "splitting points" or "spreading points."

Show committee: the members of a kennel club responsible for planning, organizing, and conducting a dog show.

Show side: the side of a dog visible to the judge (usually the dog's left side).

Sidewinding: a faulty gait in which the dog moves with its body at an angle to its line of travel. Sometimes called "crabbing."

Single tracking: when gaiting, the feet converge to strike a single line of travel at the dog's centerline. Single tracking is desirable in some breeds, and a fault in others.

Sire: the male parent of a dog.

Slab-sided: lacking in roundness and spring in the ribs.

Smooth coat: short hair that lies close to the dog's body.

Snipy: a pointed, weak, or excessively tapered muzzle.

Socialize: to expose a dog to a wide variety of situations, people and other dogs so that he will not be shy or fearful when away from his home.

Soundness: a measure or degree of overall mental and physical health. A dog that appears completely healthy is considered "sound", where as a dog that limps, for example, would be "unsound."

Special: a dog that has earned his conformation championship and now competes in the Best of Breed class. For example, "There are seven male specials entered today."

Square-bodied: a dog whose length (measured from the forechest to the base of the tail) is equal to his height (measured from the ground to the withers).

Stack: to pose a dog, either by letting him stand naturally ("free stack") or by positioning his legs ("hand stack").

Straight shoulder: (also "steep shoulder") a faulty front structure in which the shoulder blades are rotated vertically, rather than pointing back toward the dog's croup.

Steward: a person assigned assist the judge with many of the administrative tasks associated with running a show ring. A steward's tasks include giving armbands to exhibitors, calling the dogs to the ring, assuring access to the entrance, assembling the classes for the judge, and having ribbons ready for the judge to present to the exhibitors.

Stifle: the dog's knee.

Superintendent: a company or individual hired by a kennel club to handle the logistical and business aspects of putting on a dog show. Show superintendents must be licensed by the American Kennel Club.

Sway back: concave curvature of the back. Sometimes called "sagging topline."

Sweepstakes: an informal competition for young dogs ("puppy sweepstakes) or old dogs ("veteran sweepstakes) in which dogs cannot earn championship points. Sweepstakes are usually held at Specialty shows or at shows with supported entries. Placement winners are awarded prize money, usually a percentage of the money collected in sweepstakes entry fees.

Table breed: any one of the smaller breeds that is stacked on a table for the judge's exam.

Tail set: the position of the base of the tail relative to the back. A tail that begins before the back curves over the rump top is set "high," while a tail that begins after the spine curves is "low."

Topline: the outline of the back from the withers to the base of the tail.

Trot: a brisk, rhythmic 2-beat gait in which the diagonally opposite legs strike the ground at the same time.

Tuck-up: the profile of the abdomen, contrasting the depth of the loin with the dept of the chest. A dog whose chest and loins are the same depth has no tuck-up.

Unbenched: a show at which the presence of the dog on the show grounds is only required when the dog is actually being judged.

Undershot: A bite in which the lower front teeth protrude beyond the upper front teeth.

Unsound: a dog lacking in physical or mental attributes to a degree that it is unable to perform the function for which it was bred.

Variety: categories within a breed that are defined in the breed standard and which are judged as if they were separate breeds. For example, the three varieties of Poodles are Toy, Miniature and Standard.

Wet neck: loose, baggy skin on the underside of the neck. Sometimes called "throaty."

Winners Bitch: the female judged to be the best *non-champion* female in competition that day. Winners Bitch is the only female who earns championship points. *Abbreviation: WB.*

Winners Dog: the male judged to be the best *non-champion* male in competition that day. Winners Dog is the only male who earns championship points. Abbreviation: WD

Withers: area at the top of the shoulder blades.

Zigzag: to stagger or fail to move in a straight line, moving first in one direction and then in another.

Contacts

The American Kennel Club

Executive Offices
260 Madison Avenue, New York, NY 10016
(212) 696-8200

Customer Service/Registration Information
5580 Centerview Drive, Suite 200, Raleigh, NC 27606-3390
(919)233-9767

http://www.akc.org

Show Superintendents and Secretaries

Jack Bradshaw Dog Shows
P.O. Box 227303, Los Angeles, CA 90022-0178
(323) 727-0136
http://www.jbradshaw.com

Brown Dog Show Organization, Inc.
P.O. Box 2566, Spokane, WA 99220-2566
(509) 924-1089
http://www.browndogshow.com

Garvin Show Services
14622 SE Old Barn Lane, Boring, OR 97009-9267
(503) 558-1221
http://www.garvinshowservices.com

Roy Jones Dog Shows, Inc.
P.O. Box 828, Auburn, IN 46706-0828
(219) 925-0525
http://royjonesdogshows.com

MB-F, Inc.
P.O. Box 22107, Greensboro, NC 27420-2107
(336) 379-9352
http://www.infodog.com

McNulty Dog Shows
1745 Route 78, Java Center, New York 14082
(716) 457-3371
http://www.mcnultydogshows.com

Nancy J. Mathews
11423 SE Alder Street, Portland, OR 97216
(503) 253-9367

Onofrio Dog Shows
P.O. Box 25764, Oklahoma City, OK 73125-0764
(405) 427-8181
http://www.onofrio.com

Peters Dog Shows, Ltd.
P.O. Box 579, Wake Forest, NC 27588-0579
(919) 556-9516

Jim Rau Dog Shows, Ltd.
P.O. Box 6898, Reading, PA 19610-0898
(610) 376-1880
http://www.raudogshows.com

Kevin Rogers Dog Shows
P.O. Box 230, Hattiesburg, MS 39403-0230
(601) 583-1110
http://www.rogersdogshows.com

Nancy Wilson
8307 E. Camelback Road, Scottsdale, AZ 85251-1715
(602) 949-5389

Frequently Asked Questions

What's the difference between a match and a show?

A "match" is a practice show. You cannot earn points toward your dog's championship at a match. A "show" usually means an AKC-approved show, where you can earn points towards your dog's championship.

A match is usually open to puppies as young as three months old. Some matches exclude dogs that have earned major points toward their championships, and some matches do not allow professional handlers unless they are handling their own dogs.

What's the difference between a fun match and a sanctioned match?

A "sanctioned match" is a match that is run under the match rules of the AKC by a club recognized by the AKC. AKC-sanctioned matches are very similar to AKC shows.

A "fun match" is run by a group not licensed by the AKC, and is not run under AKC rules. A fun match generally has a relaxed, informal atmosphere. Fun matches are often run as fundraisers for clubs.

What's a specialty show?

A specialty show is an AKC-approved show in which the breeds that can be exhibited are limited, most often to one breed. Specialty shows are conducted by specialty breed clubs that are licensed by the AKC to hold shows, for example, the Goldenrod German Shorthaired Pointer Club specialty show would be open to German Shorthaired Pointers only. Specialty shows usually include non-regular classes (*e.g.,* veterans, stud dog and brood bitch) in addition to the regular classes, and usually have a sweepstakes (puppy and possibly veteran).

Specialty shows may be held in conjunction with an all-breed show: foe example, the classes for Doberman Pinschers at the Cactus Kennel Club show may serve as the specialty show for the Prickly Pear Doberman Pinscher Club. Specialty shows held in conjunction with an all-breed show use the same premium list and entry forms as the all-breed show.

"Independent" specialty shows are specialties that are not held in conjunction with an all-breed show. The premium list for an independent specialty is separate from the premium list for any other show. Independent specialty shows are often held the day before or the day after an all-breed show at the same show site.

What's a supported entry?

When a local breed club, licensed by the AKC, "supports" the entry at an all-breed show, the club members make a special effort to enter their dogs in order to ensure that the show is a major for both dogs and bitches. Sometimes a breed whose entry is supported at an all-breed show also offers sweepstakes. In addition, there may be more breed-specific trophies offered at the show, and the local breed club may host a social event. The premium list for an all-breed dog show lists the breed clubs that are supporting entries at the show; you enter a supported entry show just like you would enter a regular all-breed dog show.

What is "The Garden"?

This is shorthand for the Westminster Kennel Club's dog show, held each February in New York City at Madison Square Garden. It is a two-day benched show: four groups are judged one day, and three groups are judged on the other day. Best in Show is judged at the end of the second day. The Westminster Kennel Club show entry is limited to champions, so there is only one class for each breed: Best of Breed. The show attracts dogs from all over the country. Winning Best of Breed, a Group placement, or Best in Show at The Garden is very prestigious.

What are "puppy groups"?

Some all-breed shows hold a *non-regular* competition for puppies that parallels the structure of the regular group and Best in Show competition. The premium list for the show will state "Puppy Groups will be judged" or "Best Puppy in Show will be awarded". Any puppy entered in either the 6-9 month old or 9-12 month old class is automatically eligible for this competition, and no additional entry is required.

After Best of Breed is awarded in each breed, the judge then selects the "Best Puppy of Breed" from the winners of the 6-9 month old and 9-12 month old classes for dogs and bitches. (A puppy does not earn championship points for winning "Best Puppy of Breed" since this is a non-regular award.) The best puppy from each breed next competes in the appropriate puppy group (Puppy Sporting Group, Puppy Toy Group, etc). The winner of each puppy group then competes for "Best Puppy in Show."

What is a "bench show"? How does it differ from a "benched show"?

"Bench show" is an old-fashioned term for a conformation show, left over from the days when most dog shows in the United States were benched shows.

A conformation show may be either "benched" or "unbenched." At a "benched" show, the dogs are required to be on display at assigned "benches" during show hours, unless they are in the ring or being exercised. Thus a dog that is being shown at 1:00 p.m. may have to be at the show by 8:00 a.m., and cannot leave until the late afternoon. The premise is that at a benched show, it is easier for the public to see the dogs entered, since they will be on display all day rather than just when they are in the ring, and all the dogs of a given breed are benched together. Although this used to be the most common form of dog show, bench shows are now relatively rare in the United States.

At the much more common "unbenched" show—what we usually think of as a regular dog show today—the dogs are not on constant display, and only need to be at the show for judging, so a dog that is judged at 1:00 p.m. does not need to arrive at the show at 8:00 a.m. When he is at the show, he can wait in his handler's vehicle, in the grooming area, or anywhere else.

What do "show hours" mean?

The show hours define the time during the day that the rules governing AKC dog shows will be enforced on the show grounds. Show hours generally start one to two hours prior to judging, and end well after the end of judging, *e.g.* 7 a.m. to 7 p.m.

What are "Nationals"?

"Nationals" is a shorthand way of saying "The Specialty Show for the National Breed Club of….". For example, the national specialty show of the Dalmatian Club of America is often referred to simply as "Dalmatian Nationals." National specialty shows are held annually for most breeds; some national specialties are held in conjunction with all-breed shows, and some national specialties are independent. National specialty shows usually draw large entries from a wide geographic region, and often last several days. Winning Best of Breed at a national specialty show is very prestigious.

Should I look at the point schedule applying to the show's location, where I live, or where my dog was born?

The applicable point schedule is determined by the location of the show. For example, suppose you live in Pennsylvania. When you show your dog in Pennsylvania, the point schedule for Division 2 (New Jersey, Pennsylvania, Ohio, and Delaware) is used at the show. If you show your dog in Maryland, the point schedule for Division 3 (Maryland, etc.) is used. Even though Pennsylvania and Maryland are neighboring states, the point schedules might be very different in the two regions.

Do you get points only at an all-breed show?

No, you can get points at an all-breed show, at a specialty show (a show for one breed only), or at a group show (for example, a show for Terrier breeds only, or a show limited to the Toy breeds). In fact, you can earn championship points at any AKC licensed show in which your dog is eligible to compete. You cannot, however earn championship points at a match; AKC sanctioned matches are for practice only!

If I have questions at the show whom should I ask?

The answer really depends on where you are when the question arises, and what the question is.

If you are *in the ring* and you have a question about the judge's ring procedure or about what you are supposed to do—either during the individual exam or during group activities if you are first in line—politely ask the judge to repeat his instructions or to clarify what he or she wants you to do. Don't worry—asking a question for clarification won't label you as a novice or incompetent handler in the judge's eyes! Most judges would rather that their rings moved smoothly and on time, and were not held up because a handler bumbled around, unsure of what to do.

When you're in the ring, you may also ask a brief pertinent question of other exhibitors ("Are we going around once or twice?"), but do not try to engage them in lengthy discussions or expect them to direct you in the ring. Most exhibitors will gladly answer a quick question, but their focus in the ring is showing their dog, not helping you. If in doubt in the ring, just do what the person ahead of you does.

Outside the ring, the ring steward is the right person to ask questions relating to the ring. The steward's responsibility is to make sure the ring runs smoothly, and that all exhibitors are in the right place at the right time. Do not try to ask the judge a question if he or she is standing at the steward's table marking the judge's book or taking a break—if you are outside the ring, address your questions to the ring steward.

Questions that do not focus on the specific activity in your ring should be directed to the superintendent, AKC field representative, or show committee members. Your best bet is to head to the superintendent's table first and ask your question. If the superintendent can't answer your question, he can direct you to someone who can.

Who runs a dog show?

A club—all-breed, group or specialty—that is licensed to hold AKC events has the primary responsibility for "running" a dog show. The club applies to the AKC for permission to hold the event. The club also hires the judges and contracts for the show site. Many clubs hire a superintendent to manage most of the other show logistics, both before the show and on show day, including handling all show paperwork and setting up the rings.

What should I do if someone criticizes my dog or how I'm showing my dog?

Generally, you should ignore him or her; it's rude and bad sportsmanship to criticize someone else's dog or how it's being shown unless asked to do so. Of course, if you ask someone why she thinks the judge didn't like your dog, or what she thinks of your dog, don't get mad when she criticizes your dog—you asked for her opinion.

If someone approaches you with comments about your handling, and a genuine interest in being helpful, listen politely and decide if you want to follow their advice. If, for example, someone standing behind you in line noticed that your dog pops his elbows out when you allow him to swing his head around during the exam, then that's useful and kindly meant information. On the other hand, if someone else tells you to set your dog's front wider, and you know you are setting it properly, simply thank him and ignore his advice.

What do "BIS" and "BISS" mean?

The label "BIS" is not an AKC title but is used by some people to indicate a dog that has won "Best in Show" at an all-breed show. Another non-AKC abbreviation is "BISS" or "Best in Specialty Show." At a specialty show, the highest award is Best of Breed, not Best in Show. However, people will write BISS on pedigree or in an advertisement to indicate that the dog has won Best of Breed at a specialty.

Thus, if you see a dog advertised or listed in a pedigree as:

BIS Ch. Freedom's Fuzzyfoot Frederick

you can conclude that this dog earned an AKC bench championship (Ch.), and that he won Best in Show at an all-breed show (BIS).

My dog's breeder is her co-owner. What does that mean?

The co-owners, of a dog are the people listed as owners on the dog's AKC registration form. Often the first person listed is referred to as the "owner" and subsequent people as the "co-owners," but they're all equal owners of the dog in the eyes of the AKC, no matter where the dog lives or who pays the dog's bills. If a dog is registered in the names of, say, a husband and wife (e.g., John and Mary Smith), they are the dog's co-owners. If the dog is registered in the names of his breeder and the person who bought him (e.g., John Smith and Jane Brown), they are the dog's (equal) co-owners. A dog may have many co-owners (*e.g.,* John and Mary Smith, Jane Brown, and George Moore).

Co-ownership of a dog has its biggest impact on actions involving the AKC: you must have the agreement (signatures) of all co-owners of a dog or bitch before you can re-register the dog to other people (usually, selling the dog). Thus for example, if John Smith and Jane Brown co-own a bitch, and John would like to add his wife as another co-owner, he must have Jane's agreement. If Jane would like to sell the bitch to someone else, she must have John's agreement.

If the co-owned animal is a bitch, then you must have the agreement (signatures) of all the co-owners to register her puppies. Again, if John Smith and Jane Brown co-own a bitch that lives with Jane, and Jane breeds the bitch, she cannot register the puppies unless she has John Smith's signature on the litter registration papers. If he does not sign the papers, the puppies cannot be registered. Many litters have not been registered because co-owners didn't agree on the breeding.

Finally, beware: if your dog's co-owner gets in trouble with the AKC, it can affect any dogs he owns or co-owns. For example, if John Smith is suspended from AKC privileges, or banned permanently from AKC activities, any dogs he co-owns are ineligible to compete or to have their offspring registered. Thus Jane

Brown may now have a bitch that is ineligible for AKC activities because of her co-owner's actions.

What is an ILP registration?

ILP is the acronym for "Indefinite Listing Privilege." An ILP registration number may be assigned to purebred dogs who do not have regular AKC registration papers because their parentage is unknown. Dogs from Rescue programs are often assigned ILP numbers. Dogs with an ILP registration number must be spayed or neutered. With an ILP registration number, these dogs may compete in performance events (obedience trials, tracking tests, herding trials, lure coursing, agility trials, earthdog events and hunting tests).

What is limited registration?

Limited registration is a type of AKC registration that does not permit the offspring of that dog to be registered. A dog with a limited registration is eligible to compete in all AKC events except conformation.

What are non-regular classes?

Non-regular classes are classes other than Puppy, Novice, 12-18 months, American-Bred, Bred-By Exhibitor, Open, and Best of Breed. Non-regular classes are usually offered only at specialty show or very large all breed shows. Classes in which individual dogs compete include Veterans, Versatile, Field Trial, and so on. The winners of these classes are eligible to compete in the Best of Breed competition. Other non-regular classes, with entries that involve multiple dogs, include brace (two dogs shown together), team (four dogs shown together), stud dog (a stud dog and two of his get), and brood bitch (a brood bitch and two of her whelps).

What's a junior? And what is junior showmanship?

Children (anyone under 18 years old) who show dogs are often referred to as "juniors", whether or not they are competing in the Junior Showmanship competition. Thus you may hear ringside, "The breeder had a junior take Bear in today" or "Muffin was shown by Tom Morgan's junior"—the latter refers to a junior handler who is assisting the professional or semi-professional handler Tom Morgan.

"Junior Showmanship" is a competition for girls and boys in which their handling skills, rather than the quality of the dog they are showing, are judged. The children compete by age (Juniors are 10-13 years old, and Seniors are 14-17 years old) and by skill level (Novice for those who have won First Place fewer than three times in Novice Junior Showmanship classes, and Open for those who have won First Place in three Novice classes). Thus the junior handlers start out in the Novice class for their age group, and as their skills develop, they progress to the Open class.

Handlers who want to compete in Junior Showmanship must have a Junior Handler Number (it's required on the entry form) which can be obtained from the

AKC. Junior Showmanship classes are entered at the same time that regular conformation classes are entered using the same AKC entry form.

Where can I find a list of upcoming shows?

There are several places to find listings of upcoming shows. The most complete and authoritative listing, including judging panels, will be found in each month's *Events Calendar*, received as part of the annual subscription to the *AKC Gazette*. The *Events Calendar* lists shows and performance events occurring in the next four months. Upcoming shows and matches are also listed in regional dog event publications, such as the *Match Show Bulletin* (northeastern United States) and in on-line discussion lists.

Lists of upcoming shows can be found at the AKC's Web site and at the Web sites of various superintendents. At shows, superintendents often have premium lists for shows they will be running in the coming months. There may also be a list of upcoming shows on the back page of a premium list you already have.

How do I get on the mailing list for information about shows?

Contact the licensed show superintendents via mail, e-mail, or phone, to request that your name be placed on their mailing list for premium lists. Tell the superintendent the breed(s) you show, whether you show in both obedience and conformation, and which states or regions of the country you will be showing in. While some superintendents are regional, other superintendents run shows all over the country.

What can I do if I don't have an entry form for a show I want to enter?

You can use *any* AKC entry form to enter the show, as long as it has copies of both sides of a standard entry form.

If you use a form printed for another show, cross out the name, date, and location at the top of the form, and write in the name, date, and location of the show that you want to enter. If you use a generic entry form (an official AKC entry form with nothing printed at the top), write in the name, date, and location of the show you want to enter. Some computer pedigree data base and kennel management software can print AKC entry forms. You can also download a generic entry form from the AKC's Web site.

Two things are absolute musts: include copies of *both sides* of a standard entry form with your entry, and make sure the form shows the name, location, and date of the show you want to enter.

Entries close on Wednesday, and today is Sunday. What are my options?

If you're at a show on Sunday, and the superintendent is the same as the one you want to enter, you can drop your entry forms and entry fee check at the superintendent's table at the show, and your problem is solved.

You can use regular mail or Express Mail. Remember, however, that Express Mail does not have *guaranteed* delivery dates and times.

You can use a private service such as Federal Express, DHL or UPS. When you use a private courier, make sure you select the level of service that will deliver your entries by *the date and time* specified on the premium list. Also, you must use the street address of the superintendent; entries cannot be delivered to a post office box.

You can enter shows via either fax or the Internet. In both cases, you pay for your entries with a credit card, and there is a service charge ($3-$5) per dog per show. Or, you can use a telephone entry service, for which there is also a service charge of $3-$5 per entry.

Why does it cost so much to enter a dog in a show?

Simply because it costs so much to put on a dog show! For example, there are the costs of the physical facilities—renting the site for the day of the show (and the day before to set everything up) and having the site cleaned afterwards. There are expenses for the ring set-ups, including matting, gates, tables, awnings, and the labor to put it all up and take it all down. There are also administrative expenses for doing of all the paperwork involved in running the show, and, of course, expenses for hiring judges.

What is the "recording fee" mentioned on the entry form?

The AKC takes $0.50 from each entry as a 'recording fee" to cover their administrative costs for recording the results of the show, tabulating championship points, and sending out certificates.

The premium list says that there will be no classes for Basset Hounds offered at the show. Why?

If there are no classes offered for a particular breed or breeds at a show, it usually means that there is a specialty show for that breed (or breeds) in the same area on the same day. AKC rules state that there cannot be two shows within 200 miles of each other on any given day. For example, if there is a specialty show for Basset Hounds in Dallas on Sept. 12 and an all-breed show the same day in Ft. Worth—a few miles away—there cannot be classes for Basset Hounds at the Ft. Worth all-breed show.

The premium list gives the entry fee for an "additional class" and the entry form has a space for an additional class. How many classes can my dog enter?

You may enter your dog in only *one* regular conformation class at a show. "Additional" classes may be non-regular classes (such as brace class), obedience trial classes, or sweepstakes classes.

I entered shows next month, and now I've got a schedule conflict so I can't go. Can I get my money back?

You can withdraw your entry and get a refund of your entry fee (perhaps with a service fee deducted) only if you notify the superintendent *in writing* prior to the date and time that entries close.

If entries have already closed, the only way you can get a refund is if you are lucky enough to have a judge change. In this case, you can get a refund if you notify the superintendent in writing, either before the show or prior to the start of judging on the day of the show.

I just realized that I made a mistake on my entry form—what do I do?

It depends on what the mistake is. If you entered the wrong class or made a mistake in your dog's AKC number or name, then contact the superintendent as soon as possible to correct the error. If you accidentally left the dog's name, breed, class, or AKC number blank, then contact the superintendent as soon as possible. Other errors, such as misspelling the owner's name or omitting a dog's titles, do not have to be corrected. If in doubt, contact the superintendent.

What does "Reserve" mean?

"Reserve" is another way of saying second place or runner-up. The "Reserve Winners Dog" is the non-champion dog that the judge felt was the second best unfinished dog in competition that day. The "Winners Dog" was the best non-champion dog. Only the Winner's Dog earns points towards his championship; the Reserve Winners Dog does not earn points. The same definitions apply for Winners Bitch and Reserve Winners Bitch.

Many exhibitors are unhappy and discouraged when their dog "only goes Reserve" because they haven't earned championship points. But being awarded Reserve at a large entry can be interpreted as a very encouraging signal that your dog (and your handling skills) were in contention for winning and that this judge liked your dog enough to consider him or her for the points.

When is it OK for me to leave ringside? When am I finished for the day?

If you did not place in your class, or if you received third or fourth place, you may leave ringside as soon as you exit the ring.

If you received *first or second place*, you must remain ringside after your class is judged; you must be present for the judging of Winners Class. All first place class winners go back into the ring for Winners Class. When the Winners Dog or Winners Bitch is selected, the *second place* dog or bitch from the class won by Winners Dog or Winners Bitch must enter the ring for Reserve Winners judging.

After Winners Dog and Winners Bitch have been awarded, all the other class animals may leave. After Best of Breed judging, all animals except the Best of Breed winner are finished with showing for the day.

If I win a class and have to go back into the ring, behind whom should I stand? What's the order for the class winners?

If you win your class, you will have to go back into the ring for Winners Class. Dogs go into the ring in the opposite order from which the classes were judged: the Open class winner (if any) is at the head of the line and the Puppy class winner (if any) is at the end.

If you won second place in your class, and the dog (or bitch) that defeated you is awarded Winners Dog (or Winners Bitch) then as the handler is accepting his Winners ribbon, you should enter the ring and stack your dog in the place vacated by the Winner, since that is the spot for your class. For example, if Winners Dog is the 6-9 month puppy, then the second place 6-9 month old puppy will go to the end of the line to stack for the Reserve competition.

Who can show in Novice? What if my dog wins a class after entries close, but before the next show?

The Novice class is open to dogs (or bitches) more than 6 months old who have not won three First Places in Novice class, a First Place in Bred by Exhibitor class, American-Bred or Open Classes, nor have points toward their championship. The time-frame for these wins is prior to the *date that entries close*.

Suppose your dog is entered in the American-Bred class on Saturday and in the Novice class on Sunday. On Saturday, he wins the American-Bred class. Can he still be shown in Novice on Sunday? Yes, because *when entries closed 2½ weeks earlier he was eligible for Novice class*.

If he is entered in Novice class next weekend, he is still eligible despite his American-Bred win, because the entries for next weekend have already closed.

If he is entered in Novice classes at future shows for which entries *have not yet closed,* you must contact the superintendent and submit a revised entry, changing his class from Novice to something else. If you do not change his class, any placements and points he wins from Novice will be disallowed.

How can a judge pick the best dogs in a Group where there's such a wide variety of breeds?

In the Group competition, the dogs are not judged against each other. Rather, they are judged against their breed standard. The judge's job is to pick the dogs that most closely conform to the ideal described in the individual breed standards. Thus, the judge is asking himself, "Is this Newfoundland a better example of a Newfoundland than the Saint Bernard is of a Saint Bernard?" The same is true in the Best in Show competition.

What does the judge write down when he is judging?

The judge marks his "Judge's Book," which is the official record of his judging that day. He checks the armband numbers of the dogs exhibited that day against those printed in his book, noting any that were absent, excused, or disqualified. He also records the results of his judging, recording which dogs he gave placements to and which were Best of Breed, Best of Opposite Sex, and Best of Winners.

Many judges will take notes while they judge, especially if judging a very large class; for example, judges may write down the armband numbers of the dogs that they want to keep in their "cut" for further consideration.

Can the judge ask me questions about my dog? Can I tell him anything?

The judge can *only* ask you how old your dog is. You should *not* volunteer any information to the judge about your dog *unless* your bitch is in season, in which case it is polite to tell the judge this when the examination begins. You should *not* tell the judge who the parents or breeders are, how many points the dog has (or that today's show could finish his championship), or anything else about the dog.

This doesn't mean that you should be stonily silent when you are in the ring! If you have a question about ring procedure, by all means ask. If the judge makes small talk (for example, saying "good morning" to you as he begins your dog's exam) then respond with a cheery good morning, but don't chatter! If the judge asks you a question, then answer it *briefly*. The judge is bound to a strict time schedule and is in the ring to evaluate your dog, not to chat with you.

What is the difference between being "disqualified" and being "excused"?

Once in the ring, a dog may be excused by the judge for a variety of reasons: the dog may be lame that day, become ill in the ring, have stitches or be wearing a bandage, or the dog's behavior might prevent him from being judged. In any of these cases, the judge will excuse the animal from competition that day. Being excused applies only for that show.

Being disqualified is more serious than being excused; a disqualification goes on an animal's permanent record with the AKC. Most commonly, an animal will be disqualified from judging if it has a "disqualifying fault," such as being too large or too small, having color mismarking, or having fewer than two descended testes (for a male of any breed). Disqualifying faults for each breed are described in the breed's standard. A dog that tries to attack the judge will also be disqualified.

What does withholding placement mean?

Having a placement withheld is a rare occurrence. When a judge withholds a dog's placement, he is saying that the dog is of such poor quality that he cannot even consider the dog in the competition, and that other dogs should not get credit for defeating it. The dog is said to be "lacking in merit." Being deemed "lacking in merit" applies only to that show.

What is a wicket?

A wicket is the measuring device that the AKC uses to determine the height of a dog. It is made of metal and looks like a giant Π with adjustable leg length.

Suppose a breed standard calls for males to be 23"-25" tall at the shoulder. If a dog is being tested for being too tall –"over standard"—the crossbar of the wicket is set at 25" and the wicket is set across the dog's shoulders, with the legs parallel to and outside of the dog's front legs. The crossbar is positioned over the withers. If the wicket's legs touch the ground that means that the dog is 25" tall or less, and is in standard. If the crossbar of the wicket rests on the dog's withers and the legs *do not* touch the ground, then the dog is taller than 25" and, therefore, over standard.

The logic is reversed for measuring a dog that may be too small: the crossbar of the wicket is set at the bottom of the height standard.

Some breeds have weight rather than height limitations. If a judge believes a dog is heavier than the breed standard permits, the judge may request a scale so that the dog can be weighed.

When can I decide *not* to show my dog today?

You are not officially present and thus obligated to show until you pick up your armband. If you check in with the ring steward and pick up your armband, your dog is considered "present" at the show and must be shown.

What is an "intact" animal?

An "intact" animal is a bitch that has not been spayed or a dog that has not been neutered (castrated). Only intact animals may compete in AKC all-breed conformation shows. At specialty shows, animals shown in the Veteran's classes may be spayed or neutered. Animals that have been spayed or neutered are, however, eligible to compete in obedience, tracking, agility, and other performance events.

The Well Trained Dog

www.thewelltraineddog.com

P.O. Box 516
Collingswood, NJ 08108

e-mail: info@thewelltraineddog.com

The Well Trained Dog

Ship to:

Name _____

Address _____

Address _____

City _____ State _____ Zip _____

e-mail _____

phone (_____) _____

Make checks or money orders payable to "The Well Trained Dog"

Quantity	Title	unit price	Total
	Raising a Champion: A Beginner's Guide to Showing Dogs	$24.95	

- Shipping/handling: $4 for first book, $3 for each additional book
- Canadian orders must be paid in US dollars
- For orders of 6 or more books, contact us about discount pricing

Sub-total	
NJ residents add 6% sales tax	
Shipping/handling	
TOTAL	

Book Order Form

The Well Trained Dog

www.thewelltraineddog.com